Tort Law in Hong Kong

List of Abbreviations

AELO	Application of English Law Ordinance 1966 (Cap 88)
AG	Attorney General
CECO	Control of Exemption Clauses Ordinance (Cap 71)
CFA	Court of Final Appeal
CLEUD	Certificate of Lawfulness of Existing Use or Development
CPO	Crown Proceedings Ordinance (Cap 300)
ECO	Employees Compensation Ordinance (Cap 282)
EOC	Equal Opportunities Commission
HKPA	Hong Kong Academy for Performing Arts
HKSAR	Hong Kong Special Administrative Region
IIPH	Intentional Infliction of Physical Harm
ISPs	Internet Service Providers
LARCO	Law Amendment and Reform (Consolidation) Ordinance (Cap 23)
LO	Limitation Ordinance (Cap 347)
MIB	Motor 'Insurers' Bureau of Hong Kong
MPF	Mandatory Provident Fund
NPCSC	Standing Committee of the National People's Congress
OLO	Occupiers Liability Ordinance (Cap 314)
PSLA	Pain, Suffering and Loss of Amenities
PTSD	Post-Traumatic Stress Disorder
SDO	Sex Discrimination Ordinance (Cap 480)
SJ	Secretary of Justice

General Introduction

§1. General Background of the Country

I. Geography

1. Hong Kong is located in the southern part of China. It is a coastal city and well known for its deep natural port – Victoria Harbor. Hong Kong consists of three main territories: Kowloon, the New Territories and Hong Kong Island, and the land is mostly hilly. Due to its unique landscape, Hong Kong's government engages in land reclamation and has utilized the hillsides. Furthermore, the government has created a few 'new towns' in the New Territories to satisfy the high demand for housing; hence, many Hong Kong citizens lived in such 'new towns'.

II. History

2. Hong Kong, a part of China, became a British colony after the Opium Wars and the signing of several treaties with China. Hong Kong was a British colony until 1997, though Japan occupied Hong Kong for three years and eight months during World War II. Hong Kong returned to China in 1997 as a Special Administrative Region.

III. Political System

3. Hong Kong was part of the United Kingdom for about 155 years and it retained its common law system after the handover to China in 1997, making it distinct from the Chinese political and legal system. Under the Basic Law, Hong Kong has high degree of autonomy and can mostly govern its own affairs. The Chief Executive, as the head of the government, is responsible to the Chinese government. However, the Chief Executive can appoint government officials themselves and form their government. The Chief Executive is elected by an election committee with 1,200 members.

IV. Economic and Social Values

4. The rule of law, justice, equality and liberty are core values in Hong Kong. The rule of law is buttressed by a comprehensive legal system; no one is above the law and everyone is equal under it. Justice is protected through the independence of the judicial branch and the professional code of conduct of the legal practitioners. Liberties are secured by the Basic Law, Hong Kong's foremost constitutional document.

§2. Legal Systems

I. Primacy of Legislation and Codification

5. Like other common law jurisdictions, legislation, for which Hong Kong's Legislative Council is responsible, prevails over the common law. If there are statues governing a particular issue, courts have to follow the statues and overrule, contrary case law.

II. Position of the Judiciary

6. The position of the judiciary is as an independent body that interprets and implements law. The judiciary acts according to the Basic Law to solve conflicts or disputes with the aid of statues and case precedents. As required by the Basic Law, the judiciary ought not to be interfered with by any organs from the legislature or executive branches when exercising its functions, which include monitoring the government to ensure that it acts in conformity with the law.

III. Distinction Between Public and Private Law

7. The major distinction between public and private law is that the former governs issues relating to the public generally, like criminal law and the powers and functions of governmental bodies, and includes the Basic Law and other administrative law, while the latter covers areas which relate to rights and obligations that arise between citizens in Hong Kong. This governs general duties, like tort law, or other duties specially recognized by the law, such as contract and trust law.

IV. Sources of Private Law in General and of Tort Law in Particular

8. In Hong Kong, private law generally comes from the precedents in that field, including previous cases from the United Kingdom. Tort law derives most of its rules from British precedents and they are mostly still binding in Hong Kong. The Legislative Council has also made binding laws in these fields after the handover, such as the Sex Discrimination Ordinance (Cap 480) (SDO).

9. The law of torts is part of the English common law system, which has been developing incrementally since the Norman Conquest of 1066 in England. Historically, Hong Kong was once a British colony, and adopted the English common law system; hence, the development of tort law in Hong Kong is primarily based upon the English common law, rules of equity and English statutes. As a result, Hong Kong tort law has been developed from case law and legislation from both the English and Hong Kong legal systems.

10. Before the handover of sovereignty from Britain to the People's Republic of China on 1st July 1997, the sources of law in Hong Kong were: (1) case law, including the decisions of the Privy Council and Hong Kong courts; (2) legislation passed by the Hong Kong legislative council; (3) the English Acts and Orders in Council which were applicable to Hong Kong; and (4) Chinese law and custom. However, after the handover on 1st July 1997, the main sources of law in Hong Kong switched to the following: (1) the Basic Law; (2) the laws previously in force in Hong Kong; (3) the common law rules of equity, ordinances, subordinate legislation and customary law pursuant to Article 8 of the Basic Law; (4) legislation passed by the Hong Kong Special Administrative Region (HKSAR) legislature pursuant to Article 18 of the Basic Law; (5) case law, including the decisions of the Court of Final Appeal (CFA) of Hong Kong, and other Hong Kong courts; and (6) the Chinese national law, as listed in Annex III to the Basic Law.

11. Hong Kong tort law has relied on various ordinances, including the Application of English Law Ordinance 1966 (Cap 88) ('AELO') and the Bill of Rights Ordinance (Cap 383), along with the Basic Law itself. Initially, tort law as introduced to Hong Kong by the Supreme Court Ordinance (No 15 of 1844). Later on, a modified reception of the English law was implemented through the AELO to Hong Kong. As stated in section 3(1) of the AELO: '*The common law and the rules of equity shall be in force in Hong Kong... so far as they are applicable to the circumstances of Hong Kong or its inhabitants*'.

12. However, after the PRC resumed sovereignty over Hong Kong on 1st July 1997, the AELO was no longer part of the laws of Hong Kong. This change was made by the Standing Committee of the National People's Congress ('NCPSC') after considering the issue of treatment of laws previously in force in Hong Kong. This decision was made in accordance with Article 160 of the Basic Law of HKSAR, which declares that, '*... the laws previously in force in Hong Kong shall be adopted as laws of the Region except for those which the Standing Committee of the National People's Congress declares to be in contravention of this Law*'. Further, Articles 5 and 8 of the Basic Law of the HKSAR 1997 replaced the Royal Orders on Hong Kong and defined '*the laws previously in force in Hong Kong*' as '*the common law, rules of equity, ordinances, subordinate legislation and customary law*'. The Hong Kong Reunification

Ordinance (Cap 2601) finally confirmed the operation of the common law and the maintenance of laws previously in force in Hong Kong with such '*modifications, adaptations, limitations and exceptions as may be necessary so as not to contravene the Basic Law and to bring them into conformity with the status of Hong Kong as a Special Administrative Region of the People's Republic of China*'.[1] Hence, the old English common law continues to apply in Hong Kong and new case law that is developed in the Hong Kong courts will continue to add to the sources of tort law. Further, various new statutes and ordinances have the effect of supplementing, modifying or displacing tort law in Hong Kong.

§3. The Function of the Law of Torts

13. A tortious duty is primarily fixed by law and a person is liable under tort only when he breaches a duty imposed by law. One of the main purposes of tort law is *'to provide compensation to the injured'* for harm that is wrongfully suffered.[2] Tort law hence provides the claimant with an option to seek damages through the justice system against a person who has committed a wrong against him or her, whether the wrong is deliberate (as in trespass) or unintentional (as in negligence). Tortious liability can be categorized as intentional, unintentional or strict in nature. For strict liability torts, even if there is no finding of fault by the defendant, he or she is held liable once the occurrence of the damage is proved. As a result, persons conducting activities that may attract strict liability in tort usually insure others against the harm their activities may cause. Negligent torts are caused by the negligent acts of the tortfeasor, which include both deliberate and unintentional acts and omissions. The tortfeasor will only be found liable for the reasonably foreseeable consequences of his or her act or omission. The tort of negligence has wide applicability, which is shown in the landmark case of *Donoghue v. Stevenson.*[3] Intentional torts focus on the deliberate actions on the part of the defendant, such as trespass.[4] Therefore, whether a person is liable for an intentional tort depends on the mental state of the person rather than the damages caused by the person. This differentiation between strict liability torts and intentional torts applies in Hong Kong. Further, Order 18 rule 12 of the Rules of the High Court of Hong Kong states that, where a party's pleading alleges any condition of the mind of any person, he must state the particulars of fact which constitute that state of mind.

14. In a 'strict liability' claim, no fault on the part of the defendant is required to be proven by the claimant. As liability can be found without fault, the carelessness or intention of the tortfeasor is not relevant in an action over a strict liability tort. Strict liability torts can arise in a wide variety of circumstances, such as for injuries caused by dangerous animals[5] or injuries resulting from the breach of statutory duty (e.g., Employees Compensation Ordinance (Cap 282) (ECO)).[6]

---

1. Hong Kong Reunification Ordinance (Cap 2601), s. 5.
2. *Dobson v. Dobson* [1999] 4LRC 291, 293 (Cory J).
3. [1932] AC 562.
4. *Letang v. Cooper* [1965] 1 QB 232 (CA).
5. *Halsbury's Laws of Hong Kong* (2nd edn, Lexis Nexis 2012) Vol. 2, para. 20.146.
6. *World Wide Stationery Manufacturing Co Ltd v. Fong Chi Leung* [1994] 2 HKC 449 (CA).

15. The principal purpose of tort law is to reimburse plaintiffs who have suffered harm to their interests or rights due to the tortious acts or omissions of the defendant. The award of damages in a tortious action is subject to the court's discretion and is unliquidated in nature. This characteristic distinguishes tortious liability from contract or bailment, where the duty is directed towards particular persons and the amount of damages is pre-determined and liquidated.

16. The nature of tortious liability and the interests protected by tort law are diverse. The protected interests include land and reputation. Tortious liability covers a lot of different areas, such as the employer-employee relationship, use of land, professional responsibility, and trespass to person/land and products. Examples of torts are occupiers liability,[7] employers liability in negligence,[8] vicarious liability,[9] nuisance,[10] medical negligence,[11] negligence generally,[12] product liability,[13] and trespass.[14]

17. Tort serves two main functions: indemnification and deterrence. Not only does tort law protect the interests of people and compensate them for the harms they have sustained, but it also prevents future harms by developing laws requiring the reduction of the risk of harm. While awarding damages to the plaintiff to make good the loss suffered by him or her, the courts take into consideration a number of parameters in order to distribute the loss.

18. The first aim of tort law is to accomplish corrective justice by providing compensation to people who have suffered injury as a result of a tort. It is the existence of legal fault, rather than moral fault that warrants compensation. In calculating the monetary compensation, the court makes sure that the damages include both the wrongdoer's wrongful gain as well as the claimant's unjust loss. Secondly, tort law serves as deterrence to the tortfeasor through awarding exemplary damages. The imposition of exemplary damages is proven to be a useful tool to deter tortious acts and omissions as tortfeasors are required to pay monetary compensation to the claimant, especially those defendants who have *'calculated that the money to be made out of his wrongdoing will probably exceed the damages at risk'*.[15] Further, since litigation can tarnish the tortfeasor's professional reputation, the imposition of duty of care encourages people to act within the reasonably acceptable standards in their industry.

7. Occupier's Liability Ordinance (Cap 314) imposes duty and liability on the occupiers in relation to damage or injury occurred as a result of defects in the condition of the premises.
8. *Cathay Pacific Airways Ltd v. Wong Sau Lai* [2006] 2 HKLRD 586 (CFA).
9. *Lister v. Hesley Hall Ltd* [2001] UKHL 22 (HL).
10. *Rylands v. Fletcher* [1868] UKHL 1 (HL).
11. *Bolam v. Friern Hospital Management Committee* [1957] 1 WLR 582.
12. *Donoghue v. Stevenson* [1932] UKHL 100 (HL).
13. *Donoghue v. Stevenson* [1932] UKHL 100; *Lam Mo Bun v. Hong Kong Aerosol Co Ltd & Others* [2001] 1 HKLRD 540.
14. *Bird v. Jones* [1845] 115 ER 668.
15. *Rookes v. Barnard* [1964] AC 1129, 1126–1227 cited in *Lau Oi Kiu v. Man Chun Shing & Anor* [2015] 4 HKC 73.

§4. The Relationship Between Torts and Criminal Law

19. Criminal law is a branch of public law that governs relationships between individuals and the government, as well as interactions between individuals that are directly related to public duties. Criminal law serves to protect the public rights of a person from the criminal acts of the offenders. As a result, criminal actions are usually brought by public prosecutors on behalf of a state. In Hong Kong, all criminal prosecutions are instituted by the Secretary of Justice (SJ) in the name of the 'HKSAR'.[16] The outcome of the case is either a guilty or not guilty verdict, and the guilty offender is punishable by fine or imprisonment. The burden of proof lies upon the prosecution, who must prove the case beyond reasonable doubt. The defendant also has a fundamental right to access legal representation and the right to appeal against conviction and/or sentence.

20. The rationales for tort and criminal cases are different, though they are sometimes linked. In general, criminal courts are not intended to provide compensation to the victims for the harm they have suffered; nor are civil courts set up to punish the wrongdoers. However, in exceptional circumstances, such purposes may be served. For example, in cases where someone has deliberately injured another person (i.e., assault) the person committing the assault may be found guilty for the offence and be sentenced for imprisonment in a criminal court.[17] However, if the defendant's conduct shows malice, fraud, cruelty, insolence or the like that warrants the punishment of exemplary damages, the defendant may also be responsible for compensating the victim for personal injury and loss or damage of property.[18] Evidence of a criminal conviction, such as a certificate of trial, can also be the basis for proving liability in a tort case for compensation.

§5. The Relationship Between Contractual and Delictual or Tortious Responsibility

21. Certain areas of law, such as that which relates to torts, contract, property, administrative, family and revenue law fall under the ambit of civil law and share common roots. In a civil action, private rights or interests of the plaintiff are protected. The standard of proof in civil proceedings is determined on the balance of probabilities/ preponderance of evidence. The purpose of all civil proceedings, including tort and contract, is to protect rights, to recover property and to enforce obligations. Usually, civil proceedings are instituted by individuals against other individuals, corporations or the government.

---

16. *See HKSAR v. Leung Chun Wai* [2003] HKCU 1421 (unreported, HCMA 152/2002, 10 Nov. 2003). Before 1 Jul. 1997, the criminal cases were instituted in the name of Attorney General or the Crown – *R v. Chan Wing Kuen* [1995] 1 HKC 470.
17. Section 40 of the Offence Against the Persons Ordinance (Cap 212) provides that: 'any person who is convicted of a common assault shall be guilty of an offence triable either summarily or upon indictment, and shall be liable to imprisonment for 1 year.'
18. *Abid Saeed v. Secretary for Justice* [2015] 2 HKC 187, [261].

22. Historically, there has been a close connection between tort and contract, and there is an acceptance of concurrent liability.[19] Despite the closeness between tort and contract, they can be distinguished from each other based on the origins of the relevant duties, the relationship between the parties and the damages awarded. Contractual claims require privity of contract between the parties whereas no such requirement exists for tortious claims. Moreover, damages in contract claims are liquidated while in tort damages remain unliquidated until it is decided by the court. Also, while the duty of care for the purposes of tort is imposed by law, contractual duties are usually created by negotiation between the parties, as illustrated in the case of *Donoghue v. Stevenson.*[20]

23. In Hong Kong there is no written rule as there is in French law of *la règle de non-cumul*, under which, where there is a contract, the case must be brought under contract law. In certain cases there might be an overlap, as in case of employer's negligence, and an employee can claim for breach of contract as well as under the tort of negligence. Hence it is possible to find liability in both tort and contract law. In *Henderson v. Merrett Syndicate Ltd,*[21] the House of Lords held that where the plaintiff has a contract with the defendant he may choose the more advantageous action to pursue when both tort and contract law are violated by the same situation.[22] Generally, where a contract exists, priority is given to contract law and, in the absence of a contract, tort action may be commenced.

24. In cases of economic loss, the distinction between tort and contract may not be clear-cut and the plaintiff has an option to bring an action in either tort or contract. Traditionally speaking, economic loss was recoverable under contract law. However, the courts nowadays allow, in special circumstances, economic losses caused by negligent misrepresentations under tort law. In *Hedley Byrne & Co v. Heller & Partners,*[23] the House of Lords recognized the existence of a duty of care in a non-contractual context (tort) where the defendant assumes responsibility for the loss suffered by the plaintiff, unless, of course, a contract between them precludes that liability.

§6. Protected Interests (Are All Interested Equally Protected?)

25. Various policy considerations and societal factors affect protection of the plaintiff's interest under tort law. These considerations include the prevailing morality and other sociological and economic factors, as well as practical issues, such as risk of opening the floodgates, cost of litigation, etc. In general, tort law provides compensation to plaintiffs for harm caused by the actions or omissions of the defendant. A duty of care must exist and should have been breached, causing harm to the plaintiff. Generally the tort law covers areas such as negligence, employer's liability in negligence, vicarious

---

19. *Henderson v. Merrett Syndicate Ltd* [1995] 2 AC 145 (HL). *Henderson* overruled *Tai Hing Cotton Mill Ltd v. Liu Chong Hing Bank Ltd* [1985] 2 All ER 947 (PC).
20. [1932] AC 562.
21. [1995] 2 AC 145 (HL).
22. *Henderson v. Merrett Syndicate Ltd* [1995] 2 AC 145 (HL).
23. [1964] AC 465 (HL).

liability, occupier's liability, nuisance, *Rylands v. Fletcher*[24] liability, economic torts, reputation, product liability, trespass, etc.

24. (1868) LR 3 HL 330.

Part I. Liability for One''s Own Acts

Chapter 1. General Principles

§1. Unlawfulness and Fault: The Standard of Care and Its Breach

26. Courts determine whether a duty of care has been breached by the defendant by applying the objective 'reasonable person test'. The 'reasonable person' is hypothetical, created by the judiciary. The test tries to determine whether, in similar circumstances, the defendant's acts fall below a reasonable person's prudence. In other words, it is assessed whether the defendant has fallen below a certain standard of behaviour that is acceptable in the conduct of human affairs, given the considerations that ordinarily regulate society. In *Vaughan v. Menlove,*[25] the court stated that, to assess whether the defendant's conduct was honest and bona fide, it must ask itself 'whether the individual *'proceed[ed] with such reasonable caution as a prudent man would have exercised under such circumstances'*. Hence, this test provides courts with the discretion to assess the defendant's conduct from the 'reasonableness' perspective, which is adjustable depending on the type of circumstances and defendants involved, based on their experiences and skills. Therefore, reasonableness is based on particular circumstances instead of being a specific duty. In *N v. Agrawal,*[26] the plaintiff complained to the police after she was raped and buggered by a third party. The defendant medical practitioner, an accredited Rape and Child Abuse Forensic Medical Examiner, examined and submitted her findings in a witness statement. The defendant was told she would not be needed at the time but that she would be contacted in the following week, so she went on her holidays. The judge was unwilling to adjourn until her return, so the plaintiff lost her case, and sued the defendant for exacerbating her PTSD symptoms. The defendant was not held liable. Stuart-Smith LJ stated: '*If a duty of care exists at all it is a duty to take reasonable care to prevent the plaintiff from suffering injury, loss or damage of the type in question, in this case psychiatric injury. A failure to attend to give evidence could be a breach of such duty; but it is not the duty itself.*'[27]

27. As shown above, the degree of care is formulated by considering: (1) specific situations, such as those involving emergency, professional skills, etc., or (2) setting

25. (1837) 132 ER 490 (CP).
26. [1999] PNLR 939.
27. [1999] PNLR 939, 943.

the standard of care according to foreseeability of harm or magnitude of the risk, which includes the social utility of the defendant's activity and the cost of taking precautions, etc. The objective test looks at the type of activity undertaken, not the tendencies of the particular defendant. Thus, the same standard will be expected of professionals in a particular post. Lack of experience is irrelevant because, once qualified, society believes that the person is able to complete the job, and also because it is hard to determine when a professional can be considered experienced. An example would be *Nettleship v. Weston*,[28] where a learner driver was denied a lower standard of care than an average driver. The big question here is to find out how a reasonable person with a particular skill would act under certain circumstances. As per Mustill LJ in *Wilsher*, a junior doctor undertaking specialist work cannot claim a lower standard of duty due to his status as a beginner with less experience. The standard should not just be that of an average, competent, and well-informed inexperienced person, but that of a person who is part of a highly specialized service unit.[29] Similarly, an inexperienced golfer may not escape liability for injuring his caddie by claiming he must be held at a lower standard of duty for inconsistent play or failure to take appropriate precautions.[30]

28. In *Glasgow Corp v. Muir*,[31] the appellant's manageress allowed a picnic party to be hosted in their tearoom. Two men on the premises spilled hot tea from an urn, which scalded children. A case was brought on the children's behalf, contending that the appellant's manageress had been negligent in allowing the urn to be carried around on the premises. The children succeeded at trial, but the House of Lords reversed the decision. They held that liability should be limited to consequences of acts that a reasonable person would have considered. The appellant's manageress had no reason to anticipate that such an event would occur. Thus, she is not obliged to take precautions against the occurrence of such an event. An important note about the 'reasonable person' test is that courts are only concerned with how the reasonable person would have acted in the circumstances. Lord Macmillan stated:

> The standard of foresight of the reasonable man is in one sense an impersonal test. It eliminates the personal equation and is independent of the idiosyncrasies of the particular person whose conduct is in question. Some persons are by nature unduly timorous and imagine every path beset with lions; others, of more robust temperament, fail to foresee or nonchalantly disregard even the most obvious dangers. The reasonable man is presumed to be free both from over-apprehension and from overconfidence.[32]

29. As discussed above, it is clear that the standard of care required under the reasonable person test is what constitutes reasonable conduct for the defendant under the circumstances, not about the relationship between the parties. The nature of the relationship falls under duty of care, not standard. To find out whether there is a breach of duty; one must determine whether the defendant has fallen below the standard of care expected of the reasonable person under the circumstances. Hence, the objective standard of a reasonable person may not always reflect 'average' behaviour, as that

28. [1971] 2QB 691 (CA).
29. *Wilsher v. Essex Area Health Authority* [1987] QB 730 (CA) (Lord Mustill).
30. *Chau Fung Yee v. Lee Chi Ming* [2000] 2 HKLRD 690, 694–696 (CFI) (Seagroatt J).
31. [1943] 2 AC 448.
32. *Glasgow Corp v. Muir* [1943] 2 AC 448, 459.

will be determined on a case-by-case basis. In certain cases, influenced by policy reasons, meeting an 'average' standard may not be enough to avoid breach of duty. This is most evident in traffic accident cases, where a higher standard may be imposed since most defendants are insured and imposing similar standards on all drivers, irrespective of their experience, is more reasonable.[33]

I. The Common Standard of Care in Special Situations

30. The objectivity of the expected standard of care helps courts focus on types of activity without having to create a subjective standard for the particular defendant involved. The test looks at the degree of skill appropriate to an activity rather than considering the defendant's experience. The legitimate expectations of the plaintiff are given priority to make sure that the public is protected. This test also allows the standard of a reasonable person to be compared to the defendant's characteristics (e.g., experience, age or maturity).[34] However, applying this test to the elderly and infirm may be problematic. On the surface, it seems that the law is prepared to give special consideration to elderly plaintiffs suffering injuries, and not elderly defendants causing injuries. An elderly driver enjoys no free passes, as the public expects a common minimum safe standard from all drivers. In *Roberts v. Ramsbottom*,[35] Neill J regarded the age of the defendant irrelevant and stated: '*The driver will be able to escape liability if his actions at the relevant time were wholly beyond his control. The most obvious case is sudden unconsciousness. But if he retained some control, albeit imperfect control, and his driving, judged objectively, was below the required standard, he remains liable. His position is the same as a driver who is old or infirm.*'[36]

31. Furthermore, if compulsory insurance is in effect, there is no reason for free passes. In *Nettleship v. Weston*,[37] the plaintiff acted as a driving instructor for the defendant. The defendant panicked, causing the plaintiff to be injured in an accident. The Court of Appeal held that if inexperience is no defence in criminal law, there is no reason to lower the degree or standard for learner drivers under civil law.

32. For people with physical or mental incapacities, they must conform to the standard of an average person with the same disability taken into account. They are required to take greater precautions, as they should recognize the limitations caused by their conditions. For example, if a car driver with poor eyesight, who has not done anything to rectify it, causes an accident, he puts others in danger by carelessly choosing to drive in the first place. Where the defendant's incapacity was caused by factors totally beyond their control, like a stroke or heart attack, causing the defendant to lose the mental capacity to control his actions, the court may apply a lower standard due to the exceptional circumstances of the case.[38] However, if the defendant is aware of his medical condition, he will be held liable. For example, in *Lin Chun Yuen & Anor*

33. Motor Vehicles Insurance (Third Party Risks) Ordinance (Cap 272).
34. *McHale v. Watson* [1996] 115 CLR 866.
35. [1980] 1 WLR 823.
36. [1980] 1 WLR 823, 833.
37. [1971] 2 QB 691.
38. *Mok Ka Yin v. Tsang Hing On* [2007] 2 HKLRD 858, [2007] HKCU 1006.

v. Kwong Kam Chuen & Anor,[39] the defendant was a public light bus driver who killed a woman after having lost control of the bus. He claimed that he was in a state of automatism induced by a disease, and he had failed to take medication for it on the day of the accident. The court held the defendant liable as they took a risk by not taking medication, finding that the accident was a direct result of his negligence, and not a medical condition he was unaware of.

33. The objective standard of care will differ in special situations (e.g., emergency situations, sports, children, and professionally skilled persons). The defendant's liability while responding to emergencies is determined by whether his conduct can be viewed as being what a reasonable person's conduct would be under the same circumstances. In *Parkinson v. Liverpool Corporation*,[40] the defendant driver was not held liable when a passenger was thrown out of the bus due to his sudden braking to avoid a dog that suddenly appeared on the road. Similarly, in *Sze Ha Kam Carly v. Chum Chi On*,[41] the defendant hit the brakes sharply to avoid collision with another vehicle, but he lost control and hit a road divider. He was not held to have been negligent, as he was merely responding to an emergency situation that was not of his making. The judge believed that to find the defendant liable for not foreseeing and taking precautions for the cutting in would be too harsh. He accepted the defendant's evidence of there being no vehicle in front of him, and that the increase of speed by the other vehicle did not mean an indication to overtake. Under the Road Users' Code 1997 and Road Traffic (Traffic Control) Regulations (Cap 374 sub Leg G), drivers must stop at pedestrian crossings. If the circumstances of the situation force a driver to hit a pedestrian crossing at an inappropriate time, their actions will be judged from the standpoint of a reasonable person.

34. Participation in sports is somewhat similar to emergency situations, as the competitors may have to act in the spur of the moment. In sports injuries cases, the defendant is not liable for mere errors of judgment that cause injury or damage to others, as there is an implicit agreement that some scuffle will occur once someone agrees to participate in a sports game. Liability is determined by how a reasonable person would have acted in similar circumstances. Despite the implicit agreement, all participants have a duty towards each other to take all reasonable care. In *Chau Fung Yee v. Lee Chi Ming*,[42] an inexperienced golfer hit his caddie in the mouth and teeth with a ball. The defendant golfer was found negligent, since he took no precautions in light of his erratic play. The plaintiff caddie was also held contributory negligent for her own injuries, since she was aware of the defendant's inexperience. Different standards apply to accidents between fellow competitors and in spectator-competitor accidents. For example, in *Vowles v. Evans*,[43] a rugby referee (the defendant) was held liable for allowing a game to continue after the injury of the plaintiff player. However, the court emphasized that the standard for referees should be at a higher threshold for exposing participants to the risk of injury.

39. [2002] HKEC 1472.
40. [1950] 1 All ER 367.
41. HKCU [2010].
42. [2000] 2 HKLRD 690 (CFI).
43. [2003] 1 WLR 1607.

35. A child is held at a lower standard of care than an adult. A child merely has to conform to the standard of an ordinary child of his age and maturity. In *Mullin v. Richards,*[44] 15-year-old girls were playing 'fencing' with plastic rulers in class. The plastic ruler hit the plaintiff in her eye when it snapped, and caused her to go blind. The court held the defendant to be not liable, as children and teenagers commonly played the game, so the risk of injury was not foreseeable. Hutchinson LJ stated:

> Taking the view therefore that the learned judge… on his findings of fact that there was negligence on the part of both these young ladies—was wrong in his view and there was no evidence on which he could come to it, I would allow the appeal and direct that judgment be entered for the first defendant. I have to say that I appreciate that this result will be disappointing to the plaintiff for whom one can have nothing but sympathy, because she has suffered a grave injury through no fault of her own. But unfortunately she has failed to establish in my view that anyone was legally responsible for that injury and, accordingly, her claim should have failed.[45]

36. In *McHale v. Watson,*[46] a 12-year-old boy threw sharp metal at a post near where a 9-year-old girl was standing, and caused her eye an injury. The court dismissed the case, finding no breach of duty, as the conduct must be judged by the foresight and judgment of an ordinary boy of the same age. Generally, the court will consider the child's mental ability, background and maturity for the purposes of determining liability.

37. The standard of care for professionals is determined by what is normally done by reasonable, prudent professionals in that industry. For imposing liability on a defendant who possesses special skills (e.g., doctor, lawyer), the court will determine whether the person measured up to the standard of proficiency expected of him as a professional. This standard is higher than it is for a reasonable person with no such skill. However, the professional does not have to guarantee a particular result. For example, a solicitor cannot guarantee that his client will win a case. In *Bolam v. Friern Hospital Management Committee,*[47] the defendant gave E.C.T. to the plaintiff without applying any form of manual restraint, in accordance with his normal practice. The plaintiff tried to claim damages for the defendant's negligence in failing to administer any relaxant drug, and failing to warn him of the risks involved in treatment. The defendant was not held liable as he conformed to the custom of a responsible professional body. Ultimately, this case confirmed two principles, known as the *Bolam* test: (1) where the defendant has special skills, they are to be judged by the standard of a reasonable person who possesses such skills; (2) the professional defendant will not be held liable if it is shown that his conduct was regarded as proper by a responsible body in their profession.

38. In *Sidaway v. Board of Governors of the Bethlem Royal Hospital,*[48] the issue was whether a doctor had the duty to inform a patient of every single risk before an operation. Rejecting the plaintiff's claim, the court held that consent did not mean that

44. [1998] 1 WLR 1304.
45. [1998] 1 WLR 1304, 927.
46. (1965) 111 CLR 384.
47. [1957] 2 All ER 118.
48. [1985] AC 871 (HL).

an explanation of remote side effects was needed. Lord Scarman dissented, stating that the *Bolam* test should not apply to informed consent cases, and that it should be the doctor's duty to inform his patients of the inherent and material risks of the proposed treatment.

39. In a key turn of events, on 11 March 2015, the UK Supreme Court in *Montgomery v. Lanarkshire Health Board*[49] partly overturned the *Bolam* test regarding the doctor's liability in informed consent cases. Montgomery (the appellant) gave birth to a severely disabled child, and attributed the injuries to the negligence of a doctor working under the respondent company. The grounds on which she claimed negligence are: (1) she was not given any advice regarding the risk of shoulder dystocia before vaginal birth; and (2) the doctor failed to perform a C-section when cardio abnormalities were detected during labour. Instead of leaving it to medical professionals to determine what should be disclosed to patients, the Supreme Court held that the approach should be taken from a patient's perspective, since it takes personal autonomy and human rights into account. This decision was also in light of the fact that Montgomery studied molecular biology, and also had family members that were medical practitioners, so she was highly informed when it came to human body-related topics. Although Hong Kong tends to follow UK common law, the impact of this decision on future similar cases has yet to be seen.

40. There are problems with the *Bolam* test, such as how professionals can put themselves above the law and not be answerable to the plaintiff, as long as their behaviour is approved by a body of professionals, even if it is an unusual situation. The *Bolam* test was limited by *Bolitho v. Hackney Health Authority*.[50] This case concerned the cardiac arrest and death of a child with breathing difficulties. The defendants accepted that their doctor should have attended to the plaintiff, or arranged an appropriate person to do so. The court also had to consider whether the doctor should have intubated the child when they could have saved him. The doctor claimed that neither she nor any other doctor would have intubated the child. Lord Brown-Wilkinson dismissed the appeal on the grounds that the doctor was not negligent for doing what was accepted by an expert responsible body of medical opinion. However, it was also held that the court must be satisfied that the opinion has a logical basis. Judges have the discretion to reject logically indefensible opinions of expert bodies.

II. Factors Used by Courts to Assess Standard of Care (Risks and Benefits)

41. Depending on the circumstances, the court considers different factors in assessing the standard of care required by the defendant. The defendant should have foreseen the harm, and appreciate the magnitude of the risk (i.e., probability of the injury occurring, and knowledge of the severity). The social utility of the defendant's activities, the cost of taking precautions, and failure to conform to common practice would also be considered.

49. [2015] UKSC 11.
50. (1998) AC 232 (HL).

42. The standard of care expected from a defendant is such that if the harm that the plaintiff suffers is not foreseeable by a reasonable person, then the defendant will not be liable. Precautions against harm are only required for harm that is reasonably foreseeable, with reference to the knowledge that the defendant should have at the relevant time. In *Bolton v. Stone*,[51] the defendant's cricket ball managed to hit the plaintiff after going over a 17-feet-high fence that was 78 yards away from the defendant, and the fence was 100 yards away from where the plaintiff was standing. Evidence shows that balls had only strayed over the fence five or six times in the past thirty years, so it was rare for the ball to stray to begin with, let alone hit a stranger. The plaintiff lost the case, since the possibility of such an accident was not foreseeable. An important point was that, in the five or six times a ball had strayed, it had not hit anyone. The House of Lords also stated that the cricket club was not negligent in doing nothing about the risk of someone being injured by a flyaway cricket ball, because the cricket club would have to stop playing at that ground entirely to completely avoid such injuries from occurring again, when it was merely carrying out a lawful and socially useful activity. The situation in *Bolton* can be contrasted with that in *Miller v. Jackson*,[52] as the cricket balls in the latter case strayed from the grounds on eight or nine occasions per season. As the risk of harm was much higher, the cricket club was found negligent for not taking preventative actions to reduce the risk as much as reasonably possible.

43. If the magnitude of any risk reaches threatening levels, the court will consider the likelihood of harm. A reasonable man is not usually expected to take precautions against an event that only has a miniscule chance of occurring. A merely theoretical chance of an accident occurring will not be enough to prove a breach of duty of care by the defendant. In the case of *Overseas Tankship (U.K.) Ltd v. The Miller Steamship Co and Anor (The Wagon Mound No. 2)*,[53] neighbouring ships were burned due to the ignition of furnace oil negligently leaked into Sydney harbour from a vessel owned by the defendant. Had the defendants breached their duty of care by not preventing the fire? It was held by the Privy Council that the risk of was foreseeable, though small. With respect to the vessel's chief engineer, Lord Reid stated that, '*The only question is whether a reasonable man, having the knowledge and experience to be expected of the chief engineer of the Wagon Mound would have known that there was a real risk of the oil on the water catching fire in some way: if it did, serious damage to ships or other property was not only foreseeable but very likely.*' If a real risk of harm would be perceived by a reasonable person in the defendant's position, they have a duty to take steps to prevent it.[54] In the case of *Haley v. London Electricity Board*,[55] the defendants were liable for an accident in which a blind person fell into a hole that the defendants had dug. The risk was not so small that it could be ignored. Precautions should have been taken, bearing in mind the blind people residing in the area.

44. Regarding the magnitude of risk, the seriousness of injury is also considered by courts when setting a standard of care, and balancing the risks and rewards involved.

51. [1951] AC 850.
52. [1977] 3 All ER 338 (CA).
53. [1967] 1 AC 617 (PC).
54. *Mourton v. Poulter* [1930] 2 KB 183.
55. [1965] AC 778 (HL).

Even if the risk of harm is small, where the gravity of the injuries that could occur is great, then a reasonable man would be expected to take precautions. An example would be *Paris v. Stepney Borough Council,*[56] when the plaintiff was already blind in his left eye, and his good right eye was blinded by a metal chip striking it while working for the defendants. The defendants were found negligent in omitting to supply him with protective goggles, as the injuries that he could have, and did, sustain were serious. If there is a danger to life and personal safety, then the defendant is to be held as owing a higher degree of care.[57]

45. The purpose and social utility of the situation in which the accident occurs is also assessed. For example, in *Daborn v. Bath Tramways Motor Co Ltd*,[58] the plaintiff was injured in an accident with an ambulance during the Second World War. The ambulance had a sign saying 'left-hand drive no signal'. The accident occurred after the defendant attempted to turn after using a hand signal, which was not seen by the plaintiff. It was held that the defendant's conduct was reasonable in that time of national emergency and had social utility, and the defendant was not liable. This can be contrasted with *Overseas Tankship (UK) Ltd v. Miller Steamship Pty Ltd (The Wagon Mound (No. 2)),*[59] where the defendant's activity was not justified. Lord Reid stated:[60]

In the present case there was no justification whatever for discharging the oil into Sydney Harbour. Not only was it an offence to do so, but it involved considerable loss financially. If the ship's engineer had thought about the matter, there could have been no question of balancing the advantages and disadvantages. From every point of view it was both his duty and his interest to stop the discharge immediately.

46. In *Tomlinson v. Congleton Borough Council,*[61] the plaintiff visited an artificial lake within a country park under the defendant's jurisdiction. The plaintiff struck his head hard on the sandy bottom from a poorly executed dive, which broke his neck at the fifth vertebrae. This case raised issues regarding social utility on top of the "Occupiers' Liability Act 1957/1984. Lord Hoffmann considered the enjoyment against the consequences of risk, and concluded that the defendant did not have to take further steps to prevent swimming in the lake. Lord Hobhouse of Woodborough stated: *'The pursuit of an unrestrained culture of blame and compensation has many evil consequences and one is certainly the interference with the liberty of the citizen. Of course there is some risk of accidents arising out of the joie de vivre of the young, but that is no reason for imposing a grey and dull safety regime on everyone.'*[62] *Glasgow Corporation v. Taylor*[63] was considered, where Lord Shaw of Dunfermline stated: *'Grounds thrown open by a municipality to the public may contain objects of natural beauty, say precipitous cliffs or the banks of streams, the dangers of the resort to which are plain.'* Thus, it is evident that the court considers the risks and rewards of social utility at

56. [1951] 1 All ER 42 (HL).
57. *Luen Hing Fat Coating & Finishing Factory Ltd v. Wan Chuen Ming* 61 (2011) 14 HKCFAR 14.
58. [1946] 2 All ER 333.
59. [1967] 1 AC 617.
60. [1967] 1 AC 617, 643.
61. [2003] UKHL 47.
62. [2003] UKHL 47, 81.
63. [1922] 1 AC 44, 61.

leisure places that may have physical features capable of causing injury to careless persons or children alongside the protective measures already taken by the defendant. Obviously, it may not be possible to protect against all injuries, so the defendant will not be liable for not taking measures that a reasonable person would consider unnecessary. In *Hastie v. Magistrates of Edinburgh,*[64] Lord President stated that there are certain risks which the law, in accordance with common sense, does not protect people from, as they are *'just one of the results of the world as we find it'.*[65]

47. The failure to take precautions requiring a lot of resources to prevent accidents would not make the defendant liable (e.g., constructing expensive walkways). However, if the cost is not high, or the correction is necessary, the defendant would be held liable. The damp floors of a factory led to the electrocution of a worker in *Wong Tak-hing v. Tai Sang Industrial Co Ltd,*[66] and it was established that this was a common risk in factories. The defendants were held liable for not taking reasonable steps to keep the floors dry and safe for use. Similarly, in *Knight v. Home Office,*[67] the plaintiff's husband had suicidal tendencies, and tried to act on them one day in the prison hospital, and an officer working for the defendant ended up injuring the husband while trying to stop him from hurting himself. The defendant was not held liable as prisons did not have enough resources at their disposal to build a hospital wing specifically for mentally unstable people like him. A prison's duty of care is different from a mental hospital's, and it is held at a lower standard since it only has to ensure certain things, e.g., that no one escapes. The defendant was not liable this time, since it was the first time such an incident had occurred. However, generally, the risk and frequency of accidents should make the defendant more vigilant to avoid them in order to avoid being found liable for negligence (e.g., petrol stations contain flammable items, so precautions should be taken to ensure no items capable of igniting them are brought onto the premises).

48. In terms of the failure to conform to common practice, the defendant is held liable only if he fails to take reasonable precautions as taken by other fellow professionals, or if the defendant does not conform to the standards of practice expected. For example, the solicitors in *Li Fook Chu v. HH & Co*[68] were found negligent for not warning their clients that their claim for the recovery of a loan was time-barred. This was a failure to conform to the standards of the solicitor's profession.[69] Conformity to codes or statutes is within the community's reasonable expectations from professionals. However, in some exceptional cases, adherence to common practice may expose the plaintiff to unreasonable risks, which the defendant could be still liable for.[70] This is in accordance with *Bolitho v. Hackney Health Authority,*[71] where it was held that the court is entitled to hold professional opinion to be unreasonable if it has no 'logical basis'. With the development of third-party insurance, the community's expectations have expanded

64. [1907] SC 1102.
65. [1907] SC 1102, 1106.
66. [1975] HKLR 375.
67. [1990] 3 All ER 237.
68. [2006] 3 HKC 433.
69. (Vol. I, Rule 2.03).
70. *Lloyd's Bank Ltd v. Savory & Co* [1933] AC 201.
71. [1998] AC 232 (HL).

to expect liability to be imposed on all defendants, including drivers of all ages or experiences. This is because the defendants are insured; imposing similar standards on all drivers is reasonable.[72] Therefore, in motor accident cases, discussion is on whom the risk should fall on, as opposed to fault. The rise in public expectations has given rise to ingenious methods to improve safety standards.

III. Res Ipsa Loquitur (Rule of Evidence)

49. The burden of proof rests on the plaintiff to show that the defendant has more likely than not been careless on the balance of probabilities (e.g., falling objects cases). For the proof of carelessness, the plaintiff can rely on the Evidence Ordinance (Cap 8), which allows for criminal convictions to serve as admissible evidence in civil proceedings. Under section 62, it states:

(1) In any civil proceedings the fact that a person has been convicted of an offence by or before any court in Hong Kong shall, subject to subsection (3), be admissible in evidence for the purpose of proving, where to do so is relevant to any issue in those proceedings, that he committed that offence, whether he was so convicted upon a plea of guilty or otherwise and whether or not he is a party to the civil proceedings; but no conviction other than a subsisting one shall be admissible in evidence by virtue of this section.

50. If it is virtually impossible for the plaintiff to prove the exact cause of their injury, or the defendant's negligence, due to lack of substantial evidence, he can invoke the principle of res ipsa loquitur. It means 'the thing speaks for itself', so it relies on the fact of the accident occurring to suggest the defendant's negligence.[73] The court tries to determine a reasonable evidential inference to see whether to hold the defendant liable.[74] Ribeiro PJ in *Yu Yu Kai v. Chan Chi Keung*[75] clarified the meaning of res ipsa loquitur:

43. Whether one uses the label res ipsa loquitur or one speaks (as Hobhouse LJ would have preferred) of establishing a prima facie case, one is concerned with a rule regarding the proper approach to the evidence. It is an approach whereby, in cases where the plaintiff is unable to say exactly how his injury was caused but, consonant with his duty of care, one may expect the defendant to know, one asks whether the evidence has raised a prima facie case against the defendant and if it has, whether the defendant has, at the end of the day, dispelled that prima facie case by providing a

72. Motor Vehicles Insurance (Third Party Risks) Ordinance (Cap 272).
73. *Pickford v. Imperial Chemical Industries plc* [1998] ICR 673.
74. *Ho Ka Yin v. Express Security Ltd* [2011] HKCU 1398.
75. (2009) 12 HKCFAR 705.

plausible explanation for the plaintiff's injury which is consistent with the absence of negligence on his part.[76]

51. The res ipsa loquitur principle originated from *Scott v. London and St Katherine Docks,*[77] and is applied in very few cases. To prove the case with res ipsa loquitur, the court must prove from case facts whether: (i) the harm could have occurred without negligence; (ii) the defendant had control over the cause of harm; and (iii) the cause of harm was unknown to the plaintiff. If these conditions are satisfied on the balance of probabilities, the defendant would be held negligent. In *Ho Ka Yin v. Express Security Ltd,*[78] the plaintiff fell off her wheelchair twice while using the defendant's lift. For the first accident, the defendant was held liable upon the application of res ipsa loquitur. McWalters J stated:

> In my view the conditions precedent to the operation of the rule are present in this case. First, the plaintiff is unable to say exactly how her injury was caused. Secondly, consonant with his duty of care, one may expect the defendant to know. Thirdly, the evidence has raised a prima facie case against the defendant. I say this because the evidence is that the accident happened when the plaintiff's wheelchair encountered an obstruction when the plaintiff, in compliance with the instructions of the defendant's staff who were supervising her, propelled the wheelchair to exit the lift platform … .

52. In *Chung Man Yau and Anor v. Sihon Co Ltd,*[79] the plaintiffs were injured after falling from a great height off a balcony. The court held that their injuries were evidence of the defendant's negligence; the defendant was the occupier of the building. Applying res ipsa loquitur it was held that such an accident could not have occurred without the defendant's negligence. In *Gee v. Metropolitan Railway Co,*[80] the plaintiff fell off a train when a door suddenly opened. Since the door was under the supervision and control of the defendant's company, the court inferred the evidence of the defendant's negligence from it and held the defendant liable. In the CFA case of *Sanfield Building Contracts Ltd v. Li Kai Cheong,*[81] the plaintiff was injured after falling from scaffolding provided by a subcontractor; the principal contractor, the appellant, was also found liable. The accident could not have happened, in the absence of contrary proof, if the appellant had taken reasonable care. Justice Bokhary's discussion on the doctrine of res ipsa loquitur covered Hong Kong and UK authorities, and described the doctrine as a *'mode of inferential reasoning'* applying *'to accidents of unknown cause'*.[82] Res ipsa loquitur does not apply if the cause of the accident is discovered after investigation (e.g., equipment issues, tyres bursting).[83]

---

76. (2009) 12 HKCFAR 705, 720, para. 43.
77. [1865] 3 Hurl. & C 596.
78. [2011] 4 HKRLD 395.
79. [1996] HKLY 668.
80. [1873] LR 8QB 161.
81. (FACV No. 16 of 2002, 12 Jun. 2003); (2003) 6 HKCFAR 207.
82. (FACV No. 16 of 2002, 12 Jun. 2003), para. 3.
83. *Barkway v. S. Wales Transport Co.* [1950] AC 185.

§2. The Concept of Fault

53. The concept of fault is closely connected to the tort of negligence. Although it is fair to say that all torts involve some sort of wrongdoing, this is distinct from the concept of fault for the purposes of the tort of negligence. It was in the nineteenth century that the law of tort was significantly altered in order to provide compensation to victims during the industrial revolution by expanding the ambit of the tort of negligence. During the time of the King's Courts in England, although remedies were available for victims suffering harm as a result of certain forms of careless conduct, the tort known today as negligence, or the general idea of a duty of care, had not yet come into existence. While attempts had been made towards establishing general liability in negligence, these efforts were hampered because the law of contract overlapped with the general duty of care.[84] It was not until the case of *Donoghue v. Stevenson* that the general duty of care was finally separated from the scope of contract.[85]

54. Liability in negligence can arise from careless acts or omissions causing damage. It must, however, be shown that the defendant owed a duty of care to the plaintiff; that the defendant breached the duty of care (such as by failing to act reasonably within the circumstances and in relation to their position with respect to the plaintiff); and that breach caused damage to the plaintiff. Causation must be established between the defendant's breach and the harm to person or property suffered by the plaintiff.

55. The tort of negligence applies to many aspects of societal dealings and sets standards as to how a reasonable person is expected to socially interact with others[86] and, where reasonable care has not been taken,[87] a person is held liable. The acts or omissions[88] giving rise to tortious liability depend[89] on the existence of a duty of care, its breach and the causation of the claimant's injury.[90]

§3. The Duty of Care

I. Identifying a General Duty: 'The Neighbour Principle and the Caparo Test'

56. There are, as aforementioned, many categories within the law of tort and under the tort of negligence; a plaintiff must ascertain which category of liability their claim lies within. In order to establish whether a duty of care was owed and breached, the plaintiff should look at their relationship with the alleged tortfeasor and at which

84. *Williams v. Holland* [1833] 10 Bing 112.
85. *Donoghue v. Stevenson* [1932] AC 562.
86. *Grant v. Australian Knitting Mills Ltd* [1936] AC 85, 103 (PC), (Lord Wright).
87. *Vaughan v. Taff Vale Rly Co* (1860) 5 H & N 679, 688 (Willes J).
88. *Blyth v. Birmingham Waterworks Co* (1856) 11 Exch 781, (1856) 156 ER 1047, 784 (Alderson B).
89. *Fardon v. Harcourt-Rivington* [1932] All ER Rep 81, (1932) 146 LT 391, 392 (HL) (Lord Dunedin).
90. *Lochgelly Iron and Coal Co Ltd v. M'Mullan* [1934] AC 1, 25 (HL) (Lord Wright).

interests of theirs were harmed and what damage they suffered, be it physical, economic, psychiatric or otherwise. In *Donoghue v. Stevenson,*[91] the landmark case in which a third party to a contract for the purchase of a bottle of ginger beer suffered ill effects after discovering a decomposing snail inside the bottle partway through partaking of it, we see the roots of the modern conception of the tort of negligence. Lord Atkin's famous adaptation of the Biblical concept of loving one's neighbour into a limited legal duty applies, taken at its widest, to situations in which the defendant would be able to reasonably foresee that their acts or omissions could cause harm to others. Lord Atkin defined the neighbour principle in the following words:

> That rule that you are to love your neighbour becomes, in law, you must not injure your neighbour, and the lawyer's question, "Who is my neighbour?" receives a restricted reply. You must take reasonable care to avoid acts or omissions which you can reasonably foresee would be likely to injure your neighbour. Who, in law, is my neighbour? The answer seems to be – persons who are so closely and directly affected by my act that I ought reasonably to have them in contemplation as being so affected when I am directing my mind to the acts or omissions which are called in question.[92]

57. In his formulation, Lord Atkin stated two requirements for establishing the existence of a duty of care: foreseeability and proximity. In his own words:

> Proximity in this sense is not confined to mere physical proximity but extends to close and direct relations between the parties. In this case the scope of the notional duty owed by a manufacturer to a consumer was defined by the requirement that injury to the consumer be foreseeable and that there be proximity in the sense that the product was intended to reach the ultimate consumer in the form in which it left the manufacturer, with no reasonable possibility of intermediate examination.[93]

58. Reasonable foreseeability is determined by the knowledge that a person in the defendant's shoes would ordinarily be expected to have, whilst proximity depends on the broader relationship between the parties to tortious claim[94] and consists of various forms of closeness, including physical, circumstantial, causal or assumed.[95] For instance, in the case of *Donoghue*, the manufacturer owed a duty of care to the plaintiff because the former intended his product to reach the ultimate consumer, which included the plaintiff (Mrs Donoghue). The significance of this case is that it separated the law of negligence from the law of contract and it was no longer necessary to establish the privity of contract before bringing a claim in negligence.[96] It is also important to note that, although there is no exhaustive list as to the categories of

91. *Donoghue v. Stevenson* [1932] AC 562.
92. *Donoghue v. Stevenson* [1932] AC 562 para. 580.
93. *Donoghue v. Stevenson* [1932] AC 562, 580 (HL) (Lord Atkin).
94. *James Mc Naughton Papers Group Ltd v. Hicks Anderson & Co* [1991] 2 QB 113, 126, [1991] 1 All ER 134, 145 (CA) (Eng) (Neill LJ).
95. *Sutherland Shire Council v. Heyman* (1985) 60 ALR 1, 55–56 (Aust HC) (Deane J).
96. *Lee Cooper Ltd v. C. H. Jeakins & Sons Ltd.* [1967] 2 QB 1 cited in *Corsina (Far East) Ltd v. Taipen Yusen Wharf & Godown Co. Ltd.* [1976] HKCU 45.

negligence,[97] tortious liability cannot be for *'an indeterminate amount, for an indeterminate time, to an indeterminate class'* since such a *'crushing liability'* will place the parties in a position in which it would be impossible to obtain insurance.[98]

59. The modern test for the imposition of a duty of care was redefined by the leading case of *Caparo Industries plc v. Dickman.*[99] Despite the judgment being overruled, the three-fold test developed by Lord Bridge in the Court of Appeal still applies to determine whether a duty of care has arisen. According to this test, for one party to owe a duty of care to another, the plaintiff must establish that: (1) the defendant had foreseen or ought to have foreseen the injury or damage suffered by the plaintiff; (2) the defendant had a sufficient relationship of proximity to the plaintiff; and (3) that, in the circumstances, it was fair, just and reasonable to impose the duty of care upon the defendant. The courts will thereafter consider whether there is a policy factor that exists against imposing a duty on the defendant.[100] Such policy considerations may involve, but are not limited to, the floodgate principle:

> The court has to be alive to the consequences of a decision that one particular set of facts gives rise to a duty of care and to consider carefully whether there is a line to be drawn beyond which a duty of care is not recognised and, if so, where to draw the line. Floodgates arguments are not always attractive where they imply that the court is unable to express itself with sufficient precision, but the nature of the subject matter sometimes means that you cannot include one plaintiff's case without also encompassing many others.[101]

60. Historically, the courts are wary that the loose imposition of the duty of care would cause a ripple effect and give rise to indeterminate liability, leading to a hike in the amount of claims. The courts, as a result, often cite the floodgate principle as the rationale behind why liability in negligence is denied. It is noteworthy that the above criteria are applied to all situations, whatever the nature of the loss, be it economic or physical.[102] It should also be noted that, in the event that the loss to the plaintiff involves direct physical damage, the three criteria would normally be automatically satisfied, as illustrated in the case of *Murphy v. Brentwood District Council:*[103] *'In the straightforward case of the direct infliction of a physical injury... there is... no need to*

97. *Donoghue v. Stevenson* [1932] AC 562, 619 (HL) (Lord Macmillan).
98. *Ultramares Corp v. Touche* (1931) 255 NY 170, (1931) 174 NE 441 (NYCA).
99. [1990] 2 AC 605.
100. *Caparo Industries plc v. Dickman* [1990] 2 AC 605, 617–618, [1990] 1 All ER 568, 573–574 (HL), (Lord Bridge of Harwich); *Luen Hing Fat Coating & Finishing Factory Ltd v. Waan Chuen Ming* [2011] 2 HKLRD 223 and *Ho Ka Yin v. Express Security Ltd* [2011] HKCU 1398; HCPI 344/2008.
101. *Topp v. London Country Bus (South West) Ltd* [1993] 3 All ER 448, 460, [1992] RTR 254, 266 (May J).
102. *Marc Rich & Co AG v. Bishop Rock Marine Co Ltd* [1996] AC 211, 235 (HL).
103. *Murphy v. Brentwood District Council* [1991] 1 AC 398.

look beyond the foreseeability by the defendant of the result in order to establish that he is in a 'proximate' relationship with the plaintiff.'[104]

61. Considering the fact that the courts have historically been unwilling to contemplate whether liability should be imposed on the defendant in new situations, plaintiffs asking the court to recognize such liability will have to apply the three-fold test in an incremental manner, paying particular attention to whether any aspect of the proposed duty involves situations that have already been recognized by previous courts: '*It is preferable…that the law should develop novel categories of negligence incrementally and by analogy with established categories, rather than by a massive extension of a prima facie duty of care restrained only by indefinable considerations which ought to negative, or to reduce or limit, the scope of the duty or the class of person to whom it is owed.*'[105]

62. When determining whether there exists an issue of negligence to be tried, the courts will apply the three criteria test of foreseeability, proximity and fairness in an incremental manner. These factors will then assist the court in arriving at a conclusion in negligence cases. In *Lilley v. Hong Kong and Kowloon Ferry Ltd,*[106] the victim boarded a ferry at the Central pier. Upon the ferry's arrival at its destination at Lamma Island, it was discovered that the victim was no longer in the ferry. His body was later retrieved from the sea. It was later revealed by the autopsy report that the victim was drunk. Later, the administratrix of the deceased's estate sued the first defendant (the owner and operator of the ferry) and the second defendant (the captain and master of the vessel) for damages. There was no evidence to suggest how the deceased fell from the ferry.

63. After trial, the court came to the conclusion that the only reasonable inference which could be drawn was that the deceased, in his drunken state, accidentally fell from the ferry into the sea. The court concluded that it was unnecessary to determine the exact manner in which the deceased fell from the ferry, so long as the court was satisfied that the accident had indeed transpired. In conclusion, the court determined that it was satisfied that it was reasonably foreseeable to the defendants that a passenger would experience rolling and pitching of the ferry during its voyage and that such rolling and pitching may lead to passengers losing their balance or even falling off the ferry. The court concluded that it was just and reasonable that the first defendant and the second defendant owed their passengers a duty to take reasonable care to ensure their personal safety. As such, there exist public policy considerations in favour of the promotion of safety standards. The court concluded that:

It is fair, just and reasonable that the 1st defendant, as the operator of a ferry service providing public transport for passengers, and the 2nd defendant, as the master

---

104. *Murphy v. Brentwood District Council* [1991] 1 AC 398, 486–487, [1990] 2 All ER 908, 934 (HL), (Lord Oliver of Aylmerton); *Mobil Oil Hong Kong Ltd and Dow Chemical (Hong Kong) Ltd v. Hong Kong United Dockyards Ltd, The 'Hua Lien'* [1991] 1 Lloyd's Rep 309, 328–329 (PC).

105. *Sutherland Shire Council v. Heyman* (1985) 60 ALR 1, 43–44 (Aust HC) (Brennan J) (cited with approval in *Caparo Industries plc v. Dickman* [1990] 2 AC 605, 618, [1990] 1 All ER 568, 574 (HL) (Lord Bridge of Harwich).

106. [2012] 2 HKC 57.

of the Vessel deployed to carry passengers, should owe a duty to take reasonable care to ensure the personal safety of its passengers. The fact that Mr Adams may have consumed alcohol before, or after, he boarded the Vessel does not relieve the defendants from their duty of care (Charlesworth and Percy on Negligence 12th Ed p 2455, paras 4-48 to 4-50) … .

64. Note, however, that special duty cases involving omissions, psychiatric injuries, economic loss, rescuers and injuries to unwanted children are more complicated and focus is strictly laid on the issue of proximity in determining the existence of a duty of care.

II. Omissions

A. *Pure Omission: 'No Liability Principle'*

65. Generally, tort law does not impose liability where a claim is grounded solely on the failure to act (pure omission). The rationale behind this practice is the doctrine of individualism, wherein it is reasoned that, should liability be imposed solely due to an individual's passiveness, an individual's personal liberty would be affronted when one would be required to take positive action to act for another's interest. As such, where the omitted act does not arise from a legal duty to act, the courts will not impose liability for negligence. For example, if a person sees a blind person approaching a manhole, that person does not have any legal duty to prevent his injury, even though that same person may have a moral duty. However, where an omission is part of an action which is a legal duty and it is not possible to isolate it, the courts will construe it as an impure omission and impose liability.

66. Lord Atkin's speech in *Donoghue v. Stevenson*[107] stated that the duty of care can be breached by 'acts and omissions'. The rationale behind Lord Atkin's statement is that in many cases an omission could, when seen in a wider context, be construed as a part of a positive act itself; so if the defendant elects inaction in a situation where acting in a certain way is legally a part of his duty, that defendant will be liable for negligence. In such cases, the omission in question can no longer be viewed and judged in isolation from the positive acts of the defendant. For example, a car driver who fails to check whether the lanes are clear before turning and, in the process, causes an accident, cannot plead that checking lanes is not part of his duty. In this example, the checking of lanes and the accident are all part of the same transaction. Hence, the failure to check the lanes (i.e., omission) was carelessness that the defendant committed in the course of doing his positive act (i.e., driving, which he is legally obligated to do safely).

67. Another example of the above principle is illustrated in *Lou Siu Ping & Anor v. Lam Tse Man & Anor,*[108] where the court held that the second defendant, a solicitor, owed a duty of care to his clients (plaintiffs). The plaintiffs in this case purchased a house which was subject to a mortgage and that same house was later

107. [1932] AC 562 (HL).
108. [2012] 4 HKC 394.

foreclosed pursuant to the said mortgage. As the plaintiff's solicitor had failed to advise the plaintiffs of the risks of purchasing the said property and also failed to comprehensively explain the legal documents attached to the said property, he was held to be in breach of his duty of care. The rationale was that it was reasonably foreseeable that the plaintiff would suffer damages if he was not aware of these inherent risks. The second defendant's failure also constitutes breaches of the duties he owed to the plaintiffs under his contract to act on the plaintiffs' behalf in relation to the dealings and transactions over the property.[109]

B. Impure Omission, Failure to Prevent Harm (Nonfeasance) and Affirmative Duty

68. In *Smith v. Littlewoods Organisation Ltd,*[110] Lord Goff of Chieveley stated that *'the common law does not impose liability for what are called pure omissions'.*[111] The purpose of this illustration was to draw the distinction between positive acts and the failure to prevent harm as, for the latter, there is no liability. However, the law also provides for certain exceptions to this general rule. Lord Goff in *Smith* recognized that there are four situations where a duty may be imposed for omission, which are as follows: (1) a special relationship that creates an assumption of responsibility by the defendant for the claimant; (2) a special relationship between the defendant and a third party based on control by the defendant; (3) the defendant is responsible for a state of danger which may be exploited by a third party; and (4) the defendant is responsible for property which may be used by the third party to cause damage.

69. In *Littlewoods*, the defendant purchased a decommissioned cinema in order to redevelop the same. Subsequently, trespassers broke into the said premises and committed arson on the same property on two separate occasions. The defendant had no knowledge of the incidents. When the trespassers attempted to set the premises on fire again, the third occasion, a fire broke out and burned down the cinema. The fire also caused damage to the plaintiff's property. The court absolved the defendants of liability and stated that, despite the defendant having a duty to prevent their property from becoming a source of danger to others, such duty did not extend to the prevention of the trespassers' activities. The approach used by Lord Goff in this case was seen as a control mechanism that was designed to deny the existence of a duty of care on the part of the defendant where the wrongs were perpetrated by others.

70. In *Stovin v. Wise,*[112] the courts developed a specific approach to assess whether an omitted act would render professionals and public servants liable under a claim in tort.[113] In order to ascertain whether liability should be imposed upon a local authority, the courts must first distinguish whether the act is a positive act (misfeasance) or a failure to prevent harm (nonfeasance). It is worth bearing in mind that the courts have historically been conservative, as they have little intention of allowing their

109. *Clerk and Lindsell on Torts* (20th edn, Sweet & Maxwell Ltd 2010), paras 62, 64 & 66; *see also* 10-133 to 10-136.
110. [1987] AC 241.
111. [1987] AC 241, 279.
112. [1996] UKHL 15.
113. [1996] AC 923; *Stovin and another v. Norfolk County Council* [1996] UKHL 15.

decisions to be turned into new precedents. In *Stovin,* the House of Lords differentiated between an individual who had undertaken the duty to do certain acts from an individual who did not have any obligation to take any positive acts. Additionally, Lord Hoffmann cited certain public law principles to justify his refusal to interfere in the local authority's administrative decisions.

71. The above principles were later applied in Hong Kong in the case of *Yuen Kun-yeu v. Attorney General of Hong Kong,*[114] where the plaintiffs had made substantial deposits with a registered deposit-taking company that later went into liquidation. The plaintiffs brought an action against the Attorney General, who represented the Commissioner of Deposit-taking Companies. The crux of the plaintiff's claim revolved around the ground that the Commissioner had breached their obligations under the Deposit-taking Companies Ordinance 1976 (Cap 328, since repealed). On appeal, it was held by the Privy Council that the Commissioner had no duty of care in this situation as the plaintiff failed to prove sufficient proximity between the commissioner and the would-be depositors. It was found that, while the Commissioner had the statutory power to revoke the registration of a company, the Commissioner nevertheless had no control over the day-to-day operations of deposit-taking companies. The lack of proximity meant that the Commissioner had no duty to act in that situation for future would-be depositors. The plaintiff's claim failed as a result.

72. However, where a defendant has assumed responsibility for the care and guardianship of another's life or property, the courts may impose liability based on a pre-tort relationship. This concept was illustrated in the case of *Reeves v. Metropolitan Commissioner of Police,*[115] where the deceased was remanded in police custody. Despite being fully aware of the possibility that the deceased may commit suicide, the officers in charge took no action to mitigate the risks. After trial, the House of Lords noted:

> The reference to an independent act superseding the effect of the tortious conduct must, in my view, relate to an act which was out with the contemplated scope of events to which the duty of care was directed. Where such a duty is specifically directed at the prevention of the occurrence of a certain event I cannot see how it can be said that the occurrence of that event amounts to an independent act breaking the chain of causation from the breach of duty, even although it may be unusual for one person to come under a duty to prevent another person deliberately inflicting harm on himself.[116]

73. This principle was affirmed in the Hong Kong case of *Wong Wai Ming v. Hospital Authority,*[117] where the plaintiff was a male psychiatric nurse under the employ of the defendant and was injured by a person visiting the psychiatric centre. The person perpetrating the assault was a psychiatric patient who was registered with another hospital. On the day of the incident, the plaintiff was on duty at the reception of the psychiatric centre and the patient attempted to make several complaints. The plaintiff ignored the complaints and sent the patient away. This act agitated the patient, which

114. [1987] 2 All ER 705 (PC).
115. [2000] 1 AC 360 (HL).
116. [2000] 1 AC 360 (HL), 375 (Lord Jauncey of Tullichettle).
117. (CACV000086/2001, 20 Jun. 2001); [2000] 3 HKLRD 612 (affirmed by Court of Appeal at [2001] 3 HKLRD 209).

led to the patient losing control of herself. The patient subsequently threw acid onto persons around her. During the ensuing chaos, the plaintiff attempted to disperse the crowd, but was subsequently injured by the acid. This injury led to the plaintiff bringing an action against the defendant for breach of their duty of care. After trial, the courts found the defendant liable as it was the duty of a diligent employer to take every reasonable precaution to keep their employees safe. Keith J at the Court of Appeal stated:

> I accept, of course, that violence can take so unpredictable a form that no measures can be taken to reduce the risk of injury to staff, but what the installation of a panic button and the enclosure of the counter can do is to provide a measure of protection for those cases in which the conventional measures of persuasion and physical restraint would only work if there were sufficient members of qualified staff present at the time.[118]

74. The above judgment highlighted a simple concept: where a defendant has control over a third party who has known tendencies to endanger those around him/her, it is the defendant's inherent duty to prevent the third party under their care and control from harming others. In other words, once a defendant assumes care and control over a third party, they must also control the conduct of that third party and ensure that their actions will not lead to harm being caused to others around them; hence, the pre-tort assumption of responsibility. This concept is further demonstrated in the case of *Home Office v. Dorset Yacht Co Ltd,*[119] in which the UK Home Office was held liable for the failure of their borstal officers to control the conduct of borstal boys who were under their supervision at the material time. In this case, the officers went to sleep and left the borstal boys unattended. The borstal boys subsequently escaped from their supervising officer's custody and boarded a nearby yacht. Subsequently, they started the engine on the yacht and, during their navigation, collided with the respondents' yacht. The respondents then brought an action against the Home Office for damages. The House of Lords held the Home Office liable and extended the duty of care for omissions to cover third parties whose actions were under the care of the appellant.

75. In *Cheung Ping v. Siu Chung-yee & Another and American United General Insurance Ltd and Scotland Insurance Co Ltd,*[120] the plaintiff was injured by a lorry driven by the first defendant and owned by the second defendant, as a wheel had become detached. The wheel had become detached because of the poor maintenance of the lorry. The plaintiff sued both defendants for damages, but the court only held the second defendant liable for the vehicle being kept in a poor condition. Hence, if the defendant has a high degree of control over a potentially dangerous act and his effective control has been relied on, a duty of care will be imposed because the creation of the danger would be closely related to the direct infliction of the physical injury on the plaintiff.[121] Similar reasoning was adopted in the Hong Kong case of *So Kai Hau*

118. (CACV000086/2001, 20 Jun. 2001), 18.
119. [1970] AC 1004 (CA).
120. [1984] HKCU 32.
121. *Perrett v. Collins* [1998] 2 'Lloyd's Rep 255 (CA).

v. YSK2 Engineering Co Ltd.[122] Hence, the defendant could be liable for creating a source of danger, though it is the third party who causes the harm. For example, in *Haynes v. Harwood,*[123] the defendant was held liable for the plaintiff's injury, which was suffered while rescuing people from the defendant's running horse. The defendant's horse had been left unattended and a child had thrown a stone at the horse, causing it to run wildly on the street. It was made clear that a defendant could be held liable if his property is used by others to cause damage. In the case of *Clark Fixing Ltd v. Dudley Metropolitan Borough Council,*[124] a fire broke out in the neighbourhood of a vacant development site after a trespasser entered it and the court gave damages to the plaintiff for the council's failure to remove combustible material, as such failure had caused the situation to deteriorate.

76. Hence, an affirmative duty is imposed by the courts where: (1) a special relationship arises in which a party assumes responsibility protect the other party; or (2) the defendant has control over the third party in a special relationship; or (3) the defendant accounts for creating a state of danger which may pose dangers to others, etc. Therefore, it is the responsibility of the occupier of the land/premises to take steps to control any possible natural danger on the land/premises,[125] and failing to do so may attract liability. For public authorities, a duty of care may exist, and that is ascertained on a case-by-case basis. It is to be recalled that all '*public authorities function on the basis of a statute and before imposing any liability on them the cost to the community of the defensive measures that public authority may take to avoid liability must be taken into consideration.*'[126] Further it must also be noted that in all these omission cases the defendant's action must be sufficiently proximate enough to cause the plaintiff's injury and, if not, the claim would fail. For example, in *Hill v. Chief Constable of West Yorkshire,*[127] the court did not hold the police department liable for the plaintiff's daughter's death as the judge concluded that there was no duty from the police to an unidentified member of public who was attacked by another person, though that person posed a threat to women.

III. Psychiatric Injury

77. Psychiatric injury cases include special duties and involve the personal harm that the plaintiff suffers when they experience or witness a serious or horrific accident or situation. In the past, the focus of the courts was on the 'manner' in which identified harm resulted in nervous shock. It was argued that the injury was on a plaintiff's mind rather than their physical body. Prior to the recognition of psychological injury, many psychiatric injury cases went unheard and uncompensated as the courts had restricted claims to physical injuries. For example, in the case of *Victorian Railway Commissioner*

122. [2010] 5 HKLRD 278.
123. [1935] 1 KB 146.
124. [2001] EWCA Civ 1898.
125. *Goldman v. Hargrave* [1967] 1 AC 645.
126. *Stovin v. Wise* (1996) AC 923, (Lord Hoffmann).
127. [1988] 2 All ER 238 (HL).

v. Coultas,[128] the plaintiff was in a carriage that was nearly hit by a train when the gatekeeper negligently permitted the passage of the plaintiff's carriage. While the plaintiff in question suffered no physical injury from the ordeal, it did result in her suffering a miscarriage. The Privy Council dismissed the plaintiff's claims on the grounds that, if the council allowed a claim to proceed without presence of physical injury, the floodgate to 'imaginary claims' would be opened.

78. Such views have since been overturned with the recognition of Post-Traumatic Stress Disorder ('PTSD'), depression, personality disorders, schizophrenia, mental impairment, etc.[129] While claims relating to psychological harms have gained traction over the years, it is noteworthy that in the UK case of *Rothwell v. Chemical & Insulating Co Ltd,*[130] a 2008 case, it was held that simple emotional distress, anguish, and grief are not covered under the umbrella of psychiatric injury claims. However, in Hong Kong, the Fatal Accidents Ordinance (Cap 22) sections 4(1) and (2) provide that the bereaved family or the persons with whom the deceased was living prior to his/her death can claim compensation for bereavement. Since the 1990s, however, there has been a major shift in the law concerning psychiatric claims by secondary victims. Despite such developments, however, much of their claims are subjected to special restrictions on policy grounds. This is demonstrated by the cases of *Alcock*[131] and *White,*[132] which arose in the aftermath of the Hillsborough football stadium disaster in 1989. The cause of the accidents was found to be the negligence of the police officers involved.

79. In modern times, a claimant seeking damages for psychiatric injury can recover damages if: (1) he has suffered a recognized psychiatric injury; (2) is a primary or a secondary victim; and (3) causation is satisfied by reasonable foreseeability. The recognition of psychiatric injury claims arising out of physical injuries caused by fear after a victim witnesses a traumatic and sudden event (or its aftermath) is allowed. In other words, the chain has been extended to include events outside the immediate incident. A primary victim is one who is: (1) within the vicinity of potential danger; and (2) suffers psychiatric injury or both physical and psychiatric injury. In a primary victim case, the court draws no distinction between damages suffered physically or psychologically. Further, the courts are prepared to assume that, where physical injury is a reasonably foreseeable consequence of the defendant's conduct, it is only logical to include foreseeable psychiatric injuries and no separate foreseeability element is required. This stance is illustrated in the Hong Kong case of *Wong Yiu Ming v. To Chark Wah & Anor*[133] where the plaintiff suffered a slight physical injury when an aluminium window frame fell from the thirty-third floor of a building to near where he was standing. The court stated that it was foreseeable that such a dangerous incident could cause the plaintiff harm, even if only a minor physical injury was caused. The courts, as a result, held in favour of the plaintiff in their psychiatric injury claim. A

128. (1888) 13 App Cas 222.
129. 309.81 Posttraumatic Stress Disorder. In: *Diagnostic and Statistical Manual of Mental Disorders*, 424–429 (4th edn. American Psychiatric Association 1994).
130. [2008] 1 AC 281, [2007] 4 All ER 1047 (HL).
131. [1992] 1 AC 310, [1991] 4 All ER 907, [1991] 3 WLR 1057 (HL).
132. [1999] 2 AC 455, [1999] 1 All ER 1 (HL).
133. [1993] 1 HKC 510.

similar approach was taken by the Hong Kong courts in *CMY v. Tam Siu Wing* in 2008.[134]

80. In the UK, the House of Lords in *Page v. Smith*[135] further developed the law to promote protection for primary victims when Lord Lloyd stated in his judgment that where the defendant '*was under a duty of care not to cause the plaintiff foreseeable physical injury it is unnecessary to ask whether he was under a separate duty of care not to cause foreseeable psychiatric injury*'.[136] In this case, the plaintiff went into a relapse of his previous affliction of chronic fatigue syndrome after a minor car accident caused by the negligent driving of the defendant. He did not suffer any physical injury. The Court of Appeal initially rejected the claim that there was a breach of the defendant's duty of care on the basis that it could not have been reasonably foreseen that a plaintiff of reasonable fortitude would suffer psychiatric injuries as a result of such a minor accident.

81. The House of Lords later reversed the decision. The majority of the judges observed that the absence of physical injury does not necessarily mean that a different test should have been applied to ascertain whether there was any foreseeability of psychiatric injury. As such, there was no reason to treat physical and psychiatric harm differently where they were both caused by the defendant's negligence. The court then applied the 'eggshell skull rule' and stated that the defendant had to take the plaintiff as he found him.

82. Rescuers may also claim for damages for psychiatric injuries as primary victims when they are deployed into an area where dangers created by the defendant are still present. The considerations taken by the court are illustrated in the case of *White v. Chief Constable of South Yorkshire Police & Ors,*[137] where the House of Lords overturned the Court of Appeal's decision and disallowed the claim of police officers who had suffered psychiatric injuries while assisting in aftermath of the Hillsborough football stadium collapse in Sheffield. This incident involved 96 people being crushed to death and about 400 additional victims also being injured when the persons responsible for organizing the event negligently allowed excessive crowds to assemble in one part of the stadium. Amongst the plaintiffs were five police officers who had assisted the injured in the stadium and one who had been on duty in the temporary mortuary that was set up for the purpose of handling dead bodies from this event. The five officers were all directly exposed to the carnage that had arisen from this accident. At trial, the House of Lords acknowledged that it would be bad form to compensate public servants for psychiatric injuries that were suffered in the course of duty, especially when there were statutory schemes in place for certain public servants, including police officers, to be compensated via their pensions for trauma due to their work. Further, as the court had also previously denied compensation to relatives in *Alcock,*[138] which was related to same incident, a judgment in favour of the police officers may have led to an outcry. The view that would be taken of public servants being compensated when bereaved families received nothing weighed as a heavy consideration. The majority of the House

134. [2008] 4 HKLRD 604.
135. [1996] AC 155 (HL).
136. [1996] AC 155 (HL), 188.
137. [1999] 2 AC 455 (HL).
138. *Alcock v. Chief Constable of the South Yorkshire Police* [1991] 4 All ER 907 (HL).

of Lords were of the view that rescuers who were not personally endangered by the negligence of the event organizers could not claim as no duty was owed to them by the defendant. In the process of clarifying the law, the House of Lords cited the case of *Chadwick*[139] where a claimant had claimed to have sustained psychiatric injuries after entering a wrecked railway carriage to help tend to the injured. This claimant was allowed his claim since there was an element of personal danger that was involved when they entered into the fray, with the risk of carriage collapsing still existing. *White,* however, left one issue open for discussion, since it was not settled whether, when claiming as a primary victim, the rescuer must have been within the range of physical danger or whether it would already be acceptable if he reasonably believed that he was in danger.[140] In *White*, Lord Hoffmann, commenting on *Walker* case, stated that, '*The employee ... was in no sense a secondary victim. His mental breakdown was caused by the strain of doing the work which his employer had required him to do.*'[141] He further stated that, '*The control mechanisms were plainly never intended to apply to all cases of psychiatric injury. They contemplate that the injury has been caused in consequence of death or injury suffered (or apprehended to have been suffered or as likely to be suffered) by someone else.*'[142]

83. In *Walker v. Northumberland,*[143] the plaintiff suffered a nervous breakdown (with causes completely unrelated to work). In the circumstances, his employer promised him that help would be provided. However, contrary to the said promise, the employer took no action to assist the plaintiff when he suffered a second nervous breakdown. The plaintiff was dismissed. The court held the employer liable because, under these circumstances, it was reasonably foreseeable that the employer would be required to take additional steps to prevent psychiatric damage to the plaintiff (Colman J). Hence, employees who are not rescuers can also file claims against their employers in such circumstances on the grounds that their psychiatric illness was suffered at the workplace. Psychiatric injuries to employees can be caused by various means, such as bullying by colleagues,[144] increased workload despite the employee suffering from post-natal depression[145] and wrongful dismissal.[146] This area of law is also connected to employers' liability, which will be discussed elsewhere in this monograph.

84. A secondary victim is one who, while not being directly in danger himself, witnesses an accident that was caused by the negligence of the defendant in which other people were injured or died. Someone who suffers a recognized psychiatric injury may be able to file a claim in such circumstances. To see whether the psychiatric injury was a foreseeable consequence of the defendant's negligence, the plaintiff needs

---

139. *Chadwick v. British Railway Board* [1967] 1 WLR 912.
140. *McFarlane v. E.E. Caledonia Ltd* [1994] 2 All ER 1- a case concerning the Piper Alpha oil rig disaster where workers on board died due to series of explosions. In this case, the court did not allow the claim but Stuart-Smith LJ considered a rescuer's position and stated that if the rescuer believes himself to be in danger then he should be able to recover.
141. [1999] 2 AC 455, 506.
142. [1999] 2 AC 455, 504.
143. [1995] 1 All ER 737.
144. *Green v. DP Group Services (UK) Ltd* [2006] EWHC 1898 QB.
145. *Intel Corporation Intell Ltd v. Daw* [2007] EWCA Civ 70.
146. *Yapp v. Foreign and Commonwealth Office* [2013] EWHC 1098 (QB).

to prove strict proximity, including satisfying the 'aftermath test', and fulfil other criteria that were consolidated in the *Alcock*[147] test. This test now acts as a control mechanism and is subjected to special restrictions on policy grounds. Some of the criteria were adopted by courts in previous cases.

85. The claims in *Alcock*[148] were from secondary victims, including bereaved families, of the Hillsborough football stadium disaster on the day of the FA Cup Semi-Final, described above. Sixteen cases arose from the incident for psychiatric injury. Four plaintiffs were present at the scene, though they were not in the stampede area itself; the others included claimants who had seen their loved ones being crushed to death on the live television broadcast. Three cases relating to the disaster reached the House of Lords: *Alcock,*[149] *Hicks*[150] and *White.*[151] The relatives who had seen the events at a distance or through the television bought their claims in *Alcock*. Ultimately, their claims were rejected. The House of Lords applied the aftermath test, stating that a secondary victim must perceive the event or its immediate aftermath through their own senses, directly. It had to be established whether the claimant was involved as a secondary victim or merely passively witnessing the event. The defendant must have directly caused the psychiatric injury. In developing a control mechanism, the House of Lords stated that the claimant must have had a tie of love and affection with the person who was injured or killed in the accident, that the claimant was sufficiently proximate to the accident, and that they were able to perceive the accident themselves, unaided. Liability for causing psychiatric injury to secondary witnesses is not fully defined; relationships include those that are familial, but it is not clear in the context of extended family. Where there is no presumption of a relationship of love and affection, the plaintiff must establish it. In the case of *Hambrook v. Stokes Bros,*[152] the victim was pregnant and a mother of three children, who were walking to school. A lorry crashed into a bend where she had left her children, and one of the children had to be hospitalized. The victim suffered a miscarriage due to the shock, and the medical complications led to her death. A claim on behalf of the victim was sustained by the Court of Appeal, which limited its application to cases where plaintiffs incur psychiatric injury due to fear for their children's safety. Bystanders are not included, as can be seen in the case of *Bourhill v. Young,*[153] wherein the plaintiff had suffered a miscarriage after the shock caused by hearing a road collision between a motorcycle and a car. It was held by the House of Lords that the plaintiff was a bystander rather than someone who could foreseeably suffer harm.

86. Second, a claimant must also be within a high degree of proximity to the accident in 'time and space'. The plaintiff must normally witness the accident as it transpires or, alternatively, must at the very least come upon its 'immediate aftermath' within a very short span of time. The shock suffered must also be proven to have directly arisen out of the incident and its perception must be the cause of the psychiatric

---

147. *Alcock v. Chief Constable of the South Yorkshire Police* [1991] 4 All ER 907 (HL).
148. *Alcock v. Chief Constable of the South Yorkshire Police* [1991] UKHL 5, [1991] 4 All ER 907.
149. *Alcock v. Chief Constable of the South Yorkshire Police* [1991] UKHL 5, [1991] 4 All ER 907.
150. [1992] 2 All ER 65 (HL).
151. *White or Frost v. Chief Constable of South Yorkshire Police* [1999] 2 AC 455 (HL).
152. [1925] 1KB 141.
153. [1943] AC 92.

injury. In *McLoughlin v. O'Brian,*[154] the plaintiff (a mother) suffered psychiatrist injuries after she was informed that her husband and children were involved in a serious traffic accident. Upon her arrival at the hospital hours later, she witnessed her husband and three children suffering in horrific conditions and even witnessed the death of one of her daughters. While the Trial Court and the Court of Appeal rejected her claim, the House of Lords allowed it. Lord Wilberforce stated that, in order for a claimant to satisfy the proximity requirement in a claim that intended claimant must show that his/her nervous shock was the result of being close in space and time to the defendant's negligent act. As a result of this formulation, a plaintiff is not required to personally see or hear the accident, but instead is qualified so long as that plaintiff can prove that they have witnessed its 'immediate aftermath'. Applying the same principle, Lord Jauncey in *Alcock*[155] was able to hold that, as the victim's relatives did not witness the death of the immediate victims but were only invited to identify the bodies of the victims nine hours later at the mortuary, the 'immediate aftermath' requirement was not satisfied. It was further reasoned that as the claimant's visit to the mortuary was *'made no earlier than nine hours after the disaster and were made not for the purpose of rescuing or giving comfort to the victim but purely for the purpose of identification...'*[156] the admitted facts indicated that the time and circumstances of the 'entire event' were far too remote from the original accident.

87. The above principle illustrates that, for a claim to succeed, the claimants must show that they had first-hand experience of live carnage. As such, simply viewing recorded pictures or a television broadcast will not satisfy this requirement (i.e., relatives who know that they do no't have any legitimate claim cannot simply expose themselves to recorded footage in order to artificially cause themselves to be eligible for a claim). In *Alcock,*[157] it was stated that none of the broadcasted footage showed the suffering of recognizable individuals. Had that been the case, the broadcaster themselves could be held liable for the plaintiffs' psychiatric injuries. Lord Keith, in the course of arriving to his judgment in *Alcock,*[158] considered the persuasive Australian authority of *Jaensch v. Coffey*[159] where Deane J said that *'the aftermath of the accident extended to the hospital to which the injured person was taken and persisted for so long as he remained in the state produced by the accident up to and including immediate post-accident treatment'*. Again, the temporal consideration became a key determinant of whether the plaintiffs were eligible to claim. In the Australian case, plaintiffs were awarded damages as the accident had lasted several hours. In *North Glamorgan NHS Trust v. Walters,*[160] the plaintiff, the mother of an infant who was negligently treated by the defendant, watched her child suffer for thirty-six hours in her lap before he died. The court considered this incident as one single event and allowed the plaintiff's claim for psychiatric injuries. This principle was similarly echoed in *Tsang Mei Ying*

154. [1983] 1 AC 410.
155. *Alcock v. Chief Constable of the South Yorkshire Police* [1991] UKHL 5, [1991] 4 All ER 907.
156. [1991] 4 All ER 907, 937 (Lord Jauncey of Tullichettle).
157. *Alcock v. Chief Constable of the South Yorkshire Police* [1991] UKHL 5.
158. *Alcock v. Chief Constable of the South Yorkshire Police* [1991] UKHL 5.
159. [1984] 54 ALR 417.
160. [2002] EWCA Civ 1792 (CA).

& Anor v. Lam Pak Chiu & Anor[161] where the plaintiff's husband was killed as a result of the defendant's negligent acts. The plaintiff, as a consequence, had to give up her job in order to provide care for the deceased''s mother who became mentally unwell after this incident. The court dismissed this claim on the basis of lack of sufficient proximity between the incident and the mother''s mental illness, despite the fact that it was shown that the proximity of relationship was satisfied.

88. Finally, the plaintiff must prove that his personal injury resulted from direct trauma caused by sudden shock after witnessing the event or its immediate aftermath, rather than hearing about it from a third person. As such, there will be no claim if the plaintiff acquired the information merely through hearsay. In *Alcock*, Lord Ackner stated that it was necessary for there to be *'the sudden appreciation by sight or sound of a horrifying event, which violently agitates the mind'*.[162] In order to ascertain whether a shock is sudden the courts will first draw a distinction between how the news of the death was acquired with the actual witnessing of the death. In *Alcock,* the court held that the pictures of victims did not satisfy the criteria as the secondary victims did not see the carnage with their own 'unaided senses'. It was further held that the courts would take a different view in relation to cases involving transmitted images, as long as it was satisfied that the viewing of the images was not the sole reason for the psychiatric injury claim. In such cases, there was a combination of things, including subsequent reflection or prolonged exposure to distress. As illustrated in *Rothwell v. Chemical & Insulating Co Ltd,*[163] the plaintiffs, after exposure to asbestos over a long period of time, developed pleural plaques. The court held that mere anxiety and distress did not attract any compensation, as a state of anxiety falling short of a clinically recognizable psychiatric illness would not be sufficient to give rise to a cause of action.

IV. Economic Loss

89. Tortious liability for negligently causing economic loss, defined as purely financial loss which is not consequential upon any physical injury or damage to the plaintiff or loss of his property. As stated in *Murphy v. Brentwood*, economic loss is only '*recoverable in contract or in tort by reason of some special relationship of proximity which imposes on the tortfeasor a duty of care to protect against economic loss'*.[164] In establishing whether a duty of care can be established for negligently causing economic loss, the discussion can be grounded on two main heads: negligent statements or services, and negligent activity, which includes defective product economic loss. Courts are hesitant to impose liability for negligently causing economic loss and allow recovery as damages are speculative and can be burdensome on defendants, as well as the consideration that the floodgates could be opened in terms of cases that could be brought. As Lord Pearce stated in *Hedley Byrne & Co Ltd v. Heller and Partners,*[165] *'Economic protection has lagged behind protection in physical matters where there*

161. [2000] 1 HKLRD 883 (CA).
162. [1991] 4 All ER 907, 918 (Lord Ackner).
163. [2008] 1 AC 281, [2007] 4 All ER 1047 (HL).
164. *Murphy v. Brentwood* [1990] 2 All ER 908 (Lord Bridge).
165. [1964] AC 465.

is injury to person and property. It may be that the size and the width of the range of possible claims have acted as a deterrent to the extension of economic protection'.

90. In *Hedley Byrne & Co Ltd v. Heller & Partners,*[166] discussed in detail below, the House of Lords outlined situations in which recovery for financial loss caused by negligent statements can be imposed. In the absence of a contractual or fiduciary relationship between the parties, if the parties had a relationship of proximity, it was found that financial loss had to flow from injury or physical damage caused to the plaintiff for it to be recoverable. However, Lord Devlin stated that it was 'nonsense' to draw a distinction as to whether the financial loss was caused by physical injury or caused directly, stating that, '*The line is not drawn on any intelligible principle. It just happens to be the line which those who have been driven from the extreme assertion that negligent statements in the absence of contractual or fiduciary duty give no cause of action have in the course of their retreat so far reached.*'[167] After *Murphy,*[168] there has been a more clarified discussion on where purely economic loss is recoverable.

A. Negligent Statement and Services

91. The recovery of purely economic loss caused by a negligent statement was traditionally pursued under the law of contract, or as a breach of fiduciary duty. However, pursuant to *Hedley Byrne & Co Ltd v. Heller & Partners,*[169] purely economic loss is recoverable for breach of a duty of care. Under the *Hedley Byrne* principle, the duty of care for negligent statement will only arise in situations where there is a special relationship (sufficient proximity) between the plaintiff and the defendant. The neighbour principle in *Donoghue v. Stevenson*[170] was affirmed, but it was held that the plaintiff should ask, per Lord Devlin at page 28, '*Is the relationship between the parties in this case such that it can be brought within a category giving rise to a special duty?*'[171] Further, it was stated, '*A promise given without consideration to perform a service cannot be enforced as a contract by the promisee; but if the service is in fact performed and done negligently, the promisee can recover in an action in tort.*'[172] Further, '*The principle has been applied to cases where as a result of the negligence no damage was done to person or to property and the consequential loss was purely financial.*'[173] In this case the claimants, advertising agents, suffered economic loss as a result of not canceling substantial orders of advertising space on behalf of a client, acting in reliance on the respondent merchant bank's negligent financial reference about the creditworthiness of the client. In the particular case, the appeal was dismissed because of a disclaimer given by the defendants: in the words of Lord Devlin, '*A man cannot be said voluntarily to be undertaking a responsibility if at the very moment when he is said to be accepting*

166. [1964] AC 465.
167. [1964] AC 465.
168. *Murphy v. Brentwood* [1990] 2 All ER 908.
169. [1964] AC 465.
170. [1932] AC 562.
171. [1964] AC 465.
172. [1964] AC 465, 29 (Lord Devlin).
173. [1964] AC 465, 29 (Lord Devlin).

it he declares that in fact he is not.'[174] The House of Lords held that a duty of care would have been owed to the claimants had there been no disclaimer[175] attached with the supply of information by the bank. A principle developed in *Hedley Byrne* is that, where parties have a special relationship, there is a responsibility for the honesty of any information provided. The special relationship can be said to have arisen where: (1) the party (representee) seeking the advice or information was trusting the representor to act with care; (2) the representor knew or ought to have known that the representee was going to rely on his advice or information; and (3) the representee acted on the advice and suffered loss. Hence, to claim economic loss caused by a negligent statement, two requirements must be fulfilled, namely: (1) a special relationship between the parties based on which the defendant assumes responsibility to provide correct advice or information; and (2) reasonable reliance on the information by the claimant.

92. Liability is not limited to negligent statements, but also to services that have been undertaken. In *Ross v. Caunters*[176] solicitors for a testator were negligent in informing him about how a will should be attested – specifically, that the spouse of a beneficiary cannot be witness to the signing of a will – and were liable for the loss to the beneficiary, a third party. The solicitors were liable to the plaintiff despite the loss being purely financial because of their proximate relationship (the solicitors were asked to draft the will to benefit her, the testator's sister-in-law) and their knowledge that their negligence could cause her financial loss. A similar approach was adopted in *White v. Jones*[177] where the defendant solicitors' negligent delay of the task of drawing up a new will until the death of the testator caused loss to the intended beneficiaries, the plaintiffs.

93. In examining what considerations could limit what relationships the duty of care applies in, the court in *Ross* looked to the House of Lords case of *Home Office v. Dorset Yacht Co Ltd,*[178] where Lord Morris stated that, '*Policy need not be invoked where reason and good sense will at once point the way. If the test as to whether in some particular situation a duty of care arises may in some cases have to be whether it is fair and reasonable that it should so arise, the court must not shrink from being the arbiter,*'[179] and Lord Pearce stated that, '*To some extent the decision in this case must be a matter of impression and instinctive judgment as to what is fair and just.*'[180] *Donoghue*[181] was to apply unless there was a fair and just reason not to apply it.

94. Special relationships include situations where there is a contract between the plaintiff and defendant, such as between employers and employees, and applies to various professionals, including accountants, investment advisers and solicitors in their relationship with their clients.[182] There can be a special relationship in non-

174. [1964] AC 465, 29 (Lord Devlin).
175. Disclaimers must be narrowly construed – *Smith v. Eric S Bush* [1989] 2 All ER 514.
176. (1980) Ch 297.
177. [1995] 2 AC 207, (HL).
178. *Home Office v. Dorset Yacht Co Ltd* [1970] AC 1004.
179. *Home Office v. Dorset Yacht Co Ltd* [1970] AC 1004, 1039 (Lord Morris of Borth-y-Gest).
180. *Home Office v. Dorset Yacht Co Ltd* [1970] AC 1004, 1054 (Lord Pearce).
181. [1932] AC 562.
182. *Midland Bank Trust Co Ltd v. Hett Stubbs & Kemp* [1979] Ch 384, [1978] 3 All ER 571, [1978] 3 WLR 167.

contractual situations as well, even if the representor is non-professional, if they are more knowledgeable than the representee and their advice is relied on, and if the representor should have known that the negligent misstatement would be relied on. In *Chaudhry v. Prabhakar,*[183] the plaintiff was a newly qualified driver who asked the first defendant, a friend, to recommend a second-hand car. The plaintiff stipulated that the car should not have been in an accident previously. The first defendant had some knowledge about cars, though they were not a mechanic, and undertook the search gratuitously. The first defendant recommended a car from the second defendant, a car sprayer, even though the first defendant saw that the bonnet of the car bore marks of having been straightened after an accident. The trial court found both defendants guilty, and the first defendant's conviction was affirmed after appeal, as the Court of Appeal found that someone who volunteered to buy a car for someone as an agent, even gratuitously, owed a duty to exercise an objectively reasonable degree of care and skill in the circumstances. This was an affirmation of the principle in *Hedley Byrne,*[184] which was articulated in *Chaudhry* by Stuart Smith LJ as follows:

> negligent, although honest, misrepresentation, spoken or written, may give rise to an action for damages for financial loss caused thereby, apart from any contract or fiduciary relationship, since the law will imply a duty of care when a party seeking information from a party possessed of special skill trusts him to exercise care, and that party knew, or ought to have known, that reliance was being placed on his skill and judgment.[185]

95. In the Privy Council case of *Mutual Life Citizen Assurance Co v. Evatt,*[186] *Hedley Byrne* was interpreted more narrowly, as applying to relationships where: (1) the person who made the statement had done so in the ordinary course of their business or profession; and (2) the topic on which the statement was made required some kind of qualification, skill or competency that ordinary reasonable men are not expected to have, which the statement-maker was known by the recipient to claim to have by reason of their business or profession.

96. In *Caparo v. Dickman,*[187] the defendants prepared annual audit reports of a company. The plaintiffs, existing shareholders, bought further shares and executed a takeover bid on the basis of an audit report that negligently over-valued assets of the company. The question arose whether there existed any special relationship between the plaintiff and defendants. On appeal to the House of Lords, it was held that the auditors did not owe a duty to the investing public as there was no relationship of proximity, and that establishing one would create unlimited liability on auditors; individual shareholders who wished to procure further shares were in the same position as the investing public. The auditors' duty was to the body of shareholders as a whole and it was to inform them of how the company was functioning. It was held that to see whether there is a relationship in which the maker of a statement had a special

183. [1988] 3 All ER 718.
184. [1964] AC 465.
185. [1988] 3 All ER 718, 722.
186. [1971] 1 All ER 150, 155.
187. [1990] 2 AC 605.

duty of care the court must assess the proximity of the relationship, whether the damage was foreseeable and how reasonable it would be to impose a duty of care in all the circumstances, and consider whether the type of damage suffered was one which someone in the position of the defendant should have an obligation to prevent.

97. The special relationship between the parties is also affected by whether the advisor knows the purpose of the statement/service that he is providing. This is discussed in the Hong Kong Court of Appeal case of *Yue Xiu Finance Company Ltd & Another v. Dermot Agnew and Others (formerly t/a Deloitte Haskins and Sells).*[188] The defendants were joint auditors for two companies whose alleged negligent misstatement caused the plaintiffs not to exercise their contractual rights in put/call options. The defendants had been asked to do a special audit and were aware that the figures would be relied upon by the plaintiffs and the third party in exercising their rights. Exposure to liability was thereby limited to known parties, and loss was limited to that which could be suffered by the parties not exercising their rights due to the defendant's negligent misstatement. The decision of the trial judge to strike out the case was overturned by the Court of Appeal. In obiter, Litton VP warned against trying to over-refine the principle in *Hedley Byrne* 'in an area of the law where the duty-situation is identified by such broad concepts as foreseeability, proximity and fairness'. In relation to *Caparo v. Dickman*, it was affirmed that where the defendant gives advice or information when they are aware of the transaction that the plaintiff is considering, knows that the plaintiff would be communicated the advice or information and is likely to rely on it when deciding on whether to undertake the contemplated transaction, the defendant can be expected (unless they have disclaimed liability) to know that the plaintiff would rely on that advice or information. If the plaintiff has in fact relied on it for purpose stated, they are entitled to do so and the defendant is liable for loss caused.

98. In *Susan Field v. Barber Asia,*[189] the plaintiff, an inexperienced investor, consulted the defendant, an independent financial adviser, to help the plaintiff invest her savings conservatively. The defendant did not receive fees directly from the plaintiff, but received commissions/fess from the institutions in which the plaintiff was recommended to invest. By drawing the plaintiff into an investment that was inconsistent with her aim of being conservative, and by not adequately explaining the risks she was being brought into, the investment adviser breached their duty of care. The duty arose from the defendant proffering investment advice, and the breach was in the advice not conforming to the plaintiff's request for a conservative investment strategy. This was the first Hong Kong case in which an investment advisor was held liable. The court also considered the inexperience of the investor, as well as her express wish to invest prudently.

99. By applying the *Hedley Byrne* principle, the defendant becomes responsible for providing honest information or advice if the parties are in a special relationship.[190] Reliance on a negligent misstatement causing financial loss is not in itself actionable. There has to be a voluntary assumption of responsibility, though that can be shown by the defendant knowing, or being in a position where they ought to have known, that their advice would be relied on, rather than any subjective intention requirement

188. [1996] 1 HKCU 0467.
189. [2004] 3 HKLRD 871.
190. *DBS Bank (HK) Limited v. San-Hot HK Industrial Co Ltd & Anor* [2013] 4 HKC 1.

(per Litton VP in *Yue Xiu Finance Company Ltd & Another v. Dermot Agnew and Others (formerly t/a Deloitte Haskins and Sells)*.[191] This incorporates criticism of the concept of voluntary assumption of responsibility, such as by Lord Griffiths in *Smith v. Eric S. Bush*[192] and Lord Denning M.R in *Ministry of Housing and Local Government v. Sharp*.[193] In *Henderson (and others) v. Merrett Syndicate Ltd (and others)*,[194] the plaintiffs, underwriting members of certain Lloyd's syndicates, brought an action against the defendants (the Merrett Syndicate, who were the underwriting agents managing these syndicates, and the auditors). This case was one of a set of cases for the House of Lords to deal with questions relating to the liability of underwriting agents. The House of Lords affirmed *Hedley Byrne*, noting the requirement of one party assuming responsibility for another, and stated that the principles in *Hedley Byrne* apply not only to information and advice, but also to the performance of other services.

100. The reliance requirement could be fulfilled by, for example, the plaintiff's expectation that work undertaken would be completed. In essence, the plaintiff would rely on the defendant to exercise due care and skill in their conduct. An objective test was to be used for establishing whether responsibility was assumed. In *Henderson*, it was found that the managing agents had held themselves out as having expertise and had known that it would be relied upon implicitly by the underwriting members they were managing. In *Henderson*,[195] the judgment in *Tai Hing Cotton Mill Ltd. v. Liu Chong Hing Bank Ltd*,[196] a case from the Judicial Committee of the Privy Council, with respect to its limitation on liability in tort where there is a contractual relationship, was overruled and it was held that concurrent remedies should be allowed; a plaintiff who has claims in both contract and tort is not limited to their contractual rights. Plaintiffs are free to pursue the more advantageous course of action, unless it is an attempt to get around valid contractual exclusions or limitations by the use of tort law. This upheld Oliver J's judgment in *Midland Bank Trust Co Ltd v. Hett, Stubbs & Kemp*,[197] in which a solicitor was found able to be liable to clients for negligence in both contract and tort law, and the client could choose whichever one was the most advantageous to pursue. Oliver J recognized that contractual relationships may give rise to concurrent liability in tort.[198] Approving Oliver J's analysis, Lord Goff in *Henderson* found that the duty of care owed by the managing underwriters, established under the *Hedley Byrne* principle, and liability for its breach could give rise to concurrent liability even if the parties had a contractual relationship, unless the duty was validly limited or excluded by the contract. Either remedy could be pursued.

101. The plaintiff must be entitled to rely on the information or advice proffered by the defendant. As stated in *Caparo v. Dickman*,[199] the plaintiff is so entitled if the

191. [1996] 1 HKCU 0467.
192. *Smith v. Eric S. Bush* [1990] 1 AC 831, 864–865.
193. [1970] 2 QB 223, 268.
194. [1995] 2 AC 145 (HL).
195. [1995] 2 AC 145 (HL).
196. [1986] AC 80.
197. [1978] Ch 384.
198. [1979] Ch 384, 417.
199. [1990] 1 All ER 568- (HL).

defendant knows, or ought to know, the purpose for which the plaintiff intends to use the advice or information, knows that the information or advice would be (directly or indirectly) passed to the plaintiff and that the plaintiff was likely to rely on it. The plaintiff should be an identifiable and an intended (in an objective sense; the defendant knew or ought to have known) user of the information; if the plaintiff is not, individually or as part of a group, an identifiable and intended user, the *Hedley Byrne* principle does not apply. This is borne out by the facts of *Caparo*, discussed above. The court refused to impose liability on the auditor who prepared the report of a company as a statutory requirement. The auditor was not liable to potential investors or the existing shareholders who wished to procure further shares, as they were unintended users of such information. However, reasonable reliance could be inferred where the defendant has the knowledge that certain known/intended classes of plaintiffs will rely on the information (report/audit, etc.).

102. Reasonable reliance will also include implicit reliance.[200] In such circumstances, the defendant will be liable even if such information was not directly supplied to such intended recipients. In *Smith v. Eric S Bush,*[201] the House of Lords held the defendant, a surveyor, liable to the purchaser, who relied on their valuation report when obtaining a mortgage from the building society to buy a house. The lender/mortgagee, a building society, commissioned the valuation report, as required by law, and the plaintiff purchaser paid the society for it. The surveyors were aware that the mortgagee and buyer/mortgagor very likely would rely on such information. The surveyor was under a duty to exercise reasonable skill and care and that duty was owed to both parties to the mortgage for which the valuation was made. Therefore the *Hedley Byrne* principle also extends to proximate third parties. The surveyor had supplied the information with a disclaimer and the House of Lords stated that it was unreasonable and ineffective. The Lords further stated that even if the defendants had issued a waiver, it could not have fulfilled the test of reasonableness under section 11 of the Unfair Contract Terms Act 1977. In Hong Kong, reasonableness of exclusion clauses must be established under section 3 of the Control of Exemption Clauses Ordinance (Cap 71) (CECO).

103. Where the defendant is in the business of providing information/advice on an area in which they claim to have competence, they are liable if the information is inaccurate. In *Spring v. Guardian Assurance Plc,*[202] the defendant, who was a previous employer of the plaintiff, wrote a false and negligent reference for the plaintiff, due to which he was refused employment. The plaintiff brought an action for malicious falsehood, breach of contract and negligence. The court held that the defendant was liable for supplying the inaccurate reference as the defendant owed the plaintiff a duty of care based on the employer-employee relationship, and the duty to give a reference with due care existed after that relationship ended.

104. Further, section 3(1) of Misrepresentation Ordinance (Cap 284) allows damages to be awarded where economic loss is suffered after negligent misstatements are relied on. It is wider than the rule in *Hedley Byrne.* Liability arises where a person makes a misrepresentation that induces another person to enter into a contract,

---

200. *White v. Jones* [1995] 2 AC 207, 275 (HL).

201. [1989] 2 All ER 514; [1990] 1 AC 831 (HL); *Harris v. Wyre Forest District Council* [1988] QB 835 (HL).

202. [1994] UKHL 7.

notwithstanding that the misrepresentation is not made fraudulently, unless it can be shown that the maker of the misrepresentation believed, and had reasonable grounds to believe, that what they stated was true up to the time the contract was made.

105. After establishing that the defendant owes a duty of care to the plaintiff, the court considers the standard of care of a reasonable person in the defendant's position to determine whether there has been a breach. The court reviews the conduct of the defendant in the context of their particular profession (e.g., accountant/auditor/ solicitor), mainly in accordance with the normal practices and procedures of that profession. The court may refer to the codes of practice and industry standards of the profession in deciding the proper standard to apply. In *Peter P F Chan v. Hong Kong Society of Accountants,*[203] an accountant appealed the decision of the Disciplinary Committee of the Hong Kong Society of Accountants on the basis that the breaches they found in the preparation of audited accounts did not amount to negligence of a professional nature. The accounts were not prepared in accordance with the Companies Ordinance and were not up to the generally accepted accounting standards in Hong Kong, including the Standard Statements of Account Practice. The Court of Appeal considered that those standards should be followed and that deviations had to be exceptional and justifiable. Even though no loss was incurred by shareholders, creditors or the government, the fact that the accounts were not prepared correctly could not be set aside as a mere slip and did amount to professional negligence.

B. Negligent Activity and Defective Product Economic Loss

106. Liability for defects in property that do no't cause physical damage or damage to other property, but only cause pure economic loss (through the need to dispose of or remedy the defect in the property), is now difficult to impose. From the 1970s until 1990 a fair amount of confusion was injected in economic loss claims concerning negligent activities of the defendant resulting in economic loss to the claimant. This confusion was created by cases such as *Dutton v. Bognor Regis Urban District Council*[204] and *Anns v. Merton London Borough Council,*[205] where the Court of Appeal and the House of Lords respectively allowed damages for pure economic loss arising from defective premises. In *Dutton*, the plaintiff bought a house (she was the subsequent purchaser after the initial purchaser sold it to her within a year of the house being built by a developer) that had been built on defective foundations and had been approved by a surveyor commissioned by the local council. The plaintiff did not have the house re-surveyed as it was a new build, but it was passed by a surveyor to the building society that gave her a mortgage. When the defective foundations were found, caused by the house being built on an old rubbish site – which, an expert report claimed, the council's surveyor should have found – the plaintiff sued both the developer of the property and the council. The claim against the developer was settled out of court, and the claim against the council proceeded to trial. The council was found liable by the Court of Appeal for the negligence of their surveyor. Lord Denning MR stated: '*The damage done here was not solely economic loss. It was physical damage*

203. [2001] 1 HKLRD 687 (CA); leave to appeal refused in [2001] 1 HKLRD 779 (CFA).
204. [1972] 1 All ER 462 (CA).
205. [1978] AC 728 (HL).

to the house. If Mr. Tapp's submission were right, it would mean that if the inspector negligently passes the house as properly built and it collapses and injures a person, the council are liable: but if the owner discovers the defect in time to repair it – and he does repair it – the council are not liable. That is an impossible distinction. They are liable in either case. 'This approach was accepted by the House of Lords in *Anns*, where the plaintiffs were the occupants of the maisonette flats, the foundations of which were found to be defective. The plaintiffs issued a writ action against the builder and the council. The council was alleged to have been negligent in approving the construction of the foundations, which they failed to inspect. The House of Lords held the council liable for negligence in their failure to inspect the foundations and in approving them.

107. In *Spartan Steel And Alloys Ltd v. Martin & Co (Contractors) Ltd,*[206] the plaintiff's property was damaged due to the negligent cutting of a power line, which was owned by the third party, that supplied electricity to the plaintiff's factory, leading to damage to the metal that was in the furnaces at the time of the power cut. The court allowed the consequential economic loss due to the damage of the property and loss of profit that would have been made on the sale of that melt. However, the court did not allow loss of profits on another four melts that the plaintiff claimed would have been processed during the 14 ½ hours that the factory remained closed due to the power cut. The court classified the latter as pure economic loss that was not consequent upon property damage caused to the plaintiff. Further, the plaintiff did not possess any proprietary interest over the damaged property. This decision was based on the general principle created by *Cattle v. Stockton Waterworks Co.*[207] It is a long settled principle that the defendant who negligently damages the property of a third party does not owe any duty to the plaintiff who suffers economic loss due to reliance on the third party's damaged property. It is imperative that the plaintiff shows that he holds a proprietary interest over the damaged property. Therefore, clearly, the plaintiff cannot claim economic loss in relation to damaged property in which he only has a contractual interest.

108. During the 1980s, the approach to those types of cases was examined and reconsidered. For instance, in *Junior Books v. Veitchi*[208] the defendant company, which was a flooring specialist, was sub-contacted and employed by a main contractor to lay flooring in the plaintiff's factory. The main contractors were responsible for the construction but the flooring work was sub-contracted, on the request of the plaintiffs, so that special flooring would be laid which could support heavy machinery. The floor was defectively laid. The plaintiffs had no contractual relationship with the defendant company, so the plaintiffs argued that the defendant company owed a duty of care to them under negligence. The House of Lords ruled in favour of the plaintiffs on the basis that the subcontractor did owe a duty of care to the plaintiff and was liable for the cost that was incurred to rectify the defective flooring. Lord Keith held that subcontractors were nominated for special skills, giving rise to the necessary assumption of responsibility and associated reliance. As the defective floor did not affect the plaintiff in terms of giving rise to a risk or injury or damage to property, the cost of

206. [1973] QB 27.
207. (1875) LR 10 QB 453.
208. [1983] 1 AC 520 (HL).

re-laying the floor was considered economic loss. In his judgment, Lord Keith of Kinkel adopted Lord Wilberforce's test for establishing a special relationship in *Anns*. Lord Wilberforce stated that there was a prima facie duty of care that arose where there was *'a sufficient relationship of proximity or neighborhood'* between the defendant and plaintiff, *'such that, in the reasonable contemplation of the former, carelessness on his part may be likely to cause damage to the latter.'* Where such a duty of care arises, other considerations need to be looked at to affirm whether there are *'any considerations which ought to negative, or to reduce or limit the scope of the duty or the class of person to whom it is owed or the damages to which a breach of it may give rise'*.[209] In *Junior Brooks*, after applying this test as well as looking at *Dutton* and *Hedley Byrne*, it was found that the duty of care breached by the floor-layers could extend to economic loss, and those other cases, including *Spartan Steel*, should therefore be re-assessed.

109. In *Muirhead v. Industrial Tank Specialities,*[210] the plaintiff was a Scottish fishmonger who bought lobsters in the summer season and kept them in tanks for sale in the winter, as they could be sold at a higher price during the Christmas period. Seawater had to be filtered and pumped into the lobster tanks and circulated for oxygenation. Due to a failure in the electric motors in the pumps, several lobster stocks were wiped out and the plaintiff suffered damages. The three defendants in the case were the installer of the tank and pumps (against whom the plaintiff obtained judgment, but could not collect a remedy as they went into liquidation), the supplier (the second defendant) and the subsidiary of the manufacturer of the pumps (the third defendant). The claim against the third defendant was for compensation for loss caused by the damage to the lobsters, as well as economic loss. Lord Justice Robert Goff, delivering a unanimous verdict, found that this case was one of *'ordinary purchase of chattels, in which the buyer, if he seeks to recover damages for purely economic loss arising from defects in the goods, must on the law as it stands look to his immediate vendor and not to the ultimate manufacturer for his remedy'*. The killing of the lobsters was physical damage and that loss, as well as any financial loss arising from the physical damage to property, could be recovered. *Junior Books* was distinguished on the facts, with no equivalent reliance and proximity in the present case. Lord Nourse stated that, absent the features of reliance and proximity, a defendant would not be liable *'in respect of economic loss which is not consequent upon physical damage to the person or property of the plaintiff'* and that, in this situation, *Spartan Steel* would apply.

110. In *D&F Estates Ltd v. Church Commissioners,*[211] the first defendants built block of flats that with defective plasterwork. The plastering work was done by sub-contractors employed by the third defendants, the main contractors. A lease over an affected flat was given to the plaintiffs by the first defendant. The House of Lords held that remedial work to the flat was purely economic loss, not recoverable under *Donoghue*. The main contractors were also not found to have a duty of care with respect to the work of what they reasonably thought were competent contractors. *Junior Brooks* was distinguished as applying in the context of a uniquely proximate relationship. Lord Bridge drew a distinction between situations where an undiscovered dangerous defect

209. *Anns v. Merton London Borough Council* [1978] AC 728 (HL).
210. (1986) QB 507.
211. [1989] AC 177 (HL).

to chattels damages other property or causes personal harm (which is recoverable) and a situation where a dangerous defect is discovered by a user before any damages has occurred. In the latter cases, loss is still categorized as pure economic loss despite the fact that the discovered defect would have posed a threat of property damage or personal injury. As such it is not recoverable in the absence of a proximate relationship and reliance.

111. Finally, the *Anns* approach *'in so far as it affirmed a private law duty of care to avoid damage to property which causes present or imminent danger to the health and safety of owners, or occupiers, resting upon local authorities in relation to their function of supervising compliance with building byelaws or regulations'*[212] was overruled by the House of Lords in *Murphy v. Brentwood,*[213] along with *Dutton*, as it was recognized that such approaches undermine contract law, create indeterminable liability for the defendant and result in putting an unforeseen burden on the government funds. *Junior Books,* though not overruled, was justifiable based on its special facts which created an assumption of responsibility between the parties. In *Murphy,* the plaintiff bought a house from a developer that turned out to have defective foundations. The design of the civil engineers that the developers had relied on was defective. The defective plans had be submitted to, and approved by, the local council, based on the advice from independent consulting engineers. The internal walls of the house became cracked and there were serious problems with the gas and sewage pipes. The expenses were costly and, instead of undertaking them, the plaintiff sold the house at a loss. The plaintiff then brought an action to recover his losses from the defendant, Brentwood District Council. The House of Lords rejected the claim, considering it one for pure economic loss, and stating that such liability could only be recoverable where there was an assumption of responsibility based on special relationship between the parties, based on the *Hedley Byrne* principle. Lord Bridge affirmed the distinction he made in *D & F Estates*, noting that damages caused by something that is defective in quality but that does not cause physical injury or damage to property is purely economic loss caused by having to dispose of the thing or repair it, and not recoverable under *Donoghue* principles.

112. Further, in the UK, under the Defective Premises Act 1972, stricter liability is imposed on the builder/vendor for defective construction work (section 3) and maintenance or repair of premises (section 4, landlord's obligation). In *Murphy*, the House of Lords stated that liability imposed under the Defective Premise Act 1972 falls short of what was imposed by *Anns*. Hence there was no policy reason to impose higher common law duty on builders or on local authorities.[214] Parliament is better equipped than the court to take policy decisions in relation to consumer protection, where such changes are desired. However, in Hong Kong, there is no such specific law. There is, however, the Residential Property (First-Hand Sales) Ordinance (Cap 621), which was passed in Hong Kong to protect the interests of first-hand property buyers. Section 76 imposes criminal liability for fraudulent or reckless misrepresentation produced to induce another into buying residential property, and section 77 imposes civil liability.

212. [1989] AC 177, 2,(Lord Mackay of Clashfern).
213. [1990] 2 All ER 908, [1991] 1 AC 398.
214. Murphy, para. 116.

113. In Hong Kong, the *D & F* and *Murphy* approach is followed. In *Sunface International Ltd & Others v. Meco Engineering Ltd,*[215] the plaintiffs discovered and rectified defects in the electrical circuits in their homes. Meco Engineering Ltd was the sub-contractor for electrical circuits and was sued alongside other defendants responsible for the construction of the houses. Meco requested the Supreme Court of Hong Kong, as it was then, to strike out the cases of three plaintiffs on the basis that their statements of claim did not show any discernable cause of action against Meco. Meco's application was successful as the defect had not caused injury or damage to property.[216]

114. As seen in the cases above, the modern approach to dealing with defective products caused by negligence and pure economic loss is that there should be an assumption of responsibility between the parties and that they should share a proximate special relationship for recovery to be possible. With respect to damage to property, the plaintiff should hold a proprietary interest in order to be able to base a cause of action. The courts are reluctant to award damages for mere defective product economic loss.

V. Rescuer

115. There is no general legal duty under tort law to rescue people in peril, though this does not exclude a moral duty. However, if the defendant creates danger through a wrongful act which jeopardizes the life and property of others, he is liable to whoever comes to victim's assistance (i.e., rescuer), and the victim themselves.[217] In such cases, the defendant must have been reasonably able to foresee the intervention of a rescuer.[218] However, in the past, defendants did not owe any duty of care to rescuers, as the position of the law was that no protection was to be offered if they undertook to participate in a rescue operation and assumed personal risk. In *Baker v. TE Hopkins & Son Ltd,*[219] a couple was employed by the defendant to clean a well. They decided to go down the well against the defendant's instructions and were overcome with fumes before the defendant arrived. The defendant reached out to a doctor for assistance, who eventually died with the couple due to carbon monoxide poisoning after climbing down there in an attempt to save them. The Court of Appeal held that doctors usually face imminent dangers that elicit instinctive reactions and judgments in emergencies. Hence, *volenti non fit injuria* and contributory negligence did not apply. It was held to be irrational to suggest that a rescuer accepts the inherent risks in a rescue operation.

116. A defendant owes a duty to the rescuer if he negligently puts himself in danger.[220] An example would be *Fok Chik Yeung Apple v. I-Cable Telecom Ltd.*[221] The plaintiff sued for personal injuries sustained by him when he tried to catch the defendant's

215. [1990] 2 HKLR 193.
216. Also *see East Asia v. Tsien Wui Marble Factory Ltd & Ors* [2000] 1 HKLRD 268.
217. *Wagner v. International Railways Co* [1921] 133 NE 437 NY 176, 180.
218. *Videan v. British Transport Commission* [1963] 2 QB 650.
219. [1959] 1 WLR 966.
220. *Harrison v. British Railways Board* [1981] 3 All ER 679.
221. [2015] HKCU 2414.

property from falling out of the back of a van. The judge awarded damages to the plaintiff, since the defendant was negligent in ensuring the van tailgate would not cause a danger to others. The judge added that a rescue attempt is undertaken regardless of whether it is bound to fail, and saving lives or property are to be regarded as on the same level.

117. The rescuers may be found liable themselves if they are negligent. In *Lai Tai Tai v. Lam Pak Lo & Another*,[222] the plaintiff was the widow of a sampan driver who died during a junk boat rescue. While the sampan was in the process of being towed by the second defendant on the motor cruiser, it somehow pulled the free anchor lying on the first defendant's junk boat towards the sampan driver and killed him. The plaintiff brought an action against the defendants, and the court held both defendants liable for the sampan driver's death, and the court did not hold the deceased contributorily negligent.

118. The rescuer is entitled to claim damages only if the rescue is reasonably foreseeable (e.g., if there is a professional or parental responsibility to save life). According to *Phipps v. Rochester Corporation*,[223] parents have the primary responsibility to ensure the safety and control of their children. Professional rescuers (e.g., emergency services) are usually awarded damages if they suffer injury during rescue operation. The American fireman's rule, which assumes that professionals have accepted the risk, is inapplicable in the UK and Hong Kong. In *Salmon v. Seafarer Restaurants*,[224] and *Ogwo v. Taylor*,[225] occupiers of premises were held liable for the injuries to firefighters during rescue because they had caused the fires. In *Salmon*, the defendant was a fish and chips shop owner who forgot to turn off the chip fryer, and closed shop for the night. The plaintiff firefighter was injured from being thrown to the ground from the roof by an explosion. The plaintiff was allowed to claim damages, despite having to undertake the risk that comes with his duty to put out fires. Similarly, in *Ogwo*, the defendant was also being negligent, as he was trying to burn paint off from some fascia boards in his house when the fire started. The plaintiff firefighter suffered burns to his face despite wearing protective clothing, due to intensely hot steam managing to seep through it. He was able to claim damages and the court held the risk did not have to be exceptional.

119. This principle also applies to psychiatric injuries of professional rescuers as primary victims. For instance, in *Hale v. London Underground Ltd*,[226] a firefighter was awarded compensation for PTSD and depression. He had to enter the narrow King's Cross station several times to save victims from a fire. However, in *White v. Chief Constable of South Yorkshire Police & Ors*,[227] police officers at the Hillsborough disaster were not allowed to claim for compensation because they were not in physical danger, despite suffering psychiatric injury as rescuers. The House of Lords explained that the rescuer was able to claim in *Chadwick v. British Railway Board*[228] because he

222. [2000] 1 HKLRD 499.
223. [1955] 1 QB 450.
224. (1983) 1 WLR 1264.
225. [1987] 3 WLR 1145.
226. [1993] PIQR Q30.
227. [1999] 2 AC 455.
228. [1967] 1 WLR 912.

was in physical danger. Further discussion of this aspect can be found under the topic of psychiatric injury, above.

120. The standard of care of a rescuer is that of a reasonable person, so he will be liable for negligent acts that cause extra injury or damage to the property of the victim, or a third party.[229] Where a rescuer is negligent, damages for personal injury or property damage may be limited or may not be awarded and a claim may be defeated due to the following defences: *volenti non fit injuria*, which means that no injury is done to a person who consents to a voluntary assumption of risk; and contributory negligence, as damages will be lessened if the rescuer fails to exercise reasonable care for the safety of his property or self. For contributory negligence, the defendant must prove that the conduct of the rescuer was unreasonable and that they disregarded their own safety.[230] A recent example in Hong Kong is *Irving Matthew William and Anor v. Man Chun Yeung and Anor*,[231] where the second plaintiff was injured by trying to save the first plaintiff (her son), who was stuck under the gate of their house. She claimed she sustained back and mental injuries from the incident, thus suing the defendants under both occupier's and rescuer's liability.

§4. Capacity (Infants, Minors)

121. Where a child is a plaintiff, an action is brought by the parents or guardians. However where the child is a defendant the objective standard of care will be differently applied. For details *see* '§1. Unlawfulness and Fault: The Standard of Care and Its Breach'.

229. *East Suffolk Rivers Catchment Board v. Kent* [1941] AC 74 (HL); *Hyett v. Great Western Railway Co* [1948] 1 KB 345.
230. *Baker v. TE Hopkins & Son Ltd* [1959] 1 WLR 966.
231. [2016] HKCU 689.

Chapter 2. Specific Cases of Liability

§1. Liability of Professionals

122. Professional liability is discussed under former subheadings relating to standard of care and pure economic loss. The general principles of negligence are used to determine the standards of professional conduct in different areas, such as the expectations from those who work in the medical, legal, engineering, tax advising, banking, and accounting fields. If the courts have to consider whether the professional's conduct has breached the standard of care, they see if the professional was acting in accordance with the common practice of the relevant professional body. The court applies the *Bolam v. Friern Hospital Management Committee*[232] and *Bolitho v. City and Hackney HA*[233] cases to determine the liability of the professional. It is difficult to prove causation in medical negligence cases as there may be multiple causes to the plaintiff's injury and subject specific texts should be referred to.

123. In general, professionals owe a higher standard of care, though they do not need to achieve a certain result. They are not judged at the same standard as inexperienced persons. For example, in *Wells v. Cooper,*[234] a householder fixing a door only needed to meet the standard of reasonable amateur carpenters but not professionals. In *Susan Field v. Barber Asia,*[235] the defendant, the plaintiff's independent financial adviser, was liable for negligence for their financial advice. The plaintiff was not experienced and had expressed her wish to invest conservatively. The court considered the inexperience of the plaintiff and her will to invest prudently, and held that the investment adviser breached his duty.

124. Likewise, in *Midland Bank Trust Co Ltd v. Hett Stubbs & Kemp,*[236] the client was awarded damages for the solicitor's negligence in not registering the option to buy, causing the plaintiff economic loss by not being able to buy the land. Similarly, in *White v. Jones,*[237] a solicitor negligently failed to amend the plaintiff's will and therefore he was liable for the economic loss sustained by the plaintiff due to his negligence. These two cases are compared here to illustrate the special relationship that occurs with the plaintiff when the defendant is a professional, and the *Hedley Byrne*[238] principle imposes responsibility on the defendant for his professional conduct. In these cases, they did not only consider 'statements' but also professional services, which shows that courts can adopt a more flexible approach to the *Hedley Byrne* principle.

232. *Bolam v. Friern Hospital Management Committee* [1957] 2 All ER 118.
233. [1998] AC 232 (HL).
234. [1958] 2 QB 265.
235. [2003] HKCU 712; Also *see* Jose Antonio Maurellet & Adrian Lai, '*The Minibond Saga: Caveat Emptor or Financial Adviser Beware?*', Hong Kong Law. (2008 December).
236. [1979] Ch 384, [1978] 3 All ER 571, [1978] 3 WLR 167.
237. [1995] 2 AC 207.
238. [1964] AC 465.

§2. Liability of Public Authorities

125. In Hong Kong, similar to the UK, public services tortious liability is governed by general common law rules. Hence, were a public official negligently acts or omits performance of his duty resulting in an injury to the plaintiff, in addition to recourse in public law, he may be able to pursue private law actions in tort for: (1) the breach of statutory duty simpliciter (i.e., irrespective of carelessness); or (2) the careless performance of a statutory duty in the absence of any other common law right of action; or (3) the breach of common law duty of care arising either from the imposition of the statutory duty or from the performance of it; or (4) misfeasance in public office (i.e., the failure to exercise, or the exercise of, statutory powers either with the intention to injure the plaintiff or in the knowledge that the conduct is unlawful).[239]

126. However, in misfeasance in public office cases, public policy plays a significant role when determining the duty of care owed by a public authority, such as a government department or public health department, in situations of economic loss, omission, psychiatric illness,[240] and unintended births, etc. This has been discussed in detail in this text under the topics of omission, psychiatric illness, economic loss and unintended children. The court has to be mindful of the far-reaching consequences of holding a public authority liable and how it may affect the allocation of government funds and dictate how public money should be spent. It will also affect insurance costs. For example, in omission situations, if a court' imposes a duty of care onto a public authority for wrongful life[241] or for omission[242] it will lead to interference with the budgeting of the public authority and cause loss of public money.[243] Hence, in determining the liability for negligence of a public authority, the court takes into consideration that public authorities mainly operate under statute and that it may not be appropriate to impose a common law duty of care on them if the legislature did not intend it.

§3. Abuse of Rights

127. The doctrine of abuse of rights is found in civil law traditions, such as in Swiss, German and French law, and is a legal principle which prevents injury caused by the malicious exercise of legal rights or abuse of legal procedure giving rise to liability. In the common law tradition there is no similar principle. However, all of common law is based on the rule of law, justice, fairness and equity; as such, the abuse of rights will incur liability.

128. Generally, in tort law, the abuse of rights by parties, whether negligent or intentional, will incur liability. For example, a police officer who oversteps in the

239. Michael Ramsden & Dr Hsiao-Pen Chang, '*Misfeasance in Public Office*', in *Tort Law & Practice in Hong Kong* (Justice Kemal Bokhary, N. Sarony & D.K. Srivastava eds, 3rd edn., Sweet & Maxwell, 2014), Chapter 32, 32.001.
240. *Alcock v. Chief Constable of the South Yorkshire Police* [1991] UKHL 5, [1991] 4 All ER 907.
241. *Mckay v. Essex Area Health Authority* [1982] 2 QB 116.
242. *Hill v. Chief Constable of West Yorkshire* [1988] 2 All ER 238 (HL).
243. *Stovin v. Wise* [1996] AC 923 (HL).

performance of his duties can be held liable for assault/battery/false imprisonment for the use of unnecessary force.[244]

129. Specifically, under the tort of malicious prosecution, which aims at protecting citizens from abusive uses of the criminal justice system, civil liability is imposed for the abuse of criminal investigation and prosecution systems.[245] This tort is difficult to prove since a prosecutor has a special immunity and liability is limited to cases where the prosecution is brought without reasonable and probable cause or fabrication of the evidence. This tort does not extend to wrongful disciplinary proceedings.[246]

§4. Injury to Reputation and Privacy

I. General

130. The tort of defamation is committed when the defendant makes a false statement that is either libellous or slanderous, injuring the plaintiff's reputation. This tort applies when a person's reputation is lowered in the eyes of right thinking people in society by published or spoken words. Strict liability is imposed on the defendant when his defamatory statement attacks the moral character of the plaintiff, like the defendant holding plaintiff as the object of ridicule of a serious nature and communicating it to the third party, making false allegations that plaintiff was incompetent, lacking in a certain ability, or producing goods or work of an inferior quality. The limitation period on civil actions in Hong Kong is either three or six years. For defamation, it is six years from the date when the cause occurred, and it may be extended in exceptional circumstances.[247]

131. Hong Kong's Defamation Ordinance 1986 was first enacted in 1887 and it is mostly derived from the Defamation Act 1952 (UK). The Ordinance contains twenty-nine sections and a schedule. This ordinance interprets '*words*' as '*including pictures, visual images, gestures and other methods of signifying meaning*'. For the tort of defamation, the court needs to strike a balance between the right to free expression and people's reputations. As such, it is important that freedom of expression cannot be abused as an excuse to harm others' reputations. Hence, there are provisions about the extent of the right and the scope in which the Defamation Ordinance can be applied, and the detailed provision was laid down in the Bill of Rights Ordinance: '*Everyone shall have the right to hold opinions without interference... Everyone shall have the right to freedom of expression... The exercise of the rights provided for in paragraph (2) of this article carries with it special duties and responsibilities... subject to certain restrictions... for respect of the rights or reputations of others; or for the protection of national security or of public order (order public), or of public health or morals.*'[248] Therefore, legislation is used to try to maintain a balance between freedom of expression

244. *R v. Governor of Brockhill Prison, ex parte Evans (No. 2)* [2001] 2 AC 19.
245. *Kowloon Dairy Ltd v. Ku Yuk Shing* [1968] HKDCLR 57.
246. *Gregory v. Portsmouth City Council* [2000] 1 AC 419.
247. Limitation Ordinance (Cap 347) s. 4(1).
248. Cap 383 s. 16.

and protection of reputation. Article 27 of the Basic Law provides Hong Kong citizens with the freedom of speech, press, publication, association, assembly, procession, demonstration, joining or forming trade unions and also going on strike. The Basic Law also provides foundations for the enactment of Bill of Rights Ordinance.[249] Article 39 of the Basic Law states: '*The provisions of the International Covenant on Civil and Political Rights, the International Covenant on Economic, Social and Cultural Rights, and international labour conventions as applied to Hong Kong shall remain in force and shall be implemented through the laws of the Hong Kong Special Administrative Region.'* In Hong Kong, no provision is specifically made for invasion of privacy, although the Personal Data (Privacy) Ordinance (Cap 486) could provide some protection.

132. In the most serious criminal cases and some particular civil cases, like defamation, jury trials are allowed. In *Chiang Lily v. Secretary for Justice,*[250] it is stated that *'there is no right to trial by jury in Hong Kong'*. It is up to the plaintiff to decide which court to bring his action to. If he commences the claim in District Court, he could claim no more than HKD 1 million. Jury trials in defamation cases take place in the Court of First Instance of the High Court and the court allows such kinds of trials on a discretionary basis. Under the High Court Ordinance,[251] the parties in a defamation case can seek a jury trial, but it is left to the court's discretion to allow such an application, after considering whether such a request would prolong the examination of documents or accounts or any scientific or other investigation. The judge decides whether the alleged words are capable of being defamatory in the eyes of a reasonable or right thinking person before putting them in front of the jury.

133. The ordinary meaning of defamation is making slanderous or libellous statements to harm the plaintiff's reputation, character or good name. The tort of defamation aims to protect the claimant's reputation from being harmed by false statements (both written and spoken). Libel is where the defamatory statement is made and recorded permanently, such as in pictures, statues & waxworks. This tort is actionable per se and the plaintiff only needs to show that the statement is defamatory and false, and then burden shifts to the defendant. In *Youssoupoff v. Metro-Goldwyn Pictures,*[252] a film was produced about the sexual relations and murder of Rasputin, showing the allegedly false statements through the scenes and recorded speech in the film. The plaintiff (Princess Irina Alexandrovna of Russia) contended that any reasonable man would link the female character having sexual relationships with Rasputin in the film with the plaintiff. Hence, the publication would amount to defamation. In this case, it was held that the scenes in the film affected third parties' perception of the plaintiff's moral character and therefore an action in libel was founded.

134. Slander includes statements, like spoken words, gestures and mimicry, which are transitory or temporary. Generally, the plaintiff needs to prove s/he had suffered special damages in a slander case. In *Allsop v. Allsop,*[253] the plaintiff failed to prove the causation between his illness and the slanderous statement, and hence the

249. Cap 383 s. 16.
250. [2010] HKCU 698 (unreported, FAMC 64/2009, FAMC 65/2009, 26 Mar. 2010) (CFA).
251. Cap 4 s. 33A.
252. [1934] 50 TLR 581.
253. [1865] 5 H & N 534.

court held it was too remote to claim such damage. The court found that the distinction between libel and slander was that the former is actionable per se.

135. There are four situations where slanders can be actionable per se: first, if the statement is accusing the plaintiff of committing a criminal offence for which they could be sentenced to imprisonment; second, if the statement is related to a sexually transmitted disease; third, if it affects official, professional or business reputation (section 23 the Defamation Ordinance 1986);[254] and fourth, if the statement is related to the unchastity of a female.[255] In the case of *Lee Ting and Another v. Wei Sau-Hung,*[256] the plaintiffs were husband and wife. They sued the defendant for slander after he made a false statement about the wife having adulterous relationships with others in the village where defendant and plaintiffs were living. The plaintiffs claimed that they were being ridiculed by others in the village and suffered from stress and agony after such accusations, though they did not plea particular damages; they claimed for general damages and an injunction. However, the court awarded damages notwithstanding the absence of special damages. The court based its decision on section 21 (words imputing unchastity to woman or girl per se actionable) of the Defamation Ordinance.

II. Who Can and Cannot Sue for Defamation

136. Anyone, including authors, publishers, corporations or even non-business entity, can be potentially liable if they are involved in producing a defamatory statement. An employer can be liable under vicarious liability[257] for their agent's defamation during the course of employment if the agent was authorized to speak for the employer.[258] Corporations could be sued. The House of Lords case of *Jameel v. Wall Street Journal Europe SPRL (No.3)*[259] is useful in this connection. The first plaintiff, who was a wealthy Arab businessman, and the second plaintiff, a company in Saudi Arabia, sued the defendant for libel for publishing an article accusing the plaintiffs of being linked to terrorism, and the court awarded damages to both plaintiffs. The defendants, in their appeal, brought up a few issues, two of which are relevant in our present context: firstly, whether a company can sue under this tort; and, secondly, whether the *Reynolds* privilege can be used.[260] Lord Bingham, in response to these issues, commented (at paragraph 26): '*...the good name of a company, as that of an individual, is a thing of value. A damaging libel may lower its standing in the eyes of the public and even its own staff, make people less ready to deal with it, less willing or less proud to work for it. If this were not so, corporations would not go to the lengths they do to protect and burnish their corporate images.*'

254. *Tsang Hon Chu v. Wong Kwok Leung* [2005] DCCJ 3917 of 2003); In *Au Yee Ming Ivan v. Ng Fei Tip* (District Court, DCCJ 4595/2008).
255. Defamation Ordinance 1986 (Cap 21) s. 21.
256. [1977] HKDCLR 17.
257. *Riddick v. Thames Board Mills* [1977] QB 881.
258. Please refer to vicarious liability (Part II, Chapter 1) for updates.
259. [2007] 1 AC 359 (HL).
260. For the comments as to Lords views on the *Reynolds* Privilege *see* para. 164, below.

137. The general rule for a class action is that libel or defamation against a class would not lead to liability to particular individuals in that class. In the case of *Knupffer v. London Express Newspaper Ltd,*[261] an article was published by the defendant's newspaper about the Young Russian Party being unpatriotic and being willing to work under the rule of Hitler to advance fascism in Russia. The plaintiff was the head of the political party and, though the party was international, the party members were not easily identified and a right-thinking person would recognize that the statement was referring to plaintiff. Lord Atkin stated: '*The reason why a libel published of a large or indeterminate number of persons described by some general name generally fails to be actionable is the difficulty of establishing that the plaintiff was, in fact, included in the defamatory statement.*' The proper test would be whether a reasonable person would automatically recognize that the defamatory statement is referring to plaintiff; if not, the action would fail. There are two exceptions: first, if the statement is referring to a specific class of people but there is something in words or circumstances that could direct the statement to the particular plaintiff,[262] and, secondly, if the class referred to is small in number and the statement referred to each member, then such statements may still attract liability.

138. Governments cannot use the tort of defamation as it would go against the democratic process and freedom of speech, but an individual government official or councillor can sue if they are personally defamed. In *Derbyshire County Council v. Times Newspaper Ltd,*[263] the court held that the government cannot sue for defamation and this rule has already been accepted to confine the Hong Kong government. In *Derbyshire*, the plaintiff attempted to sue the defendant for its article accusing the council of mismanaging pension funds. The council argued as a corporate entity but was rejected, as the court saw that there was no 'pressing social need'. The court would rule differently if an individual councillor brought a suit for being defamed by malicious statements. On the other hand, universities can sue in defamation. In *Hong Kong Polytechnic University & Others v. Next Magazine Publishing Ltd & Another,*[264] the plaintiff sued the magazine publisher for defamation. The judge at the Court of First Instance held that the university, as a governmental body, could not sue in defamation from the *Derbyshire* ruling. The Court of Appeal later reversed the decision and held that the university was not a governmental body as it was not part of the bodies of government, nor was it democratically elected. It would be of public interest to protect the university's reputation.

139. Political parties and public bodies cannot sue in relation to their governmental functions or public offices, so as to balance freedom of speech in a democratic society. In *Tilbrook v. Parr*[265] the plaintiff, as chairman of a political party, sued the defendant, an author of blog, for accusing a party, the English Democrats, of being racist, but the court held that such words did not clearly refer to the plaintiff. Likewise, in *Goldsmith*

261. [1944] AC 116 (HL).
262. *Charles Sin Cho Chiu v. Tin Tin Publication Development Ltd & Another* (HCA 6662 of 1997) p. 1197.
263. [1993] AC 534 (HL).
264. [1997] 1 HKLRD 514, (1997) HKPLR 286, CA.
265. [2012] EWHC 1946.

v. Bhoyrul,[266] it was affirmed by Justice Buckley that democratically elected bodies, especially government bodies, shall not be allowed to prohibit public criticism.

III. Elements of General Liability in Defamation

140. The claimant must prove three things: (1) the nature of statement was defamatory; (2) the statement was referring to the claimant; and (3) it was published or communicated to a third party.

A. Statement was Defamatory

141. To consider whether the plaintiff's reputation was harmed by the defendant's statement, an objective test of how a 'right-thinking person' would understand the defamatory statement is used. This test is to see if such a statement would 'lower the reputation of the claimant'[267] and whether such a statement discredits them. The statement would cause the plaintiff to be regarded with hatred, contempt, ridicule, fear or disesteem, and would generally be regarded as lowering the plaintiff's reputation in the eyes of right-thinking people. In *Byrne v. Deane,*[268] police went to a club to raid and seize an illegal fruit machine. A notice was later posted saying, 'but he who gave the game away may he burn in hell and rue the day'. The plaintiff pleaded that the notice was referring to him and the court held that being a police informant could not be a negative statement and that any right-thinking person would act similarly and inform police about the occurrence of any illegal operations.

142. The court considers the publication as a whole in defamation cases and that is shown in *Charleston v. News Group Newspapers Ltd.*[269] The courts, while considering whether the publication of photographs was defamatory, also considered factors such as the viewing of the photos with or without the headlines. The defendant was accused of superimposing the plaintiff's face onto naked bodies in pornographic poses. In their defence, the defendant stated that the headlines clearly showed that the photo was superimposed, and hence the court did not hold the defendant liable. The test for libel is whether the ordinary person, after considering the entire defamatory material, would find them defamatory to the plaintiff and, in this case, the court saw that an ordinary person could not find that the plaintiff could be linked to participating in such acts. However, Lord Nicholls warned the newspaper that they are 'playing with fire' and had the text been printed a little further down the article or even on other page, the court would have taken a different view.[270] In *Li Yau-Wai v. Genesis Films Ltd,*[271] the plaintiff was ridiculed by his friends after his photo was shown in a comedy scene of a film. In *Au Yee Ming Ivan v. Ng Fei Tip,*[272] the defendant, as the principal

266. [1998] QB 459.
267. *See Sim v. Stretch* [1936] 2 All ER 1237.
268. [1937] 1 KB 818 (CA).
269. [1995] 2 AC 65 (HL).
270. [1995] 2 AC 65 (HL), 74.
271. [1987] HKLR 711.
272. [2013] HKCU 1079.

of the college, made a statement on the plaintiff's integrity to the Education and Manpower Bureau which was held to be defamatory.

143. In exceptional circumstances, such as where an actor was described as 'hideously ugly', commentators may also be liable for defamation. In *Berkoff v. Burchill,*[273] the defendant published two film reviews in a Sunday newspaper, commenting on the plaintiff's appearance as being ugly and exposing him to ridicule. The defendant appealed, arguing that the statement was not capable of being defamatory and that the injury to feelings and annoyance was not relevant in this case. The court held that the defendant was liable though his words did not mean to link the plaintiff's business conduct to disgrace or deficiency.

144. The issue of innuendo may arise. In law, innuendo means that the defendant has used some libellous language and the extrinsic facts or circumstances mean that the plaintiff could sue. A situation in which defamatory innuendos may be actionable is where the words are neutral but become defamatory after being combined with some extrinsic circumstances in relation to someone. In *Cassidy v. Daily Mirror Newspapers, Limited,*[274] a photographer sent a photo with a description of Mr Corrigan, saying he was engaged Miss X. The defendant newspaper company was not aware that the plaintiff, Mrs. Cassidy, was the lawful wife of Mr Corrigan. The plaintiff brought a claim in libel on the basis that the photo constituted innuendo and imputed that the plaintiff was an immoral person who was cohabiting with Mr Corrigan. The defendant argued on appeal that the article was not referring to the plaintiff; it was not defamatory to the plaintiff. However, the court held that the article concerned the plaintiff for any right-thinking person who knew the plaintiff, and the false information that Mr Corrigan was an unmarried man would affect the reputation of the plaintiff, and hence the plaintiff was awarded damages.

145. Defamatory innuendo can be inferred from the natural meaning of the words used by a reasonable person. The test is objective, based on what a reasonable person would perceive in the natural and ordinary meaning of the words.[275] In *Far East Engineering Services Ltd v. Choy Yau Chiu,*[276] the plaintiff and defendant were both involved in the construction of five schools in Tuen Mun. The defamatory statement implicated the plaintiff in corruption. The court allowed the claim and accepted that there was innuendo in the words used.

B. The Defamatory Statement Referred to the Claimant

146. Defamatory statements could use express or implied references, like name, nickname or position, etc., as long as an ordinary and reasonable person would link such statement to the plaintiff and the plaintiff was defamed. The plaintiff has to prove that the subject of the defamatory statement was him and, if the name is not in the statement, then the court would either look into the inference of the plaintiff's friends or what an ordinary reader would see from the statement.

---

273. [1996] 4 All ER 1008 (CA).

274. [1929] 2 KB 331(CA).

275. *Lewis v. Daily Telegraph Ltd* [1963] 2 All ER 151.

276. [2005] HKCU 1400 (unreported HCA 2146 of 2004, 7 Oct. 2005).

147. In *Oriental Press Group Ltd v. Hong Kong Daily News Ltd & Anor*,[277] a defamatory statement was made with reference to the Sun Group as 'the Sun Newspaper Group'. Deputy Judge Wesley Wong stated that extrinsic evidence must be provided to connect the libel to the plaintiff where the libel does not *ex facie* refer to the plaintiff. From the evidence, the article was sufficiently connected to the plaintiff and a reasonable person would conclude that such statements were referring to the plaintiff. In *Newstead v. London Express Newspapers*,[278] a newspaper published an article concerning the bigamy of a barman named Camberwell, and the plaintiff also had a business named Camberwell. The question before the courts was whether an ordinary person would connect the statement to the plaintiff. It was held by the courts that a reasonable person would have found that the statement was linked to the plaintiff and it would be immaterial whether such statement was referring to someone else; what needed to be established was whether such statement was defamatory in nature.

C. *Publication (Communicated to a Third Party)*

148. The defamatory statement must be communicated to someone other than the plaintiff, and, hence, the plaintiff can claim each and every time the defamatory statement is publicized. Publication could be in any form, including books, articles, etc. both print and digital versions. Two important issues should be considered in relation to publication: intention and dissemination. In cases where there is disputed intention, where the re-publication is not intentional, the court will apply the reasonable foreseeability test to consider whether it could have been known that such re-publication would take place. This point is illustrated by *Theaker v. Richardson*[279] where the defendant was liable for the fact that she foresaw that her husband would open the letter.

149. For dissemination, we have to first distinguish republication and mechanical distribution. The three defendants in *Bunt v. Tilley*[280] were accused of posting defamatory opinions on websites. The plaintiff also sued the Internet Service Providers ('ISPs'). The court held that it was too much to impose liability on the service provider as they could not monitor each posting, considering them akin to a telephone service provider. They facilitated a means of communication.

150. There are some common law exceptions where the communication to a third party does not amount to publication: (1) If a third party opens and reads someone's letter without authorization; (2) if the defamatory statement is communicated to a person who could not understand the language or a person with unsound mind [Official Languages Ordinance (Cap 5) 1974]; (3) if the defamatory statement is made to a blind, deaf or other person who could not comprehend that the statement was referring to the plaintiff; (4) if a post office delivers a letter to the plaintiff; (5) if a library or bookshop provides a book contain defamatory statements but does it innocently; (6) if a defamatory statement is published by person linked to the publication industry and who was doing it innocently; or (7) under the Hong Kong Defamation Ordinance

277. [1997] 3 HKC 622.
278. [1940] 1 KB 377 (CA).
279. [1962] 1 WLR 151 (CA).
280. [2007] 1 WLR 1243.

(Cap 21) section 25 the defendant could exempt his liability if the plaintiff accepts that the defendant was acting innocently and offered actions to correct such conduct.

151. Publication on the internet should also be considered, as it could widely spread defamatory statements. In Hong Kong, there are no specific statutes made or provisions in the Defamation Ordinance (Cap 21) that deal with cyber defamation. It shall be noted that in the Defamation Ordinance (Cap 21), some changes about innocent dissemination[281] are made. However, there are no similar provisions to the UK Defamation Act 2013 that provide some special protection to ISPs. The Act provides defences for operators if they did not personally post the defamatory material. This is, in effect, a codified version of *Bunt v. Tilley.*[282] Generally, service providers who upload or are agents for passing on defamatory material can be liable for defamation in Hong Kong. Storage of defamatory information can amount to publication if any subscriber entered the server and viewed it. The court would weigh the aggravating effect if the publication appears in both paper form and on the internet. In the case of *Chu Siu Kuk Yuen v. Apple Daily Ltd and Others,*[283] the defendant published the defamatory statement both in digital and paper form and the court stated that this did not aggravate the defamation as the paper copies were already in huge numbers.

152. In Hong Kong, internet publications stored on internet servers would still be defamation, as can be seen from *Godfrey.*[284] In this case, the defendants were an ISP operating a UseNet newsgroup. Someone posted something defamatory in the US, which originated from the defendants' new group, and the defendant delayed before removing such posts, and the court allowed damages for the delay.

153. Similarly, the forum operators would generally be considered subordinate distributors, as in *Oriental Press Group Ltd v. Fevaworks Solutions Ltd.*[285] The verdict was handed down to the plaintiff on the basis that the defendant was not a publisher but a 'subordinate distributor' of the defamatory statement.

154. In some cases, ISPs have been sued in the Hong Kong and courts have taken various approaches in dealing with these defamation cases. In *Investasia Ltd & Anor v. Kodansha Co Ltd & Anor,*[286] the first plaintiff was a company who had a business in Hong Kong but established it in the British Virgin Islands, while the second plaintiff was a businesswoman. The defendant was a Japanese company which published two defamatory articles, one of which was downloaded by many Hong Kong people on the internet while the other was published in magazines. Therefore, the plaintiff sued the defendant's company in Hong Kong and they succeeded in showing a sufficient link to Hong Kong to bring such claim (*See* Order 11 r. 1(1) f of the Rules of the High Court (Cap 4A).

281. Section 25 of the Defamation Ordinance concerns unintentional defamation. Subsection (1) (a) provides that if a person innocently publishes words which are defamatory of another person, he or she can make an offer of amend. If such an offer is accepted, no legal proceedings shall be taken by that another person.
282. [2007] 1 WLR 1243.
283. [2001] 1 HKLRD 1.
284. *Godfrey v. Demon Internet Ltd* [2001] QB 201.
285. [2012] 1 HKLRD 848 (CA); [2013] 5 HKC 253 (CFA).
286. [1999] 3 HKC 515.

155. It is unclear whether hyperlinks count as publications, but in Canada it was considered as a neutral reference in *Crookes v. Newton.*[287] As for tweets, in *Cairns v. Modi,*[288] the defendant was liable for a 140 character tweet accusing Chris Cairns, a New Zealand cricketer, of being connected to match mixing. For emails, the place where it was downloaded would be the place of publication. In the case of *Emperor (China Concept) Investment Ltd v. SBI E-2 Capital Securities Ltd and Another,*[289] the court granted the defendants a stay of proceedings in Hong Kong because the email was received in Singapore, though it was sent from Hong Kong.

IV. Defences to the Tort of Defamation

A. Statutory Defences (Unintentional Defamation/Innocent Dissemination)

156. Under the Defamation Ordinance (Cap 21), sections 4 and 25 provide defences of apology and unintentional defamation respectively to avoid or reduce the damages. Under section 25(1) of the Defamation Ordinance, if the publisher makes an offer to make amends and if the apology is accepted by the plaintiff and the compensation is settled, then no proceedings for libel or slander may be brought. Section 25(5) of the Defamation Ordinance provides a defence of innocent or unintentional defamation, which could be pleaded if the publisher can prove that he did not intend to publish the defamatory words concerning the plaintiff, or that all reasonable care had been taken by the publisher to avoid any defamatory material in the publication, etc. In *Oriental Press Group Ltd & Others v. Fevaworks Solutions Ltd & Others*[290] where the appellant sued the respondent, a website provider and administrator of a very popular internet discussion forum, for three defamatory statements on its website, the CFA found the respondent a 'subordinate' publisher of the defamatory statement, and held the respondent to be an innocent disseminator and that the respondent could not have known the defamation prior to its publication due to the high volume of traffic on the forum, which later removed the defamatory statements.

157. Under section 4 of the Defamation Ordinance (Cap 21), the publisher can avoid liability if he provides a reasonable apology and proves that the libel was inserted in the newspaper without actual malice or gross negligence[291] and an apology was offered before the commencement of the action or at the earliest opportunity afterwards. Generally, the apology or retraction of publication would serve as mitigating factors for the court in assessing damages, since such defamatory statements would have already caused some harm to the plaintiff.[292] Section 17 of the Defamation Ordinance allows defendants to provide evidence in mitigation, like the fact that the plaintiff has

287. [2011] SCC 47.
288. [2012] All ER 203.
289. [2005] HKLRD L13.
290. [2013] HKEC 1025.
291. *Chu Siu Kuk Yuen v. Apple Daily Ltd & Others* [2002] 1 HKLRD 1.
292. *Chan Kwong Wai v. Lo Sau King and Others* [1963] HKLR 692.

already recovered its damages, or has brought actions for damages, or has received or agreed to receive compensation, etc.

B. Privilege (Absolute and Qualified)

158. As a matter of public policy and in the public interest on certain privileged occasions, freedom of speech overrides the protection of reputation. The maker of a defamatory statement on a privileged occasion may avail themselves of absolute or qualified privilege from the defamation action.

159. Absolute privilege applies to three situations: parliamentary proceedings, judicial proceedings and executive/official proceedings.

160. Parliamentary proceedings: In Hong Kong, the Legislative Council (Powers and Privileges) Ordinance (Cap 382) provides protection to the freedom of speech of members of the Legislative Council (LegCo). This privilege includes freedom of speech and debate during LegCo sessions (section 3), immunity from legal proceedings (section 4) and freedom from arrest (section 5). No action under the tort of defamation can be taken against the members of LegCo for statements (no matter how defamatory they are) made during debates in LegCo or proceedings before a committee, and such freedom of speech and debate shall not be liable or questionable in any court or place outside LegCo.[293] Under section 14 of Legislative Council (Powers and Privileges) Ordinance (Cap 382), lawful witnesses attending and producing documents before the council also enjoy the absolute privilege. The publishers involved in the publications of LegCo papers are also protected. Section 10 of the Defamation Ordinance (Cap 21) stays judicial proceedings against persons involved in the publication of papers printed by an order of LegCo upon production of the certificate and affidavit of authority to publish. Further, newspapers can rely on absolute privilege if their report was published or broadcasted contemporaneously with the committal proceedings.[294]

161. Judicial proceedings: Statements made during the course of court proceedings are also privileged, and the people involved in court proceedings, such as witnesses, solicitors, judges and juries, are immune from an action of defamation for statements made during court proceedings or during relevant investigations. Hence, anyone involved in the process of administration of justice, such as witnesses, cannot be sued for defamation.[295] This privilege extends to proceedings before tribunals and commissions.[296] Further, fair and accurate newspaper or broadcast reports on judicial proceedings which are in public interest are protected, provided that they are published contemporaneously or as soon as practicable after the hearing.[297]

162. Executive privilege: Some government officers and government communications enjoy absolute privilege in respect of the statements made in the performance of their official duties.[298] For instance, under section 18 of the Ombudsman Ordinance (Cap

293. *Church of Scientology of California v. Johnson-Smith* [1972] QB 522.
294. *See* Legislative Council (Powers and Privileges) Ordinance (Cap 382) s. 13(2); Magistrates Ordinance (Cap 227) ss 87A(5) and (6).
295. *Taylor v. Director of the Serious Fraud Office* [1998] 4 All ER 801(HL).
296. *Wong Shui Kee Roger v. Victor LL Chu* [2000] 3 HKC 589 (CA).
297. Defamation Ordinance (Cap 21) s. 13.
298. *Li Ngan Shui Brumen v. Official Receiver* [1995] 1 HKC 133.

397), for the purposes of the law of defamation, absolute privilege shall be attached to the publication of any matter *'(a) by the Ombudsman or his staff to any person for the purpose of an investigation under this Ordinance... '*. Likewise, under section 14 of the Electoral Affairs Commission Ordinance (Cap 541), immunity is provided where *'(a) the Commission in respect of anything done, or omitted to be done, by it in good faith in the performance of a function or the purported performance of a function under this or any other Ordinance... '*. In *Chatterton v. Secretary of State for India in Council,*[299] the plaintiff brought an action in libel against the defendant in relation to a communication in writing made by the defendant, the Secretary of State, to an Under-Secretary of State in the course of the performance of his official duties. The Court of Appeal held that such cases should not be allowed, because to inquire into the motives of an officer of state with respect to an official communication made to another high state official would 'tend to take from an officer of state his freedom of action in a matter concerning the public interest'.[300]

163. Qualified privilege: Under the common law, a privilege arises in relation to a statement where the defendant has 'an interest or a duty, legal, social, or moral, to make it to the person to whom it is made, and the person to whom it is so made has a corresponding interest or duty to receive it. This reciprocity is essential'.[301] Traditionally, focus was on the relationship between the giver of information and recipient of the relevant information. However, the qualified privilege is displaced if the defendant makes a statement with malice and abuses the privileged occasion.

164. In the landmark case of *Reynolds v. Times Newspaper Ltd,*[302] Albert Reynolds (former Prime Minister of the Republic of Ireland) sued the defendant for libel for a story concerning his resignation. Lord Nicholls stated that the focus on reciprocity in *Adam v. Ward*[303] should not be allowed to obscure the rationale of the underlying public interest on which privilege is founded.[304] Lord Nicholls also set out the responsible journalism test and listed non-exhaustive factors to determine whether the publication of relevant information is in the public interest or not and listed relevant factors as including: (1) the seriousness of the allegations; (2) tThe nature of the information; (3) the source of information; (4) the steps taken to verify the information; (5) the status of information; (6) the urgency of the matter; (7) whether comment was sought from the plaintiff; (8) whether the article contained the gist of plaintiff's side of story; (9) the tone of the article; and (10) the circumstances of the publication.[305] The House of Lords in *Jameel v. Wall Street Journal Europe SPRL*[306] elaborated on the applicability of the *Reynolds* privilege. Lord Hoffmann, allowing the appeal, held that the article as a whole was a matter of public interest and that the inclusion of a defamatory statement may be justifiable so long as it made a proper contribution to the whole thrust of the publication. As to whether the publisher satisfied the test of responsible

299. [1895] 2 QB 189.
300. *Chatterton v. Secretary of State for India in Council* [1895] 2 QB 189, 190 (Lord Esher MR).
301. *Adam v. Ward* (1917) AC 309, 334 (Lord Atkinson).
302. [2001] 2 AC 127.
303. (1917) AC 309.
304. *Reynolds v. Times Newspaper Ltd* [2001] 2 AC 127, 195.
305. *Reynolds v. Times Newspaper Ltd* [2001] 2 AC 127, 205.
306. [2007] 1 AC 359.

journalism, it was held that since reasonable steps had been taken to verify the facts, the failure to obtain the claimants' response was an insufficient ground to deny this defence.

165. Hong Kong follows the UK position on qualified privilege, which is illustrated in *Ming Kee Manufactory Ltd v. Man Shing Electrical Manufactory Ltd,*[307] where the defendant falsely communicated to the plaintiff's customers that the plaintiff was selling unapproved products. The court held that no privilege arose as the defendant did not have any legal, social or moral duty to make such a communication; nor did the customers have a corresponding interest to receive such information. Likewise, in *Pui Kwan Kay v. Ming Pao Holdings Ltd,*[308] which concerned suspected football match-fixing, the Hong Kong Court of Appeal for the first time followed the *Reynolds v. Times Newspaper Ltd* approach, and found that the reporters of Ming Pao met the requirements for the defence of responsible journalism.

166. Under the Defamation Ordinance (Cap 21), the instances when the qualified privilege will apply include the reports of the legislature (section 12), reports of judicial proceedings (section 13) and, reports published in newspapers and broadcasts (section 14).

C. *Justification (Truth)*

167. The defence of truth is based on the logic that truth is not defamatory as such the claimant cannot complain of a true statement even if he thinks such a statement tends to lower his reputation. For this reason, the defendant is entitled to the complete defence of truth in an action for defamation where he publishes a statement that is true in substance and fact i.e., when statement is substantially true. In Hong Kong, section 26 of the Defamation Ordinance (Cap 21) provides the defence of justification and states that *'in an action for libel or slander in respect of words containing two or more distinct charges against the plaintiff, a defence of justification shall not fail by reason only that the truth of every charge is not proved if the words not proved to be true do not materially injure the t'plaintiff's reputation having regard to the truth of the remaining charges'*. The onus is on the defendant to prove the truth of the statement. The defendant has only to satisfy that the material content of the alleged defamatory statement is true and it is not a requirement that truth of each word must be proven. This is illustrated by *Alexander v. North Eastern Railway Co,*[309] where the defendant published that the plaintiff was charged and convicted before a magistrate for an offence of not paying proper train fares and that the plaintiff served three weeks in prison, when in reality the plaintiff had served only two weeks in prison. Blackburn J held that 'the question is whether what is stated inaccurately is the gist of the libel',[310] and, in this case, the defendant's statement was accepted as substantially true.

168. The defendant is required to demonstrate that the words are true in substance and in fact, as against having to prove that they are literally true in every detail. In

307. [1992] 1 HKC 442.
308. [2015] HKCU 2771.
309. (1865) 6 Best and Smith 340.
310. *Alexander v. North Eastern Railway Co* (1865) 6 Best and Smith 340, 344.

Kwan Siu Wa Becky v. Marla Susilo,[311] the plaintiff sued the defendant for publishing two defamatory emails to a group of cabin crew. In understanding the meaning of the emails, the court considered: (1) express meaning of the alleged defamatory words; (2) any implied or inferred meaning of those words; and (3) the context of the alleged defamatory words. After review the court found that both emails were defamatory in nature and ruled in favour of the plaintiff. The defendant failed to prove that the defamatory statements were substantially true.

169. For an action in defamation, the presence of malice or spitefulness does not defeat the defence of truth as long as the words complained of are proven to be true. This is illustrated by *McPherson v. Daniels,*[312] where the court held that the plaintiff was not entitled to recover damages if the statement was true. Littledale J. stated 'the law will not permit a man to recover damages in respect of an injury to a character which he does not or ought not to possess'.[313]

170. For a successful defence of truth, the defendant needs to prove that the 'sting' of the defamatory statement was substantially true and that will turn on the interpretation of facts of each case. For example, in *Wakley v. Healey and Cooke,*[314] the defamatory statement, which stated that the claimant was a 'liabelist journalist' was interpreted to mean that he was a habitual liabelist who had a habit of writing libels. The court's interpretation favoured the claimant argument. Further the defendant may not be absolved of defamation where he only proves the truth of unconnected statement/s. In such a situation, it is no defence for the defendant to rely on the truth of the other unconnected statements that are not related to defamatory statements that are present in the same publication.

171. Where the plaintiff does not identify a distinct statement on which to bring an action of defamation, the defendant does not have to show the truth of all the allegations, provided that 'the words not proved to be true do not materially injure the t'plaintiff's reputation having regard to the truth of the remaining'.[315] In any event, the plaintiff is not allowed to cherry pick statements if such statements are interconnected and the plaintiff knows that the defendant would not be able to prove the truth of such statements. In such circumstances, the rule is that the sting of the defamatory statement must be understood in the context of the whole article.[316]

D. Fair Comment

172. The complete defence of fair comment protects the defendant's democratic right to freedom of expression on matters of public interest as long as the comment is honestly and fairly made and based on a true statement of fact. Since the defence of fair comment allows criticism of the plaintiff on matters of public interest, it is perceived

311. [2011] HKCU 904.
312. (1829) 10 Barnewall and Cresswell 263.
313. *'M'Pherson v. Daniels* (1829) 10 Barnewall and Cresswell 263, 272.
314. (1849) 4 Exchequer Reports (Welsby, Hurlstone and Gordon) 53, 154 ER 1122.
315. *See* s. 26 Defamation Ordinance (Cap 21) Also *see China Bocom Insurance Company Limited v. Next Magazine Publishing Limited & Anor* [2010] HKCU 2647.
316. *Alice Li Miu Ling v. Hong Kong Polytechnic University* [2013] 3 HKC 221; *Oriental Daily Publisher Ltd v. Ming Pao Holdings Ltd* [1999] 4 HKC 354.

as essential for the efficient working of any public institution.[317] To succeed in the defence of fair comment it must be proven that the comments were honestly based on a true set of facts, that such comments were identifiable as remarks and that the comments were not motivated by malice. Section 27 of the Defamation Ordinance (Cap 21) offers a defence of fair comment and the test for this defence is whether the comment was based on proven facts, even if not all alleged facts can be proved.[318] This defence could be availed of as follows: (1) the statement was of the public interest; (2) the statement was a comment or opinion based upon the true facts; and/or (3) the statement was honestly held.

173. The scope of this defence is wide and the general understanding is that the opinions that are of public interest could be on the conduct of a person holding public office, including politicians, as well as on a wide range of topics, including artistic exhibitions, and the ethical standards of news media. In *London Artists Ltd v. Littler*,[319] Lord Denning M.R. defined the public interest widely, stating that it should not be confined within narrow limits. He stated: '*Whenever a matter is such as to affect people at large, so that they may be legitimately interested in, or concerned at, what is going on; or what may happen to them or others; then it is a matter of public interest on which everyone is entitled to make fair comment.*'[320]

174. The comment must be a remark based on true facts and the defendant is required to show that. Then the judge will determine the connection between the comments and facts with respect to content and the context of those facts.[321] In *Oriental Daily Publisher Ltd v. Ming Pao Holdings Ltd*,[322] a case about two articles published by Ming Pao perceived as 'an assault by Oriental Press against TVB', the court held that the statement should be considered in terms of both its content and its context, and the test is therefore whether a reasonable ordinary reader would regard the statement as a comment or fact.[323] Accordingly, the fairness is judged by the objective standard of whether any fair-minded person could honestly express the opinion in question if he would have known the facts accurately. In interpreting this standard, the courts consider comments fair only if they are relevant to the facts to which they are addressed, and the defendant must not indulge in unwarranted imputations under a cloak of criticism. Hence, the true test is whether the opinion, however exaggerated, obstinate or prejudiced, was honestly held by the person expressing it.[324] The presence of malice or lack of genuine belief in the comment defeats the defence of fair comment. Clearly the meaning of malice for the defence of honest comment and qualified privilege is different. In terms of fair comment, malice means spite, evil motive and dishonesty, whereas for the defence of qualified privilege, the meaning of malice is broader and

317. *Cheng & Another v. Tse Wai Chun* [2000] 3 HKLRD 419.
318. *China Bocom Insurance Company Limited v. Next Magazine Publishing Limited & Anor* [2010] HKCU 2647, para. 23.
319. [1969] 2 QB 375 (CA).
320. *London Artists Ltd. v. Littler* [1969] 2 QB 375 (CA), 391.
321. *China Bocom Insurance Company Limited v. Next Magazine Publishing Limited & Anor* [2010] HKCU 2647, paras 22–23.
322. [1999] 4 HKC 354.
323. *Oriental Daily Publisher Ltd v. Ming Pao Holdings Ltd* [1999] 4 HKC 354, 367 (Yuen J).
324. *Silkin v. Beaverbrook Newspapers Ltd.* [1958] 1 WLR 743, 747 (Diplock J).

the maker of statement is not required to possess an honest belief in his statement but merely show that he did not abuse the privileged occasion at which the defamatory statement was made. This could be illustrated by *Reynolds v. Times Newspaper Ltd.*[325] In this case, although the defendant abandoned the plea of fair comment, Lord Nicholls took the chance to clarify that fair comment cannot 'be used as a cloak for mere invective'.[326]

E. Consent

175. There is no cause of action under the tort of defamation if the plaintiff consents to the publication of the defamatory statement. The reasoning is straightforward, as the plaintiff in such circumstances is seen to have authorized the publication of the defamatory statement and waived his right to bring an action. As such, it is unfair to hold the defendant liable for the dissemination of such defamatory information.[327]

§5. Interference by a Third Person with Contractual Relations (Intentional Economic Loss)

176. Economic torts impose liability for infringement of the plaintiff's legitimate economic interests and compensate any intangible commercial losses caused by intentional and unlawful acts of the defendant (e.g., unlawful interference that does not include fair competition). For a further discussion on economic torts, specialist works should be referred to,[328] as they coincide with other administrative bodies and statutes (e.g., labour law, competition law, some intellectual property laws like unfair competition). This text will focus on tortious liability only. Actions for pure economic loss under the tort of negligence could sometimes perform the function of an economic tort, as demonstrated by *Hedley Byrne.*[329] However, a significant point to remember is that the reason for liability under economic torts and negligence are distinct: the former are intentional torts, and the latter is not.

177. Economic torts were developed during the early twentieth century, mainly to provide a remedy for the loss sustained by parties affected by trade unions organizing industrial disputes. Hence, most cases then were in industrial settings[330] with trade unions, or commercial disputes.[331] Nowadays, there is a statute protecting the rights of participation in trade unions/industrial action for workers, so economic torts remain

325. [2001] AC 127 (HL).
326. *Reynolds v. Times Newspaper Ltd* [2001] AC 127 (HL), 193.
327. Also *see* Defamation Ordinance (Cap 21), Sch Part II, (Statements Privileged Subject to Explanation Or Contradiction).
328. H. Carty, *An Analysis of the Economic Torts* (2nd edn, OUP 2010); P. Cane, *Tort Law and Economic Interests* (2nd edn, Clarendon Press 1996); H. Carty, '*The Economic Torts in the Twenty First Century*', 124 L.Q. Rev. (2008) 641; S. Deakin & J. Randall, '*Rethinking the Economic Torts,*' 72 Modern L. Rev. 519 (2009).
329. *Hedley Byrne & Co Ltd v. Heller & Partners Ltd* [1964] AC 465 (HL).
330. *Quinn v. Leathem* [1901] AC 495 (HL).
331. *Lumley v. Gye* [1854] 3 E & B 114; *Torquay Hotel v. Cousins* [1969] 1 All ER 522 (CA); *Merkur Island Shipping v. Laughton* [1983] 2 All ER 189 (HL).

mostly to protect against unfair competition. Historically, English judges ruled in favour of competition due to the *laissez faire* philosophy, thus restricting the application of economic torts.[332] Over the years, economic torts became increasingly significant, but also confusing. Courts viewed causing loss by unlawful means as inducing or procuring a breach of contract, unlawful interference with contractual relations,[333] intimidation or indirect ways of committing the *Lumley* tort.[334] These torts are dealt with under the unified theory. This confusion was eventually brought to an end by the House of Lords decision of *OBG v. Allan,*[335] which described it as *'un-natural union'*[336] that must be brought to an end. They stated that inducing or procuring a breach of contract and causing loss by unlawful means are different concepts. Another landmark decision, *Total Network v. Revenue,*[337] clarified the concept of unlawful means under the concept of conspiracy.

178. Currently, there are two different kinds of economic torts: (1) direct interference (e.g., inducing a breach of contract, causing loss by unlawful means and conspiracy); and (2) false representation (e.g., passing off, deceit and injurious falsehood). The second category of economic torts remains unchanged. In Hong Kong, it seems that the *OBG* and *Total Network* approaches have been adopted.[338] For example, in *Shenzhen Fuhaitong Precision Industry Co Ltd v. Byd Company Ltd,*[339] *'leading counsel for the plaintiffs and the defendants by counterclaim relies on the speech of Lord Hoffman in* OBG Ltd *case and submits that the unlawful means must be actionable by the third party or would have been actionable if the third party had suffered loss'*. In that case, the parties were competitors. The plaintiffs developed confidential information for their business operations, which the defendants procured from the plaintiff's employees, thus making them in breach of their duties. The approach was also applied in *Total Lubricants Hong Kong Ltd v. Christophe de la Cropte de Chanterac and Ors,*[340] wherein the plaintiff relied on the principle of *Total Network* in his argument, which was that conspiracy to commit criminal conduct to inflict loss on plaintiff constitutes 'unlawful means'.[341] The defendants were former employees of the plaintiff that conspired to steal confidential information from the plaintiff before defecting.

---

332. *Mogul Steamship Co Ltd v. McGregor, Gow & Co* [1892] AC 25; *Allen v. Flood* [1898] AC 1.
333. *Thomson & Co Ltd v. Deakin* [1952] 2 All ER 361 (CA); *GWK Ltd v. Dunlop Rubber Co Ltd* [1926] 42 TLR 376.
334. *Lumley v. Gye* [1854] 3 E & B 114.
335. [2007] UKHL 21 (HL).
336. [2007] UKHL 21 (HL), para. 38 (Lord Hoffmann).
337. [2008] UKHL 19 (HL).
338. *Wong Chun Tak v. The Registrar Of High Court* [2015] HKCU 1255; *Pido v. Compass Technology Company Ltd* [2010] 2 HKLRD 537 (CA), *C Y Foundation Group Ltd Anor v. Best Max Holdings Ltd & Ors* [2013] HKCU 1273; *Axa China Region Insurance Company Limited v. Lin Kwai Ying Katie* [2012] HKCU 853; *Formerly Known as v. Eton Properties Limited* [2012] HKCU 1268 etc.
339. [2010] HKCU 1813.
340. [2012] HKCU 268.
341. [2012] HKCU 268, para. 12.

I. Direct Interference Economic Torts

179. The direct interference economic torts include: (1) procuring a breach of contract; (2) causing loss by unlawful means; and (3) conspiracy to injure (lawful and unlawful). There are a couple of points to note about these torts after *OBG*. First, *Lumley* and unlawful means torts are separate. Second, in *OBG*, Lord Hoffmann stated that the *Lumley* principle differs from unlawful means torts in at least four aspects:

> First, unlawful means is a tort of primary liability, not requiring a wrongful act by anyone else, while Lumley v Gye created accessory liability, dependent upon the primary wrongful act of the contracting party. Secondly, unlawful means requires the use of means, which are unlawful under some other rule ('independently unlawful'), whereas liability under Lumley v Gye requires only the degree of participation in the breach of contract, which satisfies the general requirements of accessory liability for the wrongful act of another person... Thirdly, liability for unlawful means does not depend upon the existence of contractual relations. It is sufficient that the intended consequence of the wrongful act is damage in any form; for example, to the m'claimant's economic expectations... Fourthly, although both are described as torts of intention... the results which the defendant must have intended are different. In unlawful means, the defendant must have intended to cause damage to the claimant (although usually this will be, as in Tarleton'v 'M'Gawley, a means of enhancing his own economic position). Because damage to economic expectations is sufficient to found a claim, there need not have been any intention to cause a breach of contract or interfere with contractual rights. Under Lumley v Gye, on the other hand, an intention to cause a breach of contract is both necessary and sufficient. Necessary, because this is essential for liability as accessory to the breach. Sufficient, because the fact that the defendant did not intend to cause damage, or even thought that the breach of contract would make the claimant better off, is irrelevant.[342]

A. Inducing a Breach of Contract

180. This tort historically suffered uncertainties, and it was recognized mostly in trade and industrial disputes. However, it also applied to other contractual situations, which led to the expansion of its ambit, and its link to interference with contractual relations. This tort developed from *Lumley v. Gye,*[343] where the plaintiff theatre owner contracted a famous singer (third party) to perform at his theatre only. The defendant was a rival theatre owner who, upon finding out about the contract, offered money to the singer to break it, and she did. The court held the defendant liable, on the basis that the action for inducement can apply beyond the strict master-servant relationship. The court stated that if a defendant induces a contracting party to commit a breach of contract (or other actionable wrong), then the defendant is only liable as an *accessory*,

342. *OBG v. Allan* [2007] UKHL 21; [2008] 1 AC 1 (HL), para. 8, concurred with by Lord Nicholls [paras 168–198], Lord Walker [para. 264], Baroness Hale of Richmond [para. 302] and Lord Brown [para. 320].

343. 118 ER 749.

since the main purpose of this tort is to prove he 'joined with' the third party to breach its contract with the plaintiff. This tort is committed when the defendant intentionally interferes with the existing contractual rights between the parties, so persuasion to undertake lawful means to end a contract does not count.

181. In *Lumley* the defendant, knowing that a contract existed between a third party and the defendant, intentionally and unlawfully induced the third party to breach his contract. The defendant was liable under the 'inducing breach of contract' tort. Liability can only be established if there is an actual breach by the contracting party, so merely making statements to convince the contracting party will be insufficient.[344] Secondary liability can only occur if primary liability is found.

182. The requirements[345] that the plaintiff has to prove are: (1) knowledge of the contract's existence; (2) intention to induce or procure a breach of contract; and (3) breach of contract. To succeed it must be proven that the defendant had knowledge of the existence of the contract, as well as awareness that the inducement would lead to a breach. In *Merkur Island Shipping Corp v. Laughton,*[346] the plaintiff employed a third party. The defendants subsequently asked the third party to work for them, and their business was similar to the plaintiff's. It was presumed that the defendant knew of the existence of the plaintiff's contract. The defendant is not liable if he did not know of such a contract, or its precise terms. To prove that first requirement, the defendant must have knowledge of any possibly relevant contractual terms that might be broken if the third party acts in response to the inducement. The law will not presume the defendant to have constructive knowledge of the terms' existence if the defendant had some agreement with the third party and unintentionally failed to make appropriate inquiries about its contractual obligations. This was clarified in *Mainstream Properties v. Young,*[347] where the House of Lords stated that lack of knowledge limits the liability incurred. However, if the defendant deliberately refrains from making inquiries, because he suspects that he will be disadvantaged after information is revealed, then he will be liable under the 'blind eye knowledge' principle. In *Emerald Construction Co Ltd v. Lowthian,*[348] Lord Denning stated that it would be sufficient to prove liability if they did not know the actual terms but intentionally disregarded available means of knowledge, like the man who turns a blind eye. In *Peter Geoffrey De Krassel v. Vincent Julia Chu & Ors,*[349] a distinction was made between 'blind eye knowledge' and mere suspicion. 'Blind eye knowledge' has a legal effect on the induced, regarding his contract, through the defendant's conduct.[350] The defendant may know about the existence of the contractual terms, but not realize that the third party will be in breach of its contract by responding to the inducement. Lord Hoffmann stated, *'To be liable for inducing a breach of contract, you must know that you are inducing a breach of contract.'*[351] It was also stated in *OBG* that, *'It is not enough that you know that you*

344. *OBG v. Allan* [2007] UKHL 21; [2008] 1 AC 1 (HL), paras 39–44, esp. para. 44.
345. *Peter Geoffrey De Krassel v. Vincent Julia Chu & Ors* [2010] 2 HKLRD 937, para. 64.
346. [1983] 2 AC 57.
347. [2007] UKHL 21 (HL).
348. [1966) 1 WLR 691.
349. *Peter Geoffrey De Krassel v. Vincent Julia Chu & Ors* [2010] 2 HKLRD 937.
350. *OBG v. Allan* [2007] UKHL 21; [2008] 1 AC 1 (HL) (Lord Nicholls).
351. *Mainstream Properties v. Young* [2007] UKHL 21 (HL).

are procuring an act which as a matter of law or construction of the contract is a breach. You must actually realize that it will have this effect.'[352]

183. The second requirement for inducing a breach of contract is that the defendant knew about the existence of the contract and deliberately interfered, to the detriment of the plaintiff. In *Quinn v. Leathem,*[353] the appellant trade union wanted to enforce a closed shop agreement with the respondent butcher, by convincing one of his customers to refuse trading with respondent unless he hired employees from the union. The union representative threatened to call a strike among the customer's workers if he did not do as he was told. There was a '*conspiracy to injure*'. It was found that, '*It is a violation of legal rights to interfere with contractual relations recognized by law if there be no sufficient justification for the interference.*'[354] It is no defence for him to show that he was not malicious or spiteful, or that his motive was not to cause damage to the claimant. If the defendant had no intention, despite his knowledge of contract, he may not be found liable.[355] In *Millar v. Bassey,*[356] the defendant singer allegedly breached her contract with Dreampace, a record company, preventing their contract with the plaintiff being executed. The issue for the court was whether the conduct of the defendant was aimed directly at the plaintiff, or whether it is sufficient for the conduct to lead to the natural and likely consequence of the contract being breached. However, the distinction was disapproved of in *OBG* afterwards.[357] Lord Hoffmann noted that it was important to distinguish between '*ends, means and consequences*'.[358] Merely having a causative participation is insufficient.[359] Where ends and means are identified, except in consequential circumstances, liability could arise as they were incidental to the defendant's purpose.

184. Since the inducement is directed to the third party, it would not require any unlawful action by the defendant per se to incur liability. In *OBG*, Lord Hoffmann stated, '*the distinction between direct and indirect interference is unsatisfactory, and it is time for the unnatural union between* Lumley v Gye *tort and the tort of causing loss by unlawful means to be dissolved*'.[360] Direct interference by the defendant towards the third party to break his contract with the plaintiff is the only form that survived after *OBG*. In *Exchange Telegraph Co v. Gregory & Co,*[361] related to malicious inducement to break contracts. The defendant stole and published information that the plaintiff gave to subscribers about the stock exchange. By inducing subscribers to pass on the information, the defendant induced them to break their contracts. It should be noted that indirectly interfering with contractual relations is not included under this tort.

352. *OBG v. Allan* [2007] UKHL 21; [2008] 1 AC 1 (HL), para. 39.
353. [1901] AC 495.
354. [1901] AC 495, 511 (Lord McNaghten).
355. *Club Deluxe Ltd v. Club Metropolitan Ltd and Ors* [1995] 2 HKLR 69.
356. 1994 EMLR 44.
357. *OBG v. Allan* [2007] UKHL 21; [2008] 1 AC 1 (HL).
358. *OBG v. Allan* [2007] UKHL 21; [2008] 1 AC 1 (HL), para. 42.
359. *OBG v. Allan* [2007] UKHL 21; [2008] 1 AC 1 (HL), para. 191.
360. *OBG v. Allan* [2007] UKHL 21; [2008] 1 AC 1 (HL), para. 38.
361. [1896] 1 QB 147.

185. Lastly, since inducing a breach of contract incurs secondary liability, there is no liability if there is no breach of contract. The defendant cannot be liable if it persuades a party to a contract to terminate their contract by proper means, and the party uses lawful means. In *RCA Corp v. Pollard*,[362] the court held that making a contract less valuable is not actionable, unless there is an actual breach of contract. In *Torquay Hotel v. Cousins*,[363] the Court of Appeal took it a step too far by treating the prevention of contractual performance as an extension of the *Lumley* tort.

186. As a defence the interference may be permissible where the defendant is securing the performance of his prior contract or where an equal or superior right of performance of contract exists. In Hong Kong, the Trade Unions Ordinance (Cap 332) under section 43, protects registered trade unions from tortious actions. The defendant can also plead moral or social duty as a defence, but that is insufficient on its own.[364] The plaintiff can claim damages and injunctions as remedies.

B. *Causing Loss by Unlawful Means*

187. This is a generic tort, confirmed by *OBG*, which includes direct interference torts (e.g., interference with contractual relations/business/rights, or intimidation). All of them were seen as freestanding torts, except it was suggested by some case law[365] that interference with contractual relations was an 'indirect' form of committing the 'direct' *Lumley* tort (i.e., inducing a breach of contract). The *OBG* decision described this distinction as an 'unnatural union' to be dissolved. It was accepted that the 'indirect' manner of committing the *Lumley* tort is the same, and could be put together under 'causing loss by unlawful means'. Therefore, the earlier confusion was brought to an end by the *OBG* decision.

188. The requirements to prove that the defendant has committed unlawful means torts are that the defendant has acted and: (1) the act is unlawful; (2) the act must affect third party's freedom to deal with the plaintiff; and (3) the intention is to cause loss to the plaintiff. First, wrongful acts against a third party will count as unlawful only if they are actionable in civil law, directed towards them by the defendant, for the purposes of "unlawful means torts'. This acts as a suitable 'control mechanism'.[366] Second, the defendant must affect the third party's freedom to deal with the plaintiff, but the third party does not 'join with' the defendant to bring about a loss on the plaintiff.[367] In *RCA Corp v. Pollard*,[368] the defendant sold illegal copies of the records of Elvis Presley made at concerts, while the plaintiff had the exclusive rights to sell records by the artist. The defendant's appeal was allowed by the Court of Appeal. It was found that for the tort of wrongful interference, it must be shown that the harm

362. [1983] Ch 135.
363. [1969] 2 Ch 106.
364. *Abdul Razzak Yaqoob and Ors v. Asia Times Online Ltd and Anor* [2008] HKCU 679.
365. *Thomson & Co Ltd v. Deakin* [1952] 2 All ER 361 (CA); *GWK Ltd v. Dunlop Rubber Co Ltd* [1926] 42 TLR 376.
366. *OBG v. Allan* [2007] UKHL 21; [2008] 1 AC 1 (HL), para. 266 (Lord Walker).
367. *OBG v. Allan* [2007] UKHL 21; [2008] 1 AC 1 (HL), para. 52 (Lord Hoffmann).
368. *RCA Corp v. Pollard* [1983] Ch 135.

was in some way intended to affect the plaintiff. In that situation, the estate may have had rights to sue, but not the plaintiff.

189. Third, the defendant's intention does not have to be very specific to 'target' the plaintiff. In *OBG*, Lord Hoffmann stated that narrow interpretation would strain the concept of intention, and cause trouble in cases where the defendant has really used unlawful means. The plaintiff should be allowed to rely on the infringement of a third party's rights. For example, in *Tarleton v. M'Gawley*,[369] the shipmaster moored off by the West African coast and later used cannon shots to repel a canoe from a rival British trading ship, which also wished to trade with the West African natives. The master of the ship only intended to monopolize the local trade, but that was at the expense of causing loss to the plaintiff. An action would lie for frightening African natives, as third parties, from coming to the plaintiff's vessel to trade.

190. Lord Hoffmann clarified by reference to *Rookes v. Barnard*,[370] and *J T Stratford & Son Ltd v. Lindley*,[371] that 'unlawful' for 'unlawful means' torts have two elements: *'(a) a wrongful interference with the actions of a third party in which the claimant has an economic interest and (b) an intention thereby to cause loss to the claimant... [Or, simply put,] intentionally causing someone loss by interfering with the liberty of action of a third party in breach of a contract with him is unlawful'.*[372] As per Lord Nicholls, it would be insufficient and inadequate to suggest that ''unlawful' simply meant a wrongful act, or an act that caused a wrong to the claimant.[373]

191. Rookes created a tort of intimidation which is now part of a generic tort of 'causing loss by unlawful means'.[374] It is a reminder that in *OBG*, the court allowed intimidation to be bi- or tripartite. However, Lord Hoffmann clarified that such a fact is minor, and it would *'only add one footnote to this discussion of unlawful means'*. He further stated that, *'In defining the tort of causing loss by unlawful means as a tort which requires interference with the actions of a third party in relation to the plaintiff, I do not intend to say anything about the question of whether a claimant who has been compelled by unlawful intimidation to act to his own detriment, can sue for his loss. Such a case of 'two party intimidation' raises altogether different issues.'* Moreover, Lord Walker in *Total Network* asserted that a two-party intentional harm tort (i.e., intimidation) is an exceptional situation.[375]

192. Remedies may be awarded for all not-too-remote economic losses caused by unlawful means torts. Usually, compensatory damages are provided when the loss is exemplary.[376] Damages for pain, suffering and distress caused by the defendant's actions can be recovered. Aggravated damages may be awarded where the defendant's conduct increases the injury sustained by the plaintiff through additional distress,

369. (1790) 1 Peake NPC 270.
370. [1964] UKHL 1.
371. [1965] AC 269.
372. *OBG v. Allan* [2007] UKHL 21; [2008] 1 AC 1 (HL), para. 47.
373. *OBG v. Allan* [2007] UKHL 21; [2008] 1 AC 1 (HL), para. 146.
374. *Rookes v. Barnard* [1964] AC 1129.
375. *Revenue and Customs Commissioners v. Total Network SL* [2008] UKHL 19; [2008] 1 AC 1174 (HL), para. 100.
376. *Rookes v. Barnard* [1964] AC 1129.

embarrassment or humiliation. Injunctions may be given to stop the defendant from committing wrongful acts that are imminent but not yet in action.

C. Conspiracy

193. The tort of conspiracy is committed when two or more parties reach an agreement to engage in conduct, which can be lawful or unlawful, with the intention to cause damage to the plaintiff's economic interests.[377] The element of agreement is decided in the context of the facts of the matter, as adopted in Hong Kong from the British case of *Kuwait Oil Tanker Co SAK v. Al Bader:*[378] *'In most cases it will be necessary to scrutinise the acts relied upon in order to see what inferences can be drawn as to the existence or otherwise of the alleged conspiracy or combination. It will be the rare case in which there will be evidence of the agreement itself.'* The two main categories of the offence are lawful and unlawful conspiracy. Lawful conspiracy is committed when the conduct agreed to is intended to cause loss or damage to the plaintiff, but the means themselves do not need to be unlawful. As Lord Wright stated in *Crofter Hand Woven Harris Tweed Co Ltd v. Veitch,*[379] *'It is in the fact of the conspiracy that the unlawfulness resides.'* The elements of unlawful conspiracy require that the agreement between the defendants must be to do an unlawful act engaging in unlawful means, with the intention of causing damage to the plaintiff.

194. For lawful means conspiracy, the defendants cannot be found liable if they were acting with the dominant purpose of self-interest.[380] However, as stated by Lord Diplock in *Lonrho plc v. Fayed,*[381] *'...When conspirators intentionally injure the plaintiff and use unlawful means to do so, it is no defence for them to show that their primary purpose was to further or protect their own interests; it is sufficient to make their action tortious that the means used were unlawful.'* If the offence is ongoing or the acts conspired over have not occurred, an injunction may be granted. This tort is mainly for the recovery of financial loss – and not for injury to reputation or feelings – and damages may be granted for, among others, loss of wages and expenses incurred in finding out the conspiracy.[382]

1. Lawful Means Conspiracy

195. The tort of conspiracy became increasingly utilized due to economic growth during and after the industrial revolution. Employers brought cases against trade unions

---

377. *Mulcahy v. R* [1868] LR 3 HL 306.
378. [2000] 2 All ER (Comm) 271; this has been adopted in Hong Kong and is cited in, among others, *Sinodental Investments Ltd and Others v. Sin Chung Yin Ronald and Others* and *Hengshi International Investments Ltd v. Bayspring International Ltd and Another* (22 Jul. 2014, HCA2176/2012).
379. [1942] 1 All ER 142, 462.
380. *Crofter Hand Woven Harris Tweed Co Ltd v. Veitch* [1942] 1 All ER 142.
381. [1992] 1 AC 448, 465G-466A.
382. *Lonrho Plc. v. Fayed* (No. 5) [1993] 1 WLR 1489; *Tse's Forex Investment Co Ltd v. Man Yuk Lan & Anor* [1995] HKLY 1001, CA.

for conspiracy to injure, which is another term for lawful means conspiracy.[383] The court's approach was to hold that, if the parties' predominant intention was the protection of their own interests, they were not liable. In *Mogul Steamship Co Ltd v. McGregor, Gow & Co,* the court held that the defendants had no liability because the ship owner's main motive to formulate an association was to protect their interests and to obtain monopoly in the lucrative Chinese tea trade. Even if that drove the plaintiffs out of business, the defendants had not committed any conspiracy. Likewise, in *Crofter Hand Woven Harris Tweed Co Ltd v. Veitch,*[384] the House of Lords held that there was no conspiracy because the predominant purpose of the combination (trade union) was to promote the legitimate interests of the combiners and the means adopted were lawful because threat did not involve committing a crime or tort. Viscount Simon in at 445 stated that:

> If that predominant purpose is to damage another person and damage results that is tortious conspiracy. If the predominant purpose is the lawful protection or promotion of any lawful interest of the combiners (no illegal means being employed), it is not a tortious conspiracy, even though it causes damage to another person.

196. The requirements of lawful conspiracy are stated in *Pido v. Compass Technology Company Ltd,*[385] namely: (1) the combination or agreement between two or more individuals; (2) a predominant intention to injure the plaintiff; (3) acts that were carried out pursuant to the combination or agreement and with that predominant intention; and (4) it resulted in loss and damage to the plaintiff.[386] The presence of all of these requirements is necessary. These requirements are affirmed in *Sinodental Investments Ltd and Others v. Sin Chung Yin Ronald and Others*[387] and *Hengshi International Investments Ltd v. Bayspring International Ltd and Another,*[388] which listed the requirements for pleading a conspiracy defence.

2. Unlawful Means Conspiracy

197. In the 2010 case of *Total Network,*[389] the House of Lords clarified the meaning of 'unlawful means' for the purposes of unlawful conspiracy and adopted the 'instrumentality test' for this purpose, stating that the unlawful means should be the instrument intended for causing harm.[390] The House of Lords also stated that the unlawful means included criminal offences in statutes and common law, whether or

383. *Mogul Steamship Co Ltd v. McGregor, Gow & Co* [1892] AC 25 (HL); *Allen v. Flood* [1898] AC 1; *Quinn v. Leathem* [1901] AC 495 (HL); *Sorrell v. Smith* [1925] AC 700 (HL); *Crofter Hand Woven Harris Tweed Co Ltd v. Veitch* [1942] AC 435 (HL).
384. [1942] AC 435.
385. [2010] 2 HKLRD 537 (CA).
386. Also *see* , *Tse's Forex Investment Co Ltd v. Man Yuk Lan & Anor* [1995] HKLY 1001, CA.
387. (22 Jul. 2014, HCA2176/2012).
388. (18 Dec. 2015, HCMP1916/2015).
389. *Revenue and Customs Commissioners v. Total Network SL* [2008] UKHL 19; [2008] 1 AC 1174 (HL).
390. *Revenue and Customs Commissioners v. Total Network SL* [2008] UKHL 19; [2008] 1 AC 1174 (HL), para. 95 (Lord Walker of Gestingthorpe).

not the conduct by a single individual could be actionable under a different tort. In Hong Kong, this approach was accepted in the application of *Her e'Majesty's Revenue & Customs v. Hashu Dhalomal Shahdadpuri & Anor.*[391] For the purposes of this tort, the meaning of 'unlawful means' is broader than the 'causing loss by unlawful means torts' and includes both civil and criminal wrong (per Lord Walker, *Total Network*, paragraph 89). Lord Walker, clarifying the law, said that criminal conduct can constitute unlawful means, provided that it was indeed the means (instrument) of intentionally inflicting harm. Those who breach civil/criminal law in commercial activity can be sued under economic torts where there is a nexus between unlawful means and the loss caused to the claimant. Further, the wrong does not need to be independently actionable in its own right against at least one of the conspirators. The intention of conspirators does not need to be same but must intend to injure the claimant in the wide sense.[392]

198. As stated in *Pido* and *Sinodental*, for unlawful means conspiracy the intention to injure the plaintiff does not need to be the predominant intention. In *Peter Geoffrey De Krassel v. Vincent Julia Chu Also Known As Zhu Liang & Ors De Krassel v. Chu Vincent,*[393] it was held that for conspiracy to injure by unlawful means, the plaintiff had to prove: (1) the nature of the agreement; (2) the unlawful means alleged; (3) each of the unlawful acts relied on; (4) the fact that each act was carried out pursuant to the conspiracy; and (5) the relevant state of mind of the alleged conspirator. If a defendant believed that he had a lawful right to do what he was doing, he should not be liable. There should therefore be: (1) intention (relevant state of mind of the conspirators); (2) agreement/common design (nature of agreement, unlawful means used); and (3) concerted action (with each of unlawful acts relied on and carried out in pursuance of the conspiracy).

II. Misrepresentation and Economic Torts

199. This group of economic torts is the result of misrepresentation causing the claimant commercial loss and includes the torts of passing off, deceit and malicious falsehood.

A. Passing Off

200. The tort of passing off is actionable per se and protects the plaintiff from damage to the goodwill and reputation of their business caused by the defendant representing their own goods or services in a way that can possibly mislead the public into considering those goods or services as being from the plaintiff. This tort protects, among other things, the goods and intellectual property rights of the plaintiff.[394] The

391. [2010] 5 HKLRD 690.
392. *Revenue and Customs Commissioners v. Total Network SL* [2008] UKHL 19; [2008] 1 AC 1174 (HL), para. 56.
393. [2010] 2 HKLRD 937.
394. *Menfond Electronic Art & Computer Design Co Ltd v. Wong Wang Tat Victor* [2013] 2 HKC 259.

requirements[395] of passing off in the classical form are that: (1) the claimant must establish that they have goodwill or reputation attached distinctively, in the minds of the purchasing public, to the goods or services at issue;[396] (2) there must be misrepresentation, intentional or not, by the defendant to the public as to those goods or services supplied that would be likely to lead the public to believe that the plaintiff had supplied them; and (3) there must be actual or likelihood of damage to the claimant as a result of misrepresentation by the defendant. The extended form is typified in *J Bollinger v. Costa Brava Wine Co,*[397] in which the defendant sold a Spanish wine under the trading name 'Spanish Champagne'. The twelve plaintiffs brought an action on behalf of all champagne producers in the Champagne region of France for an injunction to stop the producers of the wine from Costa Brava using the label of 'champagne' or 'Spanish Champagne' and a declaration stating that those terms were a false trade description for wine made in, or made with grapes grown in, Spain. The wine produced in the Champagne province of France used grapes grown in the district and a special double fermentation process, and that trade and the public in the United Kingdom had long known of it, it had acquired a high reputation and any person would recognize champagne as that particular wine. The court held that the defendant had committed a tort of passing off by making the public believe that they were purchasing sparkling wine made from grapes grown in the Champagne province of France. The court found that a class producing goods in a certain place could have goodwill attached; the protection was not only of individuals.

201. Where the goodwill in the goods or services cannot be shown by the plaintiff, the defendant cannot be held to be liable. This is illustrated by *The Chamber of Hong Kong Computer Industry Company Limited v. Hong Kong Computer Association Limited*[398] where the claimant sought an interlocutory injunction to restrain the defendant from holding computer exhibitions with the name 'computer festival' in the title. The claimant was an organizer of large scale computer exhibitions in public playgrounds and exhibition halls from 2002. From 2002 to 2011, the claimant worked with the Shamshui Po District Office and Council. The claimant's festivals had names like 'Hong Kong Computer Festival', 'Shamshuipo Computer Festival,' etc., and the action was to protect 'computer festival' as a trade name was brought as the defendants had also started used the name 'computer festival' in their exhibitions. It was held that the name 'computer festival' was not distinctive to the plaintiff's exhibitions; there had been no misrepresentation by the defendant and no damages arising. Where passing off is proven, the court will consider all the circumstances of the case in assessing the amount of damages, including whether there has been an adverse effect to the plaintiff's goodwill or reputation;[399] the conduct of the defendants (such as whether it was fraudulent), how far the goods were circulated, the degree of publicity gained by the

395. *Reckitt & Colman Products Ltd v. Borden Inc* [1990] RPC 340, 406 (Lord Oliver), 880, as cited in, among others, *The Chamber of Hong Kong Computer Industry Company Limited v. Hong Kong Computer Association Limited* (6 Dec. 2013, HCA621/2010), 25.

396. *Star Industrial Co Ltd v. Yap Kwee Kor* [1976] FSR 256; *Tin Tin Yat Pao (International) Ltd (in Liq) v. Tin Tin Publication Development Ltd* [2000] 3 HKC 1.

397. [1961] 1 WLR 277.

398. (HCA 621/2010, CFI, 21 Sep. 2010).

399. *Xiang Si Hua v. Bailey Record Co Ltd* [1987] HKLY 409, [1987] HKCU 18.

defendant to the goods at issue; the fact of the defendant's financial gain from the tort and the effect on or loss of the plaintiff.[400] The court may also allow injunctions, either prohibitory or mandatory, and be either interlocutory or permanent. If there is an application for an interim injunction, Lord Diplock's four questions in *American Cyanamid v. Ethicon Ltd*[401] apply and it must be shown that there is a serious issue to be tried; that any loss suffered by the plaintiff in the interim before trial, should the injunction not be granted, would not be adequately compensable by damages; that, if the defendant is not found liable at trial, any damage they suffer is compensable; and where the balance of convenience lies, if there is any issue about whether damages would not be adequate.

B. Deceit

202. For the tort of deceit, which is when a false representation is made by the defendant knowingly, or recklessly as to its truth, with the intention that the representation would be acted upon by the plaintiff, the defendant is liable for loss to the plaintiff caused by his reliance upon the false representation.[402] This can be illustrated by *Pasley v. Freeman,*[403] where the plaintiff sought the defendant's advice as to the creditworthiness of a third party with whom the plaintiff wanted to start business. The defendant informed the plaintiff that the third party was creditworthy. The plaintiff sold goods worth GBP 2,364 to the third party, which subsequently proved not to be creditworthy. The plaintiff was successful in his claim against the defendant. This case forms the basis of the modern tort of deceit and it recognized misrepresentation as a cause of action in tort which, prior to 1789, was intertwined with an action for breach of contract and was in the past allowed when associated with false warranties and fraud. With the separation of tort and contract, Assumpsit was used for false warranties and liability for deceit was extended to non-contractual situations.

203. The requirements for the tort of deceit were provided by the landmark case of *Derry v. Peek*[404] which stated that for deceit there must be: (1) a representation of facts (words or conduct); (2) that representation was false and made with a knowledge that it is false, or recklessly as to whether it is false; (3) the representation must be made with the intention that it should be acted upon by the plaintiff; and (4) the plaintiff must act upon the false statement and have sustained loss.[405] In *Derry*, a company issued a prospectus saying that it had the power to move carriages by steam power, believing that they would get consent to do so from the Board of Trade. Relying on this prospectus, the plaintiff took up shares from the company. The Board of Trade did not give consent, and later the company was wound up. The plaintiff sued the company. The House of Lords held that an action in deceit against the directors failed

400. *Alan Tam Wing Lun & Others v. Tam Kwok Hung* [1991] HKLY 417, [1991] 2 HKC 384.
401. [1941] AC 396 (HL).
402. Clerk and Lindsell on Torts cited in *KBC Bank NV v. Automotive Communications Ltd* [2011] HKCU 1686.
403. (1789) 3 TR 51.
404. [1889] 14 App Cas 337.
405. Also *see* *Bradford Third Equitable Benefit Building Society v. Borders* [1941] 2 All ER 205; [1941] 2 All ER 205 (Viscount Maugham).

because the directors honestly but mistakenly believed that what they said would be true so there was no intention to deceive. The misstatement of fact must be active or what is said must be so fragmentary that it is rendered false by the omission.[406]

204. Clearly the lack of honest belief in the false statement invites liability under deceit. In *Langridge v. Levy,*[407] the defendant sold a gun to the plaintiff's father for use of his son. The defendant knew that the gun was defective but warranted it to be sound. The plaintiff used the gun and injured himself. The court held that the defendant was liable to the plaintiff because the father had told the defendant that the gun was intended for use by the plaintiff.

205. Section 40 of the Companies (Winding Up and Miscellaneous Provisions) Ordinance (Cap 32) imposes civil liability for misstatements in prospectuses. Additionally, it should be noted that a deliberate misstatement of law is not defensible. The case of *West London Commercial Bank Ltd v. Kitson*[408] concerned a tramway company that was incorporated by two Acts of Parliament and which had no power to accept bills of exchange. Two of the company's directors were found liable for accepting such a bill, as *'This acceptance amounted to a statement that the private Acts of Parliament gave the company power to accept this bill, and that the defendants were authorized to accept it for the company.'*[409] The defendants were found liable. While this was considered to be a representation of fact in the present case, and that a representation of law (especially when one person is no't in a position to know better than the other) was no't actionable, Bowen J in obiter opined that were it a misrepresentation of law, *'... I doubt whether, if a man ... wilfully misrepresented the law [he] would be allowed in equity to retain any benefit he got by such misrepresentation.'*[410]

206. Unlike passing off, deceit is not actionable per se: the plaintiff must prove actual damages. The plaintiff may be able to recover only such losses that were caused by direct reliance on the defendant's false statement. The plaintiff can recover only such damages that are direct, but cannot expect to make any profits out of it.[411]

C. *Malicious/Injurious Falsehood*

207. A plaintiff can recover damages under the tort of malicious falsehood if they suffer loss due to the defendant's false statement to a third party where the false statement was made with the intention of damaging the plaintiff. The requirements of this tort are that the defendant should: (1) make a false statement to a third party; (2) with malice; and (3) and this causes the plaintiff to suffer damage.[412] The statement must be calculated to cause harm to the plaintiff or to his property.[413] In terms of the defendant's malice, it was stated by the Court of First Instance in *Tai Yip Dyeing*

406. *Peek v. Gurney* [1873] LR 6 HK 377 (Lord Cairns).
407. [1837] 2 M & W 519.
408. [1884] 13 QBD 360.
409. [1884] 13 QBD 360, 363 (Brett MR).
410. [1884] 13 QBD 360, 363 (Bowen J).
411. *Polaroid Far East Ltd v. Bel Trade Co Ltd & Ors* [1990] 2 HKLR 447.
412. *Western Counties Manure Co v. Lawes Chemical Manure Co* [1874] LR 9Ex 218.
413. *De Beers Abrasive Products Ltd v. International General Electric Co of New York* [1975] 2 All ER 599.

Factory Ltd v. Kong Hoi Sang[414] that '*...If an injurious falsehood is published, which is known to be false, then, provided the statement is intrinsically injurious, even if published with no intentional desire to injure the other person, there will be malice'*. The tort of malicious falsehood is not actionable per se and hence it is important to show that the false statement has caused probable monetary loss to the plaintiff. Damages for loss of reputation cannot be claimed under malicious falsehood.[415]

208. In Hong Kong, under section 24(1) (slander of title, etc.) of the Defamation Ordinance (Cap 21) it is not important to prove special damages '*if the words upon which the action is founded are calculated to cause pecuniary damage to the plaintiff and are published in writing or other permanent form; or if the said words are calculated to cause pecuniary damage to the plaintiff in respect of any office, profession, calling, trade or business held or carried on by him at the time of the publication'*. In the British case of *International Business Machines Corporation & IBM United Kingdom Limited v. Web-Sphere Limited,*[416] which related to the English Act on which section 24 of the Defamation Ordinance is based, it was stated that 'calculated' meant that the statements would have to be likely to cause pecuniary damage to the plaintiff.

III. Breach of Confidence

209. The tort of breach of confidence provides a remedy for the plaintiff to prevent misuse of private commercial information.[417] The essence of this tort is that there must be the obligation of confidentiality relating to the information. The basis of this tort is in an equitable principle of good faith and to prevent the defendant from taking unfair advantage of information given to them in confidence. The breach of confidence can be in a non-contractual situation. Outside of business settings, the tort of breach of confidence could also assist in the protection of privacy. The tort of 'invasion of privacy' has been developed in some common law jurisdictions, including Australia. In England, the means by which privacy is protected include the Human Rights Act 1998.

210. There is no tort of 'invasion of privacy' in Hong Kong. In 2004, the Law Reform Commission of Hong Kong's Sub-Committee on Privacy drafted a 'Consultation Paper on Civil Liability for Invasion of Privacy' for the creation of a general tort of intrusion of privacy by statute. This reform is mainly based on the fact that media have been reporting in a way that has resulted in intrusion into the private lives of individuals, which does not seem to have any public benefit. Further, the Personal Data (Privacy Ordinance) (Cap 486) provides protection to the privacy rights of a person in relation to personal data. Complaints can be lodged at the Privacy Commission for 'intrusion of privacy' in violation of the six Data Protection Principles. The Ordinance also criminalizes misuse or inappropriate use of personal data in direct marketing activities

414. (21 Feb. 2007, HCA2917/2004).
415. *Wing On Travel Services Ltd v. Hong Thai Citizens Travel Services Ltd* [2001] 2 HKLRD 481 citing *Fielding v. Vaiety Inc* [1967] 2 QB 841, 850.
416. [2004] EWHC 529.
417. *William Allan v. Messrs Ng & Co. (a firm) & Anor* (HCA10844/1994, 24 Dec. 2010).

(Part VI); non-compliance with a Data Access Request (section 19); and unauthorized disclosure of personal data obtained without data 'user's consent (section 64), etc.

211. The obligation of confidence arises when confidential and entrusted information of a confidential nature is disclosed to third person, or used to the detriment of information provider, without his consent. The three ingredients for the tort of breach of confidence can be found in *Coco v. AN Clark (Engineers) Ltd*[418] and are that: (1) the information must be confidential; (2) there must be an obligation on the part of confidant to keep the information confidential; and (3) there is breach of confidence to the detriment of the confider. Hence, the information must be confidential and not public knowledge and disclosure of such information must cause the claimant loss[419] and must not be in the public interest. In *Douglas v. Hello!,*[420] a celebrity couple granted 'OK!' magazine exclusive rights to publish selected photographs of their wedding. Photography was forbidden at the wedding except by the 'couple's official photographer. An action was brought over rival magazine publishing photographs that were taken surreptitiously. The court examined whether authorized publishers have a cause of action against a rival publisher for the economic torts of unlawful interference with business or conspiracy to injure. The appeal by 'OK!' Magazine was allowed on the ground of breach of confidence, reinstating Lindsay 'J's judgment in first instance, and damages were awarded accordingly. The House of Lords also discussed the nature of what public information was. There is no protection of information under this tort when it is in the public domain, but the nature of the information has to be considered. In this case, each picture was supposed to be information 'OK!' was to publish. The scope of the intention required for this tort was also not to be artificially limited.

212. There is no liability under this tort if the confidential information was disclosed in the interest of the public security, heath and morals, even if it may amount to the betrayal of confidence.[421] This is supported by Article 27 of the Basic Law of Hong Kong, which supports the right to freedom of speech of the press and of publication. Article 14 of Hong Kong Bill of Rights Ordinance (Cap 383) deals with protection of privacy, family, home, correspondence, honour and reputation. Where the breach of confidence is not justified and causes damage to the plaintiff, the court may award damages of compensatory nature[422] and that could include aggravated damages[423] in suitable circumstances. An injunction may be awarded where the confidential information is not disclosed but there is an apprehension that it might be disclosed.

418. *Coco v. AN Clark* [1969] RPC 41.
419. *Saltman Engineering Co Ltd v. Campbell Engineering Co Ltd* [1948] 65 RPC 203; *Nicrotherm Electrical Co Ltd v. Percy* [1956] RPC 272.
420. [2007] UKHL 21.
421. *X v. Y* [1988] 2 All ER 648.
422. *Campbell v. MGN Ltd* [2003] EMLR 39.
423. *China Light & Power Co Ltd and Anor v. Michael Edward Ashton Ford* [1996] 1 HKLRD 57, (CA).

§6. Others

I. Occupiers Liability

213. The Occupiers Liability Ordinance Cap 314 (OLO) is a statute that outlines the law relating to occupiers and others with respect to injury or damage caused to the claimant due to the state of land or other property, or things that are done or omitted to be done thereon. The OLO consolidates the law on occupiers' liability in Hong Kong (sections 2(2) and (3)), and the common law principles on occupier's liability continue to apply wherever the OLO is silent. The OLO separately addresses liability under tort and liability under contract, as well as liability in tenancy agreements. The OLO draws from the Occupiers Liability Act 1957 from the United Kingdom. The 1957 Act is now superseded and amended by the 1984 Act.

214. There are two features that makes occupiers duty different from common law duty under negligence: firstly, the common duty of care under the OLO imposes upon the occupier a positive duty to take care towards his visitors; and, secondly, the OLO gives specific directions as to how this duty can be discharged and sets out defences that are available to the occupier. An occupier is liable for injury or harm caused to a lawful visitor as a result of their breach of the common duty of care or any extension of that duty by contract. In order to discharge it, the occupier must have taken reasonable care to see that a visitor would be reasonably safe in using the premises for the permitted purpose. In exceptional cases, an occupier is also liable for injury caused to a trespasser (duty of common humanity). As occupier's liability is a type of negligence, causation must be satisfied in order to hold an occupier liable. The common law principles continue to apply whenever the OLO remains silent. The OLO imposes a duty on the occupier of any premises towards his visitor to take such care as is reasonable under the circumstances, to ensure that the visitor will be reasonably safe in using the premises for the purposes that they are invited or permitted to by the occupier (section 3(2) OLO).

215. The duty imposed under occupier's liability covers liability for injuries arising out of the state of premises or things which were done or omitted by the occupier, whereas activity duty is governed by the general negligence law. The OLO is concerned with occupancy duty rather than activity duty, which is when operations or activities conducted on the premises cause injury to the plaintiff. This distinguishes whether the plaintiff's cause of action falls under the OLO or whether they must rely on another aspect of the tort of negligence. In *Chung Loi v. MTR Corporation Ltd & Another,*[424] the plaintiff was injured on a staircase by the placard of an election campaigner at the defendant's underground station. The defendant was not found liable as the plaintiff was not injured due to defects in the premises. However, the OLO has been applied in work site injuries where there has also been a breach of the duty to provide a safe system of work.

216. In *Wong Kwok Tung v. Tsang Hin Ping,*[425] the plaintiff was a scaffolding worker employed by the third defendant; the first defendant was the principal contractor

424. (2005) HCPI 939 of 2002.
425. Unrep HCPI 725/1997.

and the second defendant was a sub-contractor for scaffolding. All three were found liable, with the second defendant held liable as an occupier as well as for not providing safety equipment. In *Lam Cheuk Leung v. Erawan Co Ltd & Ors,*[426] the cement contractor was held liable upon injury of the plaintiff (a cement worker) under the OLO. The plaintiff fell from defective scaffolding at a time when he was not wearing a safety harness. The Court held the defendant liable for adopting an unsafe system of work and the common duty of care required him to take measures to remedy the unsafe situation. Breaches of the OLO and negligence can be found in conjunction. In *Lee Yam Kan v. Ng Pui Kuen t/a Wing Sun Scaffolding Engineering and Another,*[427] the defendants in that case, the principal contractor and scaffolding contractor, were found liable for breach of the OLO. In terms of liability for negligence, the plaintiff was also found contributory negligent for the unsafe method of work.

217. The breach of such statutory duty gives rise to a civil cause of action for damages on behalf of the lawful visitor suffering injury or damage to property. The major advantage in bringing the action as a breach of statutory duty under the OLO is perhaps in proving the standard of care, which is clearly provided by the provisions.

A. Occupier's Duty and Duty to Visitors

218. Sections 3 and 4 of the OLO regulate liability under tort law and were put in place of the common law rules in relation to the duties owed by an occupier of premises towards lawful visitors with respect to the dangers caused by the state of premises or things done or omitted to be done on them (section 2, OLO). Pursuant to section 2(3)(a) of the OLO, the duties that apply to an occupier of premises, both in statute and under common law, and the duties they owe their visitors, are the same as the common law duties owed between occupiers and their invitees or licensees, and they apply to persons occupying or having control of fixed or movable structures. The statutory and common law rules apply alike with respect to the obligations owed by an occupier or person with control over premises with respect to damage caused to property, including property that does not belong to lawful visitors.

219. An occupier of premises owes a duty to visitors in respect of dangers arising from the condition of premises or things done or omitted to be done on them (section 2(1) OLO). In *Lee Fu Wah v. Michael Lee Hoffman,*[428] the second and third defendants were held liable for the injuries caused to the plaintiff, a decoration worker, when he was chased by a dog owned by the first and second defendants, resulting in him falling and sustaining injuries. Judge Alex Lee held that the plaintiff was there for the work required by the second and third defendants, and that they breached their common duty of care by not making the premises reasonably safe for the purposes he was invited or permitted to be there for, and cited from *Street on Torts*, 9th edition: *'The Act plainly regulates the duty of the occupier in relation to structural defects or other dangers due to the state of the premises themselves, or indeed 'things' on the premises such as vicious dogs roaming free in the garden.'*

426. [2004] 1 HKLRD 778.
427. (15 Mar. 2016, HCPI196/2014).
428. [2013] HKCU 1452.

220. In *Yang Yee Man, the Administratrix of the Estate of Lam Lok Kin, Deceased v. Leung Hing Hung,*[429] the defendant's medium sized goods vehicle hit a signpost inside a car park, which fell on and killed another car park user. The defendant brought third party contribution proceedings for indemnity against the Commissioner for Transport and Hong Kong Parking Limited on the basis that they were partly liable for the accident as occupiers of a faulty car park under the OLO and were responsible for its design and management. The court accepted that the parking signposts in the car park that authorized vehicles to park in the parking spaces provided were inviting the public to park there and whosoever parks was an invitee and visitor under the meaning of the OLO. Hence, if a lawful visitor entered a car park the Commissioner would owe a duty of care to him. Judgment was entered in favour of the defendant and against the Commissioner for 20% of the damages. Hong Kong Parking Limited was not found liable because, even though they were occupiers, they were not responsible for the faulty design.

221. It should be noted that, under the common law, a highway authority is not an occupier of a public road and owes no common duty of care under the OLO towards road users who cannot be seen as invitees of the government when they are in fact exercising a right to access. A public highway user is not a visitor within the meaning of the OLO as stated in *Cheung Fung Ying (as administratrix of the estate of Wong Ming Mui, deceased, plaintiff) v. Attorney General & Anor.*[430] The doctrine which absolves highway authorities from liability as occupiers had been abolished in England and Wales by the Highways (Miscellaneous Provisions) Act of 1961. However, in Hong Kong, there is no equivalent legislation; hence, the Commissioner is not an occupier of a public road in Hong Kong. Hence, if an accident occurs on a road or in the aisle of the car park which is treated as the public road leading to the parking space, the Commissioner will owe no duty of care to the plaintiff.

222. Under the OLO the occupier owes a common duty of care to its visitors: OLO sections 2(1), 3(1) & (3)(2). The nature and extent of the common duty of care is assessed in all the circumstances of the case (sections 3(1) & (2), OLO). An occupier of premises owes the same duty, the 'common duty of care', to all his visitors, other than in so far as he is free to and does extend, restrict, modify or exclude his duty to any visitor or visitors by agreement or otherwise. The common duty of care can be modified by agreement (section 3(1), OLO), but cannot be limited with regard to strangers to the contract, who are defined as persons who are neither parties to the contract nor benefiting as a successor by assignment or otherwise from a party to the contract (section 4(1), (3)). If the duty towards strangers to the contract has been extended by that contract that extended duty must also be fulfilled (section 4(1)).

223. Section 3(2) of the OLO defines the common duty of care as the duty to take such care as in all the circumstances of the case is reasonable in order to see that the visitor will be reasonably safe in using the premises for the purposes for which he is invited or permitted by the occupier to be there. In *Cunningham v. Reading Football Club,*[431] the occupier was held liable when unruly spectators at the football match threw pieces of concrete loosened from the structure at supervising police officers, as

429. HCPI 443/2010.
430. HCA 2476/1975.
431. (1992) PIQR P 141.

they had been aware that the crowd had behaved this way in the past and they had not taken any reasonable steps address it.

224. 'Premises' for the purposes of the OLO includes land and both fixed and movable structures (section 2(3)). The terms 'occupier' and 'visitor' are not defined in the OLO and common law rules relating to who owes duties and who is owed are expressly retained in section 2(2) of the OLO. An occupier, following the judgment of Lord Denning in *Wheat v. E Lacon & Co Ltd,*[432] is someone with sufficient control over premises that they ought to realize that any failure on their part to use reasonable care could result in injury to a person coming there lawfully. The person coming there lawfully, Lord Denning went onto state, is a 'visitor'. 'Visitors' for the purposes of sections 3 and 4 are stated to be the same as invitees or licensees under common law (section 2(2), OLO)). As per Lord Denning in *Slater v. Clay Cross Co Ltd,*[433] *'The duty of the occupier nowadays is simply to take reasonable care that the premises are reasonably safe for people lawfully coming onto them: and it makes no difference whether they are invitees or licensees.'* Persons who enter premises with the legal right to do so are treated as permitted to do so by the occupier (section 3(6), OLO). The common duty of care is also an implied term in contracts with those who enter, bring or send goods to premises pursuant to contractual rights with the occupier (sections 6(1) & (2), OLO).

225. Section 3(3)(a) of the OLO specifically states that occupiers must be prepared for children to be less careful than adults. An occupier will be liable where children are injured because of a trap or an allurement set by the occupier. The factors to be taken into consideration in determining if a trap or allurement is an object with a quality that is fascinating and fatal are: the nature of object, fencing, warnings, lighting and age of the child. In *Jolley v. Sutton London Borough Council,*[434] a 14-year-old boy was left paraplegic after an accident suffered while attempting to fix up an abandoned and rotting boat on the premises of the defendant (a local authority). In the House of Lords, Lord Hoffmann allowed the appeal and found the defendant liable on the basis of want of care, establishing that it would not have caused any extra work than it should have taken under it normal duties to address the danger and the occupier must not underestimate children's ingenuity to find unexpected ways of doing mischief. In *Taylor v. Glasgow Corporation,*[435] the defendant owned a public park and grew various botanic plants. The plaintiff, aged 7, ate some poisonous berries while visiting the park and died. The poisonous plant was not fenced off and did not have any warning signs to identify the danger. The House of Lords held the defendant liable as poisonous berries were tempting and interesting to children, and posed a concealed danger. However, in the Hong Kong case of *Fu Cheung Chun Tom v. MTR Corp Ltd,*[436] it was stated that, *'If the danger or trap is not unusual to children as opposed to adults, no liability should attach to the occupier for failing to take any step to alleviate such danger other than what would have been reasonable in the case of an adult.'* Parental

432. [1966] AC 552.
433. [1956] 2 All ER 625, 627 (Denning J).
434. [2000] 1 WLR 1082.
435. [1922] 1 AC 448 (HL).
436. [2009] HKCU 336.

responsibility should also be considered. In *Phipps v. Rochester Corp,*[437] the defendant was not held liable for the injury of a 5-year-old child who fell into a trench while trespassing onto the defendant's premises with his 7-year-old sister. It was held that reasonable parents would not allow children to go out into danger, and that the parents had sufficient knowledge and should have supervised their children.

226. Section 3(3)(b) of the OLO allows the occupier to assume that a visitor who enters premises for the purpose of performing a task which calls for a special skill, expertise or experience will guard against risks ordinarily attendant on such tasks. If the visitor is a skilled worker and the risk or injury is incidental to the visitor's occupation or trade, the occupier would not incur liability. However, where the plaintiff's injury is caused due to a defect/danger in the premises or negligent use of the premises by the occupier, then the occupier is liable. In *Salmon v. Seafarer Restaurants Ltd*[438] a fireman was injured due to an explosion caused by a gas leak. In the circumstances, where it was found that the fire was started negligently, it was of the type that would require the services of firemen and would put them at risk even when they exercised care and skill, the fireman could be compensated for his injuries. The duty towards workers on lawful business on the premises extends to the accessory employment of testing and applies to the servant of the workman employed if they are delegated the work.

227. An occupier's liability for the work of independent contractors is addressed in section 3(4)(b) of the OLO. Where damage is caused to a visitor by a danger caused by the faulty execution of any work done by an independent contractor employed by the occupier, the occupier is not liable for the danger if, in all the circumstances, he had acted reasonably in entrusting the work to an independent contractor and had taken such steps (if any) as he reasonably ought in order to satisfy himself that the contractor was competent and that the work had been properly done. In *Salsbury v. Woodland,*[439] one of the defendants was a homeowner who hired a workman to cut down a large tree. In the process, the tree brought down telephone wires. The plaintiff went to assist in the gathering the wires out of the road, but fell onto a bank while trying to avoid a collision with an oncoming car. The homeowner was not found liable. Lord Widgery summarized the prevailing legal approach, stating:

> It is, of course, trite law that an employer who employs an independent contractor is not vicariously responsible for the negligence of that contractor… those cases – and there are some – in which an employer has been held liable for injury done by the negligence of an independent contractor are in truth cases where the employer owes a direct duty to the person injured, a duty which he cannot delegate to the contractor on his behalf.

In *Yeung Kam Fuk v. Len Shing Construction Co Ltd*[440] Hunter J stated that the independent contractor is not regarded as a servant of the occupier, but that the whole circumstances must be assessed to see whether the occupier has taken reasonable care with respect to the work done by the independent contractor. The four steps in *Yeung*

437. [1955] ALL ER 129.
438. [1983] 1 WLR 1264.
439. [1971] QB 324.
440. [1986] HKC 160.

Kam Fuk were adopted and summarized in *Jiang Zhong v. Yeung Chun Leung (formerly t/a Dream Home Workshop, and Others)*:[441] '*(i) has the occupier acted reasonably in entrusting the work to an independent contractor; (ii) has the occupier used reasonable care in selecting the contractor; (iii) has the occupier taken reasonable steps (if any are possible) to supervise the carrying out of the work; (iv) has the occupier used reasonable care to check (if possible) that the work has been done properly.*' Liability under the OLO is not only concerned with misfeasance (illegally performing something legal) but nonfeasance (omission of some acts that are expected to have been performed).

228. Under section 3(4)(a) of the OLO, if damage is caused to a visitor by a danger of which he had been warned by the occupier, the warning is not to be treated, without more, as absolving the occupier from liability, unless in all the circumstances it was enough to enable the visitor to be reasonably safe. The warning must be specific. In *Chan Kwai Ngor v. Leung Fat Hang (t/a Fu Restaurant)*,[442] the plaintiff's injury was caused due to a greasy ramp. The court held that as a specific notice about there being greasy ramp was not displayed, the existing warning was not sufficiently specific. It was also not placed in the right location to be of use. In any case, the court stated that a general notice in the right place is insufficient. '*Nothing short of a specific warning not to step onto the ramp will suffice in view of the greasy state of the metal surface.*'[443] A warning for usual risks will also not be sufficient if the risk becomes unusual.

229. Under section 7 of the OLO, the government is also bound by the ordinance but its liability in tort is limited to the extent specified in the Crown Proceedings Ordinance (Cap 300) ('CPO'), and section 4 of the CPO applies to duties in sections 2–5 of the OLO as statutory duties. Following section 4(2) of the CPO, if the government and its officers are bound by statutory duties binding others, the government is also subject to any liability in tort to which it would be subject if it were a private person of full age and capacity.

230. Finally, pursuant to section 5 of the OLO, if the landlord under a tenancy with an occupier is obligated to the occupier to maintain or repair premises, the landlord's duty extends to all persons and their goods that may lawfully be on the premises (without contract). The landlord is treated as an occupier of the premises and the people or goods that can lawfully be there are there by invitation or permission. This is the same situation in sub-tenancies. This liability extends to mesne landlords and those who owe the same obligation to mesne landlords. However, persons who enter premises under a tenancy for reasons that are not permitted, and when the landlord is not barred from entering their objection (e.g., due to estoppel), those persons would be considered unlawful visitors.

B. Duty to Trespassers (Duty of Common Humanity)

231. The OLO does not directly recognize a duty of care towards trespassers. It was not traditionally recognized by the common law, either.[444] However, the Occupier's

441. (5 Feb. 2016, DCEC1267/2010), para. 73(12).
442. [1992] 1 HKC 408.
443. [1992] 1 HKC 408, 410.
444. Also *see* *Robert Addie & Sons (Collieries) Ltd. v. Dumbreck* [1929] AC 358.

Liability Acts of 1957 and 1984 in the United Kingdom do, as part of a duty of common humanity owed towards those who are not lawful visitors. Additionally, in *British Railways v. Herrington,*[445] the House of Lords changed the common law position. A 6-year-old boy was electrocuted due to a detached fence. It was held that, as a general rule, a person who trespasses on the land of another did so at his own risk but it did not mean that there was no duty to protect a trespasser from potential danger; consequently, the defendant owed the common duty of humanity to the plaintiff for failing to maintain and enforce a reasonable system of inspection and repair of the fence. It was noted that the occupier of the premises did not owe a trespasser reasonable care to see that the trespasser is reasonably safe for the reasons for which they are trespassing; however, if the presence of the trespasser is known or ought reasonably to be anticipated, the occupier owes the trespasser a duty of care. It is less onerous than the duty owed to lawful visitors; it only requires the occupier to treat trespassers with ordinary humanity. This duty cannot be excluded by occupiers.

232. When examining the application and scope of the duty of common humanity, the courts will look at a variety of factors, including where and when the accident happened, the trespasser's age, whether the occupier knew of the dangers and could have rectified them and whether the occupier knew about the presence of trespassers, as well as the danger itself, whether it was concealed and the chances and extent of injury it could cause.

233. In Hong Kong, the principle in *Herrington* was considered in the case of *Chan Yan Nam v. Hui Ka Ming & Others.*[446] The plaintiff was an electrical and plumbing subcontractor employed by the first defendant (a contractor) to install toilet facilities in first floor premises. The plaintiff used a canopy to connect pipes from the flat he was working on to the common pipes. This area was under the control of the second defendant, owner of ground floor. The plaintiff fell and was injured. It was held that no common duty was owed by the second defendant as the plaintiff's presence on the canopy was not reasonably foreseeable. At paragraph 19, the Court of Appeal noted the accuracy of the trial judge's summary of the Herrington principle, stating that *'to become liable [the 2nd defendant] would have to know that the condition of platform was such that it would be dangerous to a trespasser who went on to it and it would have to know or expect that someone would go on to it.'*

234. In *Chan Yan Nam*, the Court of Appeal distinguished *Herrington*, stating that it applied where there were well-known and obvious special circumstances. In *Wong Wing Ho v. The Hong Kong Housing Authority and Another,*[447] the Court of Appeal considered the Herrington principle as part of Hong Kong law, though the Court of Appeal considered in the particular case that the plaintiff was owed the duty as a visitor rather than as a trespasser. The Court of Appeal noted the uncertainties in finding the *ratio decidendi* of the *Herrington* case.[448]

445. [1972] AC 877.
446. [2003] 1 HKC 341 (CA).
447. (28 Dec. 2007, CACV28/2007).
448. (28 Dec. 2007, CACV28/2007) paras 16–20.

C. Defences

235. Section 3(1) of the OLO provides that an occupier of premises owes same duty – the common duty of care – to all his visitors, except in so far as he is free to and does extend, restrict, modify or exclude his duty to any visitor or visitors by agreement or otherwise. As noted, those who enter premises in pursuance of their work are expected to guard against any special risks ordinary incident to it (section 3(3)). As addressed above, a warning can only discharge the occupier's liability if it is enough, in all the circumstances, to make the visitor reasonably safe, and the occupier has to take reasonable care in the circumstances with regard to the work of independent contractors in order not to be liable for faulty work done by independent contractors (section 3(4)). Pursuant to section 3(5) of the OLO, the common duty of care does no't place any obligations on an occupier in relation to the risks knowingly accepted by the visitor. Exclusion of liability is regulated by the CECO.

236. In relation to the assumption of risk by a visitor (section 3(5) OLO), when the risk is willingly accepted, the occupier bears no liability. In *Titchener v. British Railways Board,*[449] a 15-year-old girl who entered onto the railway line through a gap in the fence was hit by a train. The House of Lords dismissed the claim because the girl voluntarily and knowingly assumed the risk. In *Tomlinson v. Congleton Borough Council,*[450] the plaintiff dove into the shallow water and broke his neck. There were warning signs against swimming in the lake and in the lake, as well as safety leaflets and oral warnings by rangers in the area. The House of Lords held that the plaintiff had injured himself by his own decision to by diving into shallow water, not due to the state of the defendant's premises. The premises could not be held to be dangerous just because they were used for a dangerous activity. The risk inherent in a dangerous activity that is knowingly entered into is taken on by the visitor. However, in *Wong Wing Ho v. The Hong Kong Housing Authority and Another*[451] Le Pichon JA, giving the unanimous verdict for the Court of Appeal, stated in obiter that, *'I do not read* Tomlinson *as laying down any general principle that no duty can ever be owed by an occupier to a potential trespasser. The decision was based entirely on the 1984 Act which has no counterpart in Hong Kong...* 'before distinguishing *Tomlinson* from the facts of the particular case.

237. In relation to exclusion of civil liability for breach of contract, negligence and other breaches of duty, 'CECO' applies. Section 7 of CECO affects occupiers and restricts their ability to modify their common duty towards lawful visitors in the following ways: an occupier cannot exclude or modify his liability for death or personal injury arising from his negligence in any circumstances, but he may exclude or restrict his liability for other loss or damage, so long as such exclusion or restriction satisfies the test of reasonableness (found in section 3 of CECO); however, even where a person has agreed to or was aware of an exemption or notice, such agreement or awareness by itself is not a sufficient indication of his voluntary acceptance of the risk; the consent must be real.

449. [1983] UKHL 10.
450. [2004] 1 AC 46, HL.
451. (28 Dec. 2007, CACV28/2007), para. 21.

238. Contributory negligence for workmen is covered by section 3(3)(b) of the OLO. An occupier can assume that a workman will guard against risks ordinarily attendant on such tasks. In *Hsu Li Yun v. Incorporated Owners of Yuen Fat Building,*[452] the plaintiff's husband (deceased), an electrician and plumber, designed and installed a plumbing system on the defendant's premises. He was electrocuted while repairing the system. The defendant, the owner of building, was found negligent for not making sure that the work was done properly. The court held that the deceased was electrocuted due to the defendant's negligence as well as his own contributory negligence, which was put at 75%. In *Bhana, Angela Mary v. Ocean Apex Trading Limited,*[453] the District Court considered the case of a 69 year old, the plaintiff, who was in a shop and stepped backwards from a mirror that she was looking into and accidentally caught her leg on a shop assistant walking directly behind her, causing them both to fall. The plaintiff fractured her left radius and wrist. In considering the case, Judge Chan stated that the occupier had not taken due reasonable care towards the visitors of the shop, due to the layout of the shop and what the occupier should have known as a retail business owner, and that it was in breach of the duty. However, as the judge found that she should have looked before she stepped back, given the busy state of the shop and the narrowness of the aisles, and the plaintiff was held 15% contributory negligent.

II. Product Liability

239. Manufacturers of products that cause injury to the consumer or damage to property face a variety of consequences under the law of product liability. There can be liability in contract, the tort of negligence and legislation. Some common law jurisdictions have a statutory regime to govern product liability, though Hong Kong does not. The United Kingdom has the Consumer Protection Act 1987, creating statutory product liability and making it a strict liability offence. In Hong Kong, product liability is not a strict liability offence. In fact, the Consultative Paper by the Law Reform Commission of Hong Kong, (Product Liability Sub-Committee) proposed a reform on Civil Liability for Unsafe Products 1997, to create strict civil remedy for defective products in order to Hong Kong to adapt to the changing methods of manufacturing, which are more complicated than ever before, but this change has not yet taken place.

240. Generally consumer protection in Hong Kong in relation to product liability includes the protection afforded by the Consumer Council,[454] contract law,[455] and civil and criminal legislation.[456] There is no comprehensive statutory regime to protect

452. [2000] 1 HKLRD 900 (CA).
453. DCPI 1732/2009.
454. Consumer Council Ordinance (Cap 216).
455. Sales of Goods Ordinance (Cap 26); Control of Exemption Clauses Ordinance (Cap 71); Supply of Services (Implied Terms) Ordinance (Cap 457); Unconscionable Contracts Ordinance (Cap 458).
456. Consumers Goods Safety Ordinance (Cap 456); Gas Safety Ordinance (Cap 51); Part V of the Public Health and Municipal Services Ordinance; (Cap 132); Pesticides Ordinance (Cap 133); Antibiotics Ordinance (Cap 137); Pharmacy and Poisons Ordinance (Cap 138); Toys and Children's Product Safety Ordinance (Cap 424).

consumers and Hong Kong consumers have to rely on common law principles of product liability if the plaintiff does not have a contract with the manufacturer. As in other areas of tort, the duty of care and breach of the duty by the defendant must be shown, with causation. Product liability is a special category of duty of care under the law of negligence and deals with the damage caused by defective/unsafe/dangerous goods. Before *Donoghue,*[457] the third party, i.e., consumers who had no direct contract with the manufacturer, had no remedy against the manufacturer due to restrictions from the principle of the privity of contract. After *Donoghue*, the law of tort acquired a significant position and allowed a remedy to consumer who did not have a contract with the manufacturer. In *Donoghue,* the majority of the House of Lords rejected the distinction between dangerous and non-dangerous chattels and also discarded *'the privity of contract fallacy'*.

241. It was held that the more dangerous an act is the more care that has to be taken in doing it. The requirement to take reasonable care applies to product liability cases; the manufacturer has to exercise reasonable care in preparing and putting up a product for sale, and owes a duty to consumers. The manufacturer must ensure against defects that can cause injury to consumers, and that goes beyond manufacturing itself; for example, if defects are discovered after distribution, the manufacturer must act. The duty goes beyond complying with government regulations. There is, however, no obligation to prevent any and all risk; merely what is reasonable and foreseeable. Hong Kong does not have a strict liability regime based on legislation yet.

242. In *Lam Mo Bun v. Hong Kong Aerosol Co Ltd. & Ors,*[458] the consumer was injured due to the gas from an aerosol insecticide, which he sprayed in his kitchen, becoming trapped in the washing machine and igniting from a spark from the machine. Judge Muttrice articulates the Hong Kong position as follows:

> If a consumer sustains personal injury and/or loss and damage that is attributable to a defect in a manufactured product, an action lies in tort against its negligent manufacturer (Donoghue v Stevenson [1932] AC 562). If there is a foreseeable danger in the use of a manufactured product, the manufacturer must warn any user of the product against it. The manufacturer must produce proper instructions for the safe use of the product.[459]

243. The parties to the tort of product liability are the manufacturer and consumer. A manufacturer, someone who has a hand in creating a product, has a wide definition in law, and can include distributors, suppliers, retailers, assemblers, architects, beauticians, installers, repairers, second-hand dealers, etc. In *Andrews v. Hopkinson,*[460] a second-hand car dealer was found liable for negligence and breach of warranty because of injuries caused by a car that had longstanding defects. It was within the duty of a car dealer to ensure that the car was fit for use.

457. [1932] AC 562.
458. [2001] 1 HKLRD 540.
459. [2001] 1 HKLRD 540, 547E.
460. [1956] 2 All ER 422.

244. In *Stennett v. Hancock*[461] the plaintiff was injured by a piece of a wheel of a moving lorry that struck him. The repairer of the lorry, who had negligently reattached the wheel, was found liable while the owner of the lorry was not. The repaired lorry should not be only fit for the owner but also safe for people who could come in physical proximity of the product. In *Wong Wai Hing and Another v. Hui Wei Lee,* Hong Kong's Court of Appeal recognized *Stennett* and stated that:

Where the duty is to take reasonable care, the standard is determined objectively. The subjective intent and belief of the defendant as found by the judge are irrelevant. How that duty is discharged depends on the facts of the particular case. If technical skill or knowledge is involved, the ordinary man will discharge his duty by entrusting its performance to an apparently competent contractor.[462]

245. Multiple defendants may be sued as manufacturers. In *Lam Mo Bun*, above, the first defendant (the manufacturer from Shenzhen) and the second defendant (the distributor in Hong Kong) were both found liable for the defective insecticide spray. In *Kristan Bowers Phillips v. Initial Environmental Services Ltd and Ors,*[463] the plaintiff was a musician who was injured due to inspect spray used near the Hong Kong Academy for Performing Arts ('HKPA'). The HKPA was liable, alongside the company responsible for pest control, and the manufacturer and distributor of the spray, as well as the orchestra that the plaintiff worked at.

246. Product liability is concerned with protecting the ultimate consumer, who is the intended user of the product. The category of the ultimate consumer has been broadened to include anyone who sustains injury as a result of the defective product, as long as causation is proven. In *Barnett v. H&J Packer & Co Ltd,*[464] a confectionary manufacturer was found liable to a seller, who was injured by a piece of wire in the sweets from the manufacturer. In *Kristan Bowers Phillips,*[465] the musician was not the intended user of the pesticide, but the toxic substance caused the injury. The reason for this wide definition of the ultimate consumer is to protect persons who are not parties to a contract with the manufacturer.

247. The word product has a wide definition in law. It includes anything that is manufactured for the use of the ultimate consumer, consumable or non-consumable. In *White v. Jones,*[466] the preparation of a will without reasonable care with respect to time led to liability on the part of the solicitor. Product liability arises as a result of a defect in the product causing harm to a consumer or their property. Broadly, defects can be categorized as manufacturing, design and warning defects.

248. Manufacturing defects are errors that occur as a result of the manufacturing process, such as a failure of the quality control mechanisms that ensure that such defects do not exist. The standard of care does not require that the goods need to be perfect but that the products are reasonably safe. A design defect is a defect in design

461. [1939] 2 All ER 578.
462. (16 Mar. 2001, CACV136/2000), 114.
463. [1996] HKCU 594.
464. [1940] 3 All ER 575.
465. [1996] HKCU 594.
466. [1995] AER HL 691 (HL).

that is inherited by the product when it is manufactured according to its defective design and all the products that are manufactured are defective. The law provides a remedy for manufacturing defects, and not so much for design defects, which are difficult to ascertain and are inherently linked to the product itself rather than its manufacturing process. This is seen in the cases that relate to the thalidomide tragedy, caused by the use of thalidomide in morning sickness medication, which led to deformations in children. The manufacturer could not have reasonably foreseen the injury to consumers as the products contained design defects.

249. In order to impose product liability on manufacturers, it must be shown that the manufacturer intended his products to reach the ultimate consumer; there was no reasonable possibility of intermediate examination of the product; and there was an absence of reasonable care in the preparation or putting up of the products; this resulted in a manufacturing/design defect; and this has caused the plaintiff's injuries or damage to property. As stated by Lord Atkin in *Donoghue v. Stevenson:*[467]

A manufacturer of products, which he sells in such a form that he intends them to reach the ultimate consumer in the form in which they left him with no reasonable possibility of intermediate examination and with the knowledge that the absence of reasonable care in the preparation or putting up of the products will result in injury to the consumer's life or property, owes a duty to the consumer to take that reasonable care … .

250. The product must have reached the plaintiff with same defect as it had at the time it left the control of the manufacturer. In *Grant v. Australian Knitting Mills,*[468] the plaintiff bought underwear from a retailer that was manufactured by the defendant. The underwear caused dermatitis to the plaintiff due to a high concentration of bisulphite of soda. The defendant was found liable. However, if the plaintiff uses products for other purposes not intended by the defendant then the plaintiff will have no cause of action against the defendant.

251. The manufacturer of chemicals in *Kubach v. Hollands*[469] sold them to the distributor and told them to test the chemicals before selling. The defendant distributor did not, and also did not tell the plaintiff buyer to do so, and the plaintiff was injured by an explosion caused by the chemicals. Their claim succeeded against the distributor, but not against the manufacturer, as there had been a reasonable possibility of intermediate examination of the products, and the distributor, by ignoring the manufacturer's warning, broke the chain of causation.

252. If the plaintiff knew the risks and consented to them, then *volenti non fit injuria* – 'no injury is done to a person who consents' – applies to their voluntary assumption of risk. The defendant would have to show that the plaintiff had knowledge of the risk of danger from the goods and had agreed to that risk. The Court of Appeal in *Nettleship v. Weston*[470] stated that, '*The plaintiff must agree, expressly or impliedly, to waive any claim or any injury that may befall him due to the lack of reasonable care by the defendant.*'

467. [1932] AC 562.
468. [1936] AC 85.
469. [1937] 3 All ER 907.
470. [1971] 2 QB 691, 701.

253. The defendant may plead contributory negligence if the plaintiff fails to exercise reasonable care for his own safety or the safety of his property. In *Jones v. Livox Quarries Ltd,*[471] the plaintiff, without informing the driver, hitched a ride on the back of a slow-moving vehicle against the instructions of his employer, and was injured in an accident, when a dumper truck hit the vehicle he was travelling on. The defendant was liable but the plaintiff was one-fifth contributory negligent. The court held that *'A person is guilty of contributory negligence if he ought reasonably to have foreseen that if he did not act as a reasonably prudent man he might hurt himself.'*[472]

III. Tort of Nuisance

254. Nuisance refers to invasive conduct that interferes with the claimant's legitimate use/enjoyment and comfort/convenience in relation to his property. Liability is based on the harm to the claimant's safety, enjoyment, comfort or use of his property caused by the defendant's indirect activities. The range of acts and omissions covered by the tort of nuisance is wide and involves private nuisance, public nuisance and the *Rylands v. Fletcher*[473] rule. They all aim to protect the claimant's land or safety from defendant's unreasonable interference. The historic development of private nuisance can be traced back to the thirteenth century. Nuisance was rooted in trespass and was developed to ease infringement. Private nuisance applies where indirect, continuous, substantial and unreasonable interference affects the claimant's enjoyment of his land.[474] The House of Lords in *Cambridge Water Co v. Eastern Counties Leather Plc,*[475] made it clear that the *Rylands v. Fletcher* rule is 'an extension of the law of nuisance to isolated escapes from land' (per Lord Goff).[476] Further 'foreseeability of harm' is necessary to recover damages in public nuisance,[477] private nuisance and under the *Rylands v. Fletcher* rule.[478] At this stage it must also be remembered that under private nuisance and the *Rylands v. Fletcher* rule, claims for personal injury cannot be recovered. However, personal injury loss is recoverable in public nuisance cases as the law aims to protect public safety.

255. In contemporary times, the court needs to balance the interests of the plaintiff and defendant. The law balances the interests of the landowner/users and then sees if defendant's conduct is reasonable. In cases of private nuisance, liability is not fault-based like in negligence cases, as there is no proof of fault or of failing to meet standards of care. Standards of liability in private nuisance are based on fairness and reasonableness. For public nuisance, it is based on the seriousness of the conduct. Hence, generally, the nature of the burden under nuisance can be classified as that of mixed liability. The defences could also vary, and include statutory authority and

471. [1952] 2 QB 608.
472. [1952] 2 QB 608, 615.
473. (1868) LR 3 HL 330.
474. *Cunard v. Antifyre* [1933] 1 KB 551.
475. [1994] 2 AC 264 (HL).
476. [1994] 2 AC 264 (HL).
477. *Wagon Mound (No. 2)* [1967] 1 AC 617, 640 (Lord Reid).
478. *Cambridge Water Co v. Eastern Counties Leather Plc* [1994] 2 AC 264 (HL).

contributory negligence. The courts also accept that in some cases liability in nuisance could be raised after a negligence case.[479]

A. Private Nuisance

256. In *Wong Wai Tak Belinda & Anor v. Smart Team International Investment Ltd,*[480] private nuisance described as follows: '*...An act or omission which is an interference with, disturbance of or annoyance to a person in the exercise or enjoyment of his ownership or occupation of land is an actionable private nuisance...* '[481] If the interference is continuous, substantial, unreasonable and indirect and it affects the enjoyment or rights relating to land, the defendant would be liable in private nuisance.[482] In *Lau Tat Wai v. Yip Lai Kuen Joey,*[483] the court identified three forms of private nuisance: encroachment, direct physical injury and interference with enjoyment of land. Thereby the law addresses physical damage caused by flooding, noise,[484] smoke,[485] fumes, vibration and smells, etc.; substantial interference, which reduces the amenity value of the land; and overhanging branches encroaching onto neighbours' land[486] or spreading roots, etc. Hence, interferences such as smells, fumes, noise, etc. that emanate from the defendant's land are actionable. Sir Knight-Bruce V.C. in *Walter v. Selfe*[487] clearly stated that private nuisance does not protect mere personal discomfort unless it is '*materially interfering with the ordinary comfort physically of existence, not merely according to elegant or dainty modes and habits of living*'.[488] The plaintiff in that case, however, could sue against their neighbour's brick-burning business as it was polluting the air.

257. In order to successfully prove a claim for private nuisance, the first issue is to identify who can sue (claimant) and who can be sued (defendant), as well as the reasonableness of the defendant's use of his land. The court has to balance several factors: whether the interference was continuous, substantial and unreasonable; the plaintiff's abnormal sensitivity; the nature of the locality; the utility of the defendant's acts; and whether the defendant was acting out of malice. Then the court would consider the foreseeability, defences and remedies.

---

479. *Dymond v. Pearce* [1972] 1 All ER 1142 (public nuisance); *Cambridge Water Co Ltd v. Eastern Counties Leather Plc* (1994) 2 AC 264 (In CA claim for nuisance succeeded, which in House of Lords finally decided the case in favour of the defendant).
480. [2011] 3 HKC 322.
481. [2011] 3 HKC 322, para. 35 (Judge Mimmie Chan).
482. *Cunard v. Antifyre* [1933] 1 KB 551, 557.
483. [2013] 3 HKC 361.
484. *De Keysers Royal Hotel Ltd v. Spicer Bros Ltd* (1914) 30 TLR 257.
485. *Walter v. Selfe* [1851] 4 De G & Sm 315.
486. *Burton v. Winters* [1993] 3 All ER 847 (CA).
487. (1850) 20 LJ Ch. 433.
488. (1850) 20 LJ Ch. 433, 435.

1. Who Can Sue (Claimant) and Who Can be Sued (Defendant)?

258. The claimant needs to have a proprietary interest in the land affected by nuisance. In the landmark case of *Hunter v. Canary Wharf Ltd,*[489] the House of Lords stated that the claimant should have an interest in order to bring a nuisance claim. *Khorasandjian v. Bush*[490] provides that a licensee could also sue in private nuisance. In *Hunter*, the plaintiffs (local residents, their families and other licensees) complained that the construction of the Canary Wharf Tower interfered with their television reception, but some of the plaintiffs had no proprietary interest. The House of Lords held that only those plaintiffs who had a proprietary interest could have the right to claim for damages, as the law aims to protect interest in land only. This also demonstrates that personal injuries cannot be recovered under private nuisance. In *Malone v. Laskey,*[491] a claim for personal injury under private nuisance was rejected when the claimant was injured due to a falling object from defendant's premises. The claimant was just a licensee and had no proprietary interest.

259. According to *Lai Sai Kee & Anor v. Yim Ping Wai,*[492] a landlord can claim in nuisance if it can affect the enjoyment of land. This case even allows tenants to sue in nuisance. In *Lau Tat Wai v. Yip Lai Kuen Joey,*[493] the court rejected the claimant's claim in nuisance even though the defendant's act was seriously affecting the life of the claimant; he did not prove his proprietary interest. In this case the court relied on *Ng Hoi Sze v. Yuen Sha Sha & Anor,*[494] wherein it is stated that a plaintiff can claim in nuisance if he has exclusive possession or has occupied the land with a license, and no matter whether he is the owner, tenant or even licensee.

260. The defendant is liable in private nuisance for things emanating from his land. Hence, anyone who is a creator[495] of nuisance could be sued. The defendant can be vicariously liable if the interference of an independent contractor is foreseeable. Anyone who adopts or continues[496] the predecessor's nuisance would be liable if he fails to stop it and whoever authorizes nuisance would also be liable. In *Harris v. James,*[497] a landlord was liable for authorizing his tenants' nuisance. In 2014, the UK Supreme Court in the case of *Coventry v. Lawrence*[498] stated that a landlord could be held liable for private nuisance if he personally caused the nuisance or authorized such actions.

489. [1997] AC 677 (HL).
490. [1993] QB 727.
491. [1907] 2 KB 141; *Read v. Lyons* [1947] A C 156, 183.
492. [1997] HKLY 578, HC.
493. [2013] 3 HKC 361, paras 48–52.
494. [1999] HKCU 1583, CACV 93/1999.
495. *Sedleigh-Denfield v. O'Callaghan* [1940] UKHL 2.
496. *Sedleigh-Denfield v. O'Callaghan* [1940] UKHL 2.
497. [1876] 45 LJQB 545.
498. [2014] UKSC 13.

2. Nature of Liability: Unreasonable Interference and Unreasonable User

261. Defendants would be liable in private nuisance for their unreasonable interference[499] with the claimant's enjoyment of his land. For all actions of private nuisance, the test of reasonableness that applies is that of a reasonable user. The court can thereby balance the interests of the claimant and the defendant. Private nuisance law regulates the interference that the defendant's conduct can cause to the enjoyment of the land of the claimant. As such, a defendant is free to enjoy his land as long as it does not deprive others from enjoying theirs. Physical damage from ordinary use may not be judged as unreasonable interference.[500] However, where interference is caused, it is irrelevant that defendant has taken measures to avoid such interference. George Bramwell J. in *Bamford v. Turnley,*[501] developed a principle of '*give and take, live and let live'*, under which reasonableness and fairness are considered in private nuisance cases. In judging the reasonable use of the land, courts take into consideration the duration/frequency of the activity, locality, the hypersensitivity of the plaintiff, the utility of the defendant's activity, etc. However, if the nuisance was caused by public authorities under statutory regulations, then the courts do not have the authority to determine such issues.[502]

a. Duration, Frequency and Extent of Interference

262. The other aspect of unreasonable interference is the degree of interference. That can be determined from whether the interference was indirect, continuous, substantial and a persistent state of affairs.[503] For example, in *Ng Yuen Han v. Lam Fei* Fui *and Another,*[504] the defendant was liable for causing nuisance from continuous water seepage and noises. Likewise, in *ACL Electronics (HK) Ltd v. Bulmer Ltd*[505] the Court of Appeal held that cold air from the defendant's system damaging plaintiff's property could be substantial interference. In *De Keysers Royal Hotel Ltd v. Spicer Bros Ltd,*[506] the company was liable for nuisance from operating in forbidden hours. On the other hand, in *Capital Prosperous Ltd & Anor v. Sheen Cho Kwong,*[507] the court did not hold the defendant liable for using the shower from 11 pm till midnight, as that is reasonable and ordinary in Hong Kong.

499. *Hunter v. Canary Wharf Ltd* [1997] AC 677 (HL).
500. *Ellison v. Ministry of Defence* [1997] 81 BLR 101.
501. [1860] 3 B & S 62.
502. *Marcic v. Thames Water Utilities Ltd* [2004] 1 All ER 135 (Also *see* Breach of Statutory Duty under Part III of this text).
503. *Cunard v. Antifyre* [1933] 1 KB 551.
504. [2013] 3 HKLRD 608.
505. [1992] 1 HKC 133 (CA).
506. (1914) 30 TLR 257.
507. [1999] 1 HKLRD 633, CFI.

b. Nature of the Locality

263. When judging the reasonable use of the land, the nature of the locality can help to determine the reasonableness of actions. The importance of locality was demonstrated in *Sturges v. Bridgman,*[508] where Thesiger LJ stated, '*What would be a nuisance in Belgravia Square would not necessarily be so in Bermondsey.'* In an industrial area, some degree of interference of air quality, noise or even value of property is expected. However, if a physical injury to the land is involved, then the nature of locality is not relevant. This can be illustrated by the *St. Helen's Smelting Co v. Tipping*[509] where the plaintiff's trees and hedges were damaged by noxious fumes from the defendant's factory. The defendant argued that there was no unreasonable interference as it took place in an industrial area, and that it was a reasonable use of land in an industrial area. The court ruled that where physical damage to property is involved, the locality principle is irrelevant. The courts distinguish nuisance causing discomfort and nuisance causing damage, and the latter one is a stronger basis for the plaintiffs claim.

264. The claimant has to prove that defendant's actions have added, for example, substantial noise or vibrations. The claimant will be successful if the defendant's conduct is not reasonable in that particular locality. In such cases, expert witnesses could determine the acceptable standard. This can be illustrated by the Hong Kong case of *Reality Harvest Ltd v. Gold Margin Development Ltd*[510] where the defendant was liable for disturbing the operation of the plaintiff's office. In *Bliss v. Hall,*[511] the pre-existing nature of the nuisance was rejected as a defence. The defendant was liable for its fumes and smells even though the claimant's factory was in that region before plaintiff moved in.

265. A locality may change upon the grant of planning permission for major developments. In *Gillingham Borough Council v. Medway (Chatham) Dock Co Ltd,*[512] rejecting the plaintiff's claim for public nuisance, the court stated that the planning permission had changed the character of the neighbourhood and the question of the defendant's nuisance should be considered under the changed neighbourhood where more interference should be expected. On the other hand, in *Wheeler v. JJ Saunders Ltd,*[513] Staughton LJ held that the grant of planning permission to the defendant to expand the pig farm did not change the locality and, hence, the defendant was liable.

266. Hence, generally speaking, in the UK as well as in Hong Kong, the grant of planning permission does not provide a licence to cause nuisance. However, the grant of planning permission to the defendant for a particular use, which the plaintiff subsequently complains caused nuisance, is relevant in finding whether the nuisance exists. In *Coventry v. Lawrence,*[514] this issue was discussed in some detail. In 2006, the appellants purchased and moved into a house near a stadium and track, which was

508. [1879] 11 Ch D 852 (CA).
509. [1895] 11 HL Cas 642.
510. [2000] HKEC 588.
511. (1838) 4 Bing NC 183.
512. [1993] QB 343.
513. [1995] 3 WLR 466.
514. [2014] UKSC 13.

used for speedway racing and associated activities. Subsequently, the appellants complained to the local council about noises from the track, resulting in the issuance of Noise Abatement notices requiring works to mitigate noise. In 2008, the appellants brought proceedings for an injunction to stop the activities of the operators and landlords of the stadium and the track (the respondents) due to the noise. Prior to 2006, two planning permissions and a Certificate of Lawfulness of Existing Use or Development (CLEUD) was issued to the respondents for the stock car and banger racing. The trial court held in favour of the appellants and allowed the injunction, limiting the level of noise from these activities. In 2012, however, the Court of Appeal reversed the decision, holding that the activities at the stadium and track did not constitute a nuisance. Finally, the Supreme Court reversed the Court of Appeal's decision and restored trial court's decision. It was held that the respondents were liable for private nuisance, whereas the landlords were not held liable. The court awarded damages and an injunction against the respondents limiting the level of noise.

267. In 2014, the UK Supreme Court in *Coventry v. Lawrence*[515] considered a number of legal issues related to planning permission, especially the extent to which a defendant can argue that the grant of planning permission can be taken into account when considering the character of the locality. Lord Neuberger stated that the grant and terms of planning permission are not irrelevant but, in many cases, they may be of little, or even no, evidential value.[516] Although the court did not provide any clear guidance as to when planning permission would carry evidential value, detailed planning permission, which specifies that a particular noisy activity is permissible after a certain time, or at a certain decibel level, might be of some value.[517]

268. The grant of permission may affect the courts' discretion in awarding injunctions and they may award damages in lieu of an injunction in some nuisance cases. Lord Neuberger and the majority in *Coventry* agreed that the legal burden is on the defendant to show why damages were appropriate, rather than an injunction. The majority was also against mechanically following the *Shelfer* principle from *Shelfer v. City of London Electric Lighting Co.*[518] In *Coventry*, Lord Neuberger stated that *'(i) an almost mechanical application of A L Smith LJS's four tests, and (ii) an approach which involves damages being awarded in only 'very exceptional circumstances', are each simply wrong in principle, and give rise to a serious risk of going wrong in practice'.*[519]

c. Hypersensitivity of the Plaintiff

269. The abnormal sensitivity of the plaintiff or other particularities of his person may make it difficult to maintain an action, since the interference must be unreasonable to an ordinary person. In other words, a hypersensitive plaintiff will find it difficult to prove his case as the standard of tolerance that nuisance law adopts is that of the normal and reasonable neighbour. In *Consider Capital Prosperous Ltd & Anor v. Sheen Cho*

515. [2014] UKSC 13.
516. [2014] UKSC 13 [at 96].
517. [2014] UKSC 13 [at 96].
518. [1895] 1 Ch 287.
519. [2014] UKSC 13 [at 119].

Kwong[520] the plaintiff (a tenant of the twenty-third floor) brought an action against the defendant (an owner of a flat on the twenty-fourth floor) to prohibit him from using the water pump after 11 pm and argued that such noises disturbed his children's sleep. The court did not hold the defendant liable for the hypersensitivity of the plaintiff. Likewise, in *Robinson v. Kilvert,*[521] the plaintiff's brown paper was damaged due to the rise in temperature of the floor but the court held that the plaintiff's brown paper was part of a delicate trade, and the paper itself was unusually susceptible to heat. However, in some circumstances, it is possible for the plaintiff to recover damages for exceptionally delicate use of land, which is illustrated by *McKinnon Industries Ltd v. Walker.*[522] In this case, the plaintiff was able to recover damages for his delicate orchid crop as he could prove that ordinary crops could be similarly affected.

d. Utility of the Defendant's Conduct

270. In determining whether the defendant's conduct was unreasonable, the court may take the utility of his conduct into account. However, the utility of the defendant's conduct may not negate liability, but may be relevant to remedies. In *Miller v. Jackson,*[523] the defendants organized cricket games that were alleged to prevent the plaintiffs from enjoying their garden. The court was of the view that playing cricket after many residential buildings were constructed around the pitch constituted a nuisance in the changed circumstances. The defendant was held liable in nuisance and negligence. Lord Denning dissented, stating that cricket has utility to society and that the plaintiff's claim should not be granted, but other judges disagreed. However, due to the utility argument, the court awarded damages instead of granting an injunction. Likewise, in *Dennis v. Ministry of Defence,*[524] the plaintiff, who lived near the RAF training facility, claimed under private nuisance and the court only granted damages as such facilities are there for the public interest.

e. Malice

271. The interference would be unreasonable if the defendant acted deliberately and maliciously. In *Christie v. Davey*[525] the defendant was provoked by the plaintiff's music lessons and banged on the walls and shouted in revenge every time such lessons were had. An injunction was granted to stop such malicious conduct. Likewise, in *Hollywood Silver Fox Farm v. Emmett,*[526] the defendant was found liable for firing a gun out of malice, to scare the plaintiff's silver foxes during breeding season.

272. On the other hand, if the plaintiff does not have a proprietary interest, he cannot sue under private nuisance, even if malicious interference is present. This is

520. [1999] 1 HKLRD 633, CFI.
521. (1889) 41 Ch D 88 (CA).
522. [1951] 3 DLR 577 PC.
523. [1977] 3 WLR 20 (CA).
524. [2003] EWHC 793.
525. [1983] 1 Ch 316.
526. [1936] 2 KB 468.

illustrated by *Bradford Corporation v. Pickles,*[527] where the defendant was not held liable for diverting water away from the plaintiff's property as the plaintiff had no right to the water supply.

3. The Standard of Liability (Causation and Remoteness)

273. In Cambridge *Water Co Ltd v. Eastern Counties Leather Plc,*[528] Lord Goff stated that the damage must be reasonably foreseeable at the time of the interference. Hence, under remoteness, the defendant could be liable for nuisance only if the damage is reasonably foreseeable. However, the liability hinges on reasonable use of land from both parties. Negligence is based on fault, which is based *Wagon Mound (No 1).*[529] In *Wong Wai Tak Belinda & Anor v. Smart Team International Investment Ltd,*[530] the court held the defendant liable for vibrations from his construction, which was reasonably foreseeable. Also, the thin or eggshell skull rule, as well as res ipsa loquitur (the thing speaks for itself), apply to nuisance.[531]

4. Defences

274. In Hong Kong, the limitation period for claiming in private nuisance, pursuant to section 4(1) of the Limitation Ordinance (Cap 347) (LO), is six years. But it could be extended or excluded under sections 22–33 (Part III) in certain special circumstances.

a. Statutory Authority

275. Statutory authority could be a defence for industrial, construction or other works that would otherwise cause nuisance. The defendant would have a complete defence over the interference if it is authorized by an ordinance in express words or by implication[532] and the plaintiff has to prove that the defendant's act goes beyond statutory authorization. In *Lam Yuk* Fong *v. A-G of Hong Kong,*[533] the plaintiff argued that the illegal dumping at a refuse collection point close to his premises was a nuisance. Section 9 of the Waste Disposal Ordinance (Cap 354) provided for collection points but the defendants fail to prevent unreasonable interference by illegal dumping. The defendant did not meet the requirements under the ordinance and was held liable.

276. Statutory authority is different from planning permission, as illustrated by *Gillingham.*[534] Planning permission can sometimes show indications as to the nature

527. [1985] AC 587.
528. [1994] 2 AC 264.
529. [1961] AC 388.
530. [2011] 3 HKC 322.
531. *Wong Ching Chi & Anor v. Full Yue Bleaching & Dyeing Co Ltd* [1994] 3 HKC 606, HC (Water escape from the defendant's premises to the plaintiff was seen as sufficient to determine former's liability).
532. *Allen v. Gulf Oil Refining Ltd* [1981] 1All ER 353.
533. [1987] HKLR 263.
534. *Gillingham Borough Council v. Medway (Chatham) Dock Co Ltd* [1993] QB 343.

of locality. In *Wheeler v. JJ Saunders Ltd*,[535] the defendant was permitted to expand his pig farm. Staughton LJ held that the grant of planning permission was not a statutory authority and it did not change the locality and, hence, it was still a nuisance. *See* paragraph 267 above for recent developments with respect to planning permission.

b. Prescription

277. The defence of prescription contends that the defendant has a prescriptive right to use the plaintiff's land. However, this is difficult to establish. In *Sturges v. Bridgman*,[536] the defendant used large machinery in manufacturing, resulting in noise for twenty years, but no one had complained during that time. The plaintiff, a doctor, had their rights interfered with by the noise as his clinic was in the vicinity. The plaintiff successfully sought an injunction against the defendant, since the noise was unreasonable. Further, *'coming to the nuisance'* is no defence. This is illustrated by *Bliss v. Hall*[537] where the defendant had manufactured candles for three years before plaintiff moved into the adjacent spot. The court held the defendant liable.

5. Remedies

278. Damages, injunctions and abatement (self-help) are available remedies under private nuisance. The damages could be for damage to land, pure economic losses by depreciating the value of property (including loss in profits) or interference with plaintiff's comfort and enjoyment of his land. Nominal, punitive and exemplary damages could be awarded after considering the extent of the plaintiff's suffering. Damages for personal injuries cannot be recovered under this tort, as it only relates to the plaintiff's interest in his land.[538] If the nuisance is continuous in nature, the court may also grant an injunction.[539] As discussed under defences above, the planning permission could be a factor for the court to consider in granting damages in lieu of an injunction.[540] Abatement is the plaintiff removing the nuisance himself, but this is not encouraged. However, such an action can be allowed if the plaintiff is facing imminent harm and a quick solution is needed.

B. Public Nuisance

1. Nature of Liability

279. The law of public nuisance aims to protect public rights (such as use of highway, noise or pollution) and is generally regarded as a crime instead of a tort.[541] In the UK, it is prosecuted by the Attorney General and the remedy is a criminal

535. [1995] 3 WLR 466.
536. [1879] 11 Ch D 852 (CA).
537. (1838) 4 Bing NC 183.
538. *Malone v. Laskey* [1907] 2 KB 141.
539. *Billion Star Development Ltd v. Wong Tak Chue* [2012] 2 HKC 369.
540. *Coventry v. Lawrence* [2014] UKSC 13 (Lord Neuberger).
541. *R v. Rimmington* [2006] 1 AC 459.

punishment according to statutory provisions. In *Attorney General v. PYA Quarries,*[542] Romer LJ stated that: '... *Nuisance is 'public' which* materially *affects the reasonable comfort and convenience of life of a class of Her Majesty's subjects'.* Parties affected can bring an action in the name of the AG (equivalent of the SJ in Hong Kong), and obtain an injunction. In *PYA Quarries*, an injunction was requested to stop the noise and dust. A civil action for an injunction[543] could be brought only if it can be proven that the plaintiff suffered more than others from the defendant's acts.[544] All public nuisance claims are considered in terms of three elements: namely, the degree of interference, the substantiality of discomfort or inconvenience, and the number of parties or particular damages suffered. Unlike in private nuisance, a single act causing discomfort and inconvenience is sufficient and the plaintiff can claim for personal injuries suffered, as well as for pecuniary or business loss, etc.

280. For public nuisance claims, the law is only concerned with the effect and lawfulness of the act. In *Gillingham Borough Council v. Medway (Chatham) Dock Co Ltd,*[545] the defendant dock company was granted the right to turn an old dock into a commercial port under lease, but it affected the neighbourhood. The court held in favour of the defendant. Buckley J held that the planning permission had changed the character of the neighbourhood and the issue of public nuisance should be discussed in the changed context.

281. In *Southport Corp v. Esso Petroleum Co Ltd,*[546] Lord Denning asserted that *'the term public nuisance covers a multitude of sins, great and small'*. This law covers a wide range of interferences, like pollution and waste disposal. Nowadays, public nuisance is mostly covered under statutes, like the Public Order Ordinance (Cap 245) and Road Traffic Ordinance (Cap 374) etc. Statutory nuisance aims to protect public health in general. They provide either a criminal sanction or preventative remedy through an administrative body or by the courts, but not private compensation.

282. In some instances, both private and public nuisance can be claimed. For instance, in *Halsey v. Esso Petroleum Co Ltd,*[547] the plaintiff succeeded in claiming damages for smell and noise in private nuisance, as well as the damages to his car, parked on a public road, in public nuisance.

283. Public nuisance is a strict liability tort which aims to protect citizens' health, and which sometimes may also regulate artificial structures projecting onto the highway,[548] such as balconies or tree branches. In such situations, a defendant would be held liable even he did not intend to commit any wrong.[549] For strict liability, there is no need to prove fault or the failure to take precautions or not acting in good faith. Additionally, the defendant can still be liable under nuisance. In *Wringe v. Cohen,*[550] strict liability was imposed on the defendant in relation to the collapse of an artificial

542. [1957] 2 QB 169.
543. *Attorney General v. Chaudry* [1971] 1 WLR 1614 (CA).
544. *Lam Yuk-fong v. Attorney General* [1987] HKLR 263 HC.
545. [1993] QB 343.
546. [1954] 2 QB 182, 196.
547. [1961] 2 All ER 145.
548. *Liao Kuo Chun v. Win Capital (HK)* Ltd [2010] 4 HKLRD 257.
549. *Wringe v. Cohen* [1940] 1KB 229.
550. [1940] 1KB 229.

structure (wall) which the defendant was not aware of. Likewise, in *Ideal Construction Ltd v. Maeda Corp*[551] the defendant was responsible for constructing a flyover and roadworks. Further, during the 2014 Occupy Central Movement in Hong Kong, private individuals, including cross-border bus services minibus managers, etc.[552] brought public nuisance claims related to the protester's obstructing public roads and the Hong Kong courts granted ex parte injunctions against the un-named defendants.

2. The Standard of Liability

284. Reasonable foreseeability is also significant in public nuisance cases. The standard of liability varies in negligence and strict liability cases, depending on the category that the interference falls into. *Wagon Mound No 2*[553] includes both immediate and indirect causes. In *Wagon Mound No 2,* the question for the Privy Council to decide was whether a reasonable engineer would have known that there was a '*real risk*' of the oil catching fire. The court stated that it was no excuse, even if it had a low probability to cause fire, to allow leaks of furnace oil. In addition, Lord Reid stated that, although negligence is not required in nuisance cases, fault was almost always necessary and would be connected with foreseeability. Therefore the standard of liability and foreseeability are crucial factors in determining public nuisance cases.

285. The courts in the public nuisance claims, such as obstruction of highways, consider whether there was a 'nuisance hazard' created by defendant, which caused a 'real risk of harm'.[554] The CFA in the case of *Leung Tsang Hung v. Incorporated Owners of Kwok Wing House*[555] clarified the law on public nuisance. In this case the appellant sued on behalf of a hawker, who died after a heavy piece of concrete fell from a balcony. The claim was brought against the defendants, the flat owners, the tenants and the owners of the building. The CFA held that where the defendant ought to know that his act or omission would pose a foreseeable '*real risk*', they could be liable for public nuisance.

C. The Rylands Versus Fletcher Rule

286. The strict liability principle of *Rylands v. Fletcher* is '*an extension of the law of nuisance to isolated escapes from land.*'[556] This rule provides a remedy to land

551. [1992] 1 HKC 528 (HC).
552. *Kwoon Chung Motors Co Ltd (冠忠遊覽車有限公司) v. Kwok Cheuk Kin & Ors* [2014] HKCU 2750 (CFI); *Lai Hoi Ping (黎海平) & Anor v. Persons Occupying Portions Of Nathan Road Near To And Between Argyle Street And Dundas Street To Prevent Or Obstruct Normal Vehicular Traffic From Passing And Repassing The Occupied Areas & Ors* [2014] HKCU 2726 (CA); *Chiu Luen Public Light Bus Co Ltd (潮聯公共小型巴士有限公司) v. Persons Unlawfully Occupying Or Remaining On The Public Highway Namely, The Westbound Carriageway Of Argyle Street Between The Junction Of Tung Choi Street And Portland Street And/Or Other Persons Hindering Or Preventing The Passing Or Repassing Of Argyle Street* [2014] HKCU 2435 (CFI).
553. *Overseas Tankship (UK) Ltd v. The Miller Steamship Co and Anor (The Wagon Mound No-2)* [1967] 1 AC 617.
554. [2007] 10 HKCFAR 480, paras 17–18.
555. [2007] 10 HKCFAR 480.
556. *Cambridge Water Co v. Eastern Counties Leather Plc* [1994] 2 AC 264 (HL).

owners whose land was damaged by the escape of an artificial substance from the neighbouring landowner, who was engaging in non-natural use of his land. This rule developed from the case of *Rylands v. Fletcher,*[557] where the defendant (Mr Fletcher), the owner of a piece of land, decided to construct a water reservoir for supplying water to a mill, which the defendant did not properly manage. This caused flooding on the plaintiff's land. This case was rather difficult for the court to deal with since the defendant was not at fault; nor was the act direct or intentional, and it was a single act, therefore neither negligence/private nuisance nor trespass was applicable.

287. Initially, the plaintiff's claim failed at the Court of First Chamber, but subsequently it succeeded in the Court of Exchequer Chamber and Blackburn J stated that, '*The person who for his own purposes brings on his land and collects and keeps there anything likely to do mischief if it escapes must keep it in at his own peril, and if he does not do so is prima facie answerable for all the damage which is the natural consequence of its escape.*' The House of Lords approved the decision and Lord Cairns LC stressed that the defendant's use of the land was non-natural. Foreseeability of harm was added by Lord Goff in his leading opinion in *Cambridge Water Co. v. Eastern Counties Leather Plc.*[558]

288. For the *Rylands* rule, it must be proven that: (1) the defendant brought and accumulated a substance that is likely to cause mischief; (2) the substance escaped; (3) it was a non-natural use of land; and (4) it caused foreseeable damage of.

289. In some jurisdictions, the *Rylands* rule has been absorbed into the tort of negligence.[559] However in the UK, as well as in Hong Kong, the *Rylands* rule has a small range of application. This is clear in the House of Lords cases of *Cambridge Water Co v. Eastern Counties Leather Plc*[560] and *Transco Plc v. Stockport Metropolitan Borough Council*[561] where the Lord Goff and Lord Hoffman respectively considered the Australian approach as adopted in the case of *Burnie Port Authority.*[562] The House of Lords concluded that abolishing *Rylands* would be too radical a move to take, though Lord Goff in *Cambridge Water* did accept that there are few occasions where *Rylands* may apply.

1. Who Can Be Sued and Who Can Sue?

290. The potential defendants who could be sued under *Rylands* are the land owner or occupiers who store or accumulate substances which cause damage. In the case of *Rainham Chemical Works Ltd v. Belvedere Fish Guano Co*[563] a licensee who artificially accumulated harmful substances was liable even though he was not the owner or occupier of the land. The general principle is that if the dangerous substance is brought with the occupier's permission or for his purposes, the occupier should be liable.

557. [1868] LR 3 HL 330.
558. [1994] 2 AC 264.
559. *Burnie Port Authority v. General Jones Pty Ltd* (1994) 179 CLR 520.
560. [1994] 2 AC 264 (HL).
561. [2003] UKHL 61.
562. *Burnie Port Authority v. General Jones Pty Ltd* (1994) 179 CLR 520.
563. [1921] 1 AC 465 (HL).

291. The potential plaintiffs under the *Rylands* rule are similar to those for private nuisance. Therefore it is important to identify the plaintiff's interest in the land, as stipulated in *Hunter v. Canary Wharf Ltd.*[564] Further the House of Lords in *Transco Plc*[565] added a clarification that the claimants could only sue if they have rights to the land. To bring a claim under *Rylands*, the substance must escape and should have caused physical harm to plaintiff's land. There is no liability for physical injury as it only protects against interferences with the use of land. Further, the damaging agent must escape and cause damage. In the case of *Ponting v. Noakes,*[566] the defendant's yew tree grew within his property. The plaintiff's wandering horse ate the poisonous leaves and died. The court did not hold the defendant liable as the substance did not escape.

2. Nature of Liability

292. The *Rylands* rule is an extension of private nuisance. The creator uses the land for non-natural purposes, artificially brings and accumulates mischief-causing substances and they escape, and causing foreseeable damage to the plaintiff's land.

a. Unnatural/Artificial Accumulation

293. The defendant under the *Rylands* rule is liable for bringing or accumulating mischief-causing substances that subsequently escapes onto the plaintiff's land. The accumulation does not include natural things present on that land. In *Smith v. Kenrick,*[567] water from one mine flowed into another during the ordinary course of work. The defendant was not found liable. It should be noted that the materials need not be dangerous but can be things that can turn dangerous upon escape. In *Chan Ying Wah v. Bachy Soletanche Group Ltd,*[568] liability under the *Ryland's* rule was proven against the defendant because he had accidentally diverted sea water into the plaintiff's irrigation water.

294. The artificially accumulated materials must have escaped and caused damage to the plaintiffs land. Per Lord Goff in *Cambridge Water Co,* escape is similar to interference in private nuisance, but there is no requirement for foreseeability. In *Read v. Lyons,*[569] an explosion caused injury to the plaintiff (the inspector of ammunition factories). The House of Lords held that, as there was no escape of hazardous materials, the defendant was not liable under the *Rylands* rule. Likewise, in *Rigby v. Chief Constable of Northamptonshire,*[570] the police fired a gas canister. The court held that *Rylands* liability does not exist as the 'escape' of gas was intentional (Taylor J).

564. [1997] 2 All ER 426 (HL).
565. [2003] UKHL 61.
566. [1894] 2 QB 281.
567. [1849] 7 CB 515.
568. [2004] HKEC 1483.
569. [1946] 2 All ER 471 (HL).
570. [1985] 2 All ER 985.

b. Non-natural Users

295. The non-natural use of land is a question of fact. The meaning of non-natural use of land was interpreted to be '*some* special *use bringing with it increased danger to others, and must not merely be the ordinary use of the land or such use as is proper for the general benefit of the community*' (per Lord Moulton).[571] This approach significantly restricted the scope of *Rylands* liability. The House of Lords in *Transco Plc v. Stockport Metropolitan Borough Council*[572] dismissed the appeal of the plaintiff, who claimed costs for repairing the gas pipes. The gas pipes were exposed due to the fracture of water pipes. The House of Lords held that having water pipes was not an unusual use of land.

296. In the past, an assessment of the benefit to the community could be used to determine whether the land was being put to non-natural use. For instance, in *Read v. Lyons*[573] it was stated that running a munitions factory during wartime could be a natural use of land as it was beneficial to the community. However, in modern times, the general benefit to the community is not conclusive. The meaning of non-natural user is narrowed down by scientific developments. For example, in the early twentieth century, storing a full tank of petrol in a car was seen as a non-natural use of land,[574] while storing chemical compounds on industrial premises could be a natural use of land.[575] In contemporary times, non-natural use is understood as extraordinary use. Therefore, storage of substantial quantities of chemicals on industrial premises could be regarded as an almost classic case of non-natural use. Creating jobs and benefiting the community cannot make industrial activity a natural use of land.[576] Although the nature of neighbourhood could be taken into consideration,[577] where the defendant stores excessive and substantial quantities of mischief-causing substances, they could be held liable under the *Rylands* rule. For example, in *Wong Ching Chi & Anor v. Full Yue Bleaching and Dyeing Co Ltd*,[578] the construction of excessive water tanks in an industrial area was considered as a non-natural use of land. In case of fire, liability can be imposed under the *Rylands* rule if the defendant stores things that could spread fire to the plaintiff's land and, in that case, the use of land would be non-natural.[579]

3. The Standard of Liability

297. For the purposes of the *Rylands* rule the test of reasonable foreseeability is whether something is 'likely to cause mischief'. In *Cambridge Water Co Ltd v. Eastern Counties Leather plc*[580] Lord Goff stated that to impose *Rylands* liability

571. *Rickards v. Lothian* [1913] AC 263.
572. [2003] UKHL 61.
573. [1947] AC 156.
574. *Musgrove v. Pendelis* [1919] 2 KB 43 (CA).
575. *Cambridge Water Co v. Eastern Counties Leather Plc* [1994] 2 AC 264 (HL).
576. *Cambridge Water Co v. Eastern Counties Leather Plc* [1994] 2 AC 264 (HL).
577. *Wayfoong Credit Ltd v. Tsui Siu-man Plastics* [1984] HKLR 259.
578. [1994] 3 HKC 606.
579. *Mason v. Levy Auto Parts* [1967] 2 QB 350.
580. [1994] 1 All ER 53.

'*foreseeability of damage of the relevant type*' is a requirement. In *Cambridge Water*, the defendant was a leather tannery and it used a chlorinated solvent (PCE) to degrease the pelts. The plaintiff used water for domestic purposes. The water became contaminated by PCE and became unfit for human consumption. Subsequently, the plaintiff claimed damages for negligence, nuisance and breach of the *Rylands* rule. The House of Lords rejected the plaintiff's case as he could not prove that the contamination was foreseeable. Likewise, Lord Bingham in *Transco Plc v. Stockport Metropolitan Borough Council*[581] held that *Rylands* liability was not applicable because '*it must be shown that the defendant has done something which he recognised, or judged by the standards appropriate at the relevant place or time, or ought reasonably to have recognised, as giving rise to an exceptionally high risk of danger or mischief if there should be an escape, however unlikely an escape may have been thought to be*'.[582]

4. Defences

298. The defences, such as statutory authority, unforeseeable acts of a stranger, fault of the plaintiff, consent and act of God, applies to the *Rylands* rule. Statutory authority is the same as that which is applicable for nuisance. The unforeseeable act of a stranger is also a defence for *Rylands*. In *Rickards v. Lothian*[583] the defendant was not held liable under *Rylands* when a stranger blocked a basin, flooding the plaintiff's flat below. However, if the defendant should foresee such a stranger's act and could control the premises, he would be held liable.[584]

299. The defendant can also plead that the plaintiff is at fault for the escape of the substance.[585] Consent on part of the plaintiff to the presence of the source of the mischief-causing agent is a defence. In *Kiddle v. City Business Properties Ltd*,[586] there was an escape of water. The courts found that the tenants, by reaping benefits, were impliedly consenting to the consequences.

300. The defendant can also plead in their defence that the facts at issue are from an act of God, arguing that the escape was caused by unforeseen natural events. Lord Westbury, in *Tennent v. Earl of Glasgow*,[587] stated that these were events that '*no human foresight can provide against, and of which human prudence is not bound to recognise the possibility*'. An act of God is hard to delineate and depends on whether the land was being put to natural use. For example, if the defendant failed to keep his tank safely and it subsequently became flooded by rainwater, an act of God defence would fail as the defendant could foresee such consequences and could have taken reasonable skill to avoid it. In *Star Ferry Co Ltd v. The Owners of The Ship or Vessel 'Argonaut' & Anor*,[588] severe weather conditions resulted in the collision between the 'Argonaut' and the plaintiff's pier. The plaintiff brought an action to claim cost of

581. [2004] 2 AC 1, (HL).
582. [2004] 2 AC 1, (HL), para. 33.
583. [1913] AC 263.
584. *Hale v. Jennings Bros* [1938] 1 All ER 579 (CA).
585. *Eastern and South African Telegraph Co Ltd v. Cape Tramways Co Ltd* [1902] AC 381 (PC).
586. [1942] 1 KB 269, 274.
587. [1864] 2 M (HL) 22, 26–27.
588. [1980] HKLR 921, HC.

repairs against the defendant (Attorney General) by relying on paragraph 11 of the Schedule to the Star Ferry Company (Services) Ordinance (41 of 1951), which stated the plaintiff will not be liable for the cost of repair caused by an act of God. The defendant conceded that there was no negligence on the part of the plaintiff so the government was liable.

5. Remedies

301. The remedies are similar to private nuisance. The owner of the land can claim damages for any physical harm to their land or other property. Damages for personal injury cannot be recovered under *Rylands*.[589] The remedies of injunction and abatement also apply.

IV. Intentional Torts

302. Trespass is the oldest tort, created to protect against direct and intentional physical interference with persons or property (goods and land). Currently, there are three forms of trespass: trespass against the person, land and goods. All kinds of trespass violate the civil rights/liberties of the plaintiff, and, as such, they are actionable per se. There are other torts that also protect against interference against persons, including the tort of intentional infliction of physical harm (IIPH) and sexual harassment/ discrimination. Such torts safeguard the civil rights of all Hong Kong residents, as they are also constitutionally[590] and statutorily[591] protected. In the UK, during the nineteenth century, economic torts were developed as part of trespass to protect the economic interests of plaintiffs. Furthermore, statutory torts were developed as part of trespass to the person for protecting the claimants from harassment, as it may result in mental stress and even psychiatric harm.

A. Trespass to the Person

303. Trespass to the person protects the claimant from interferences with his/ her personal integrity. For the claim to succeed, the defendant's intention and the directness of the injury need to be shown. However, in the past, it was thought that trespass to the person could be committed both negligently *(Fowler v. Lanning)*[592] and intentionally. The meaning of intention is similar to that under criminal law, so it refers to the defendant's knowledge (actual or presumed) only, excluding motive. In *Letang v. Cooper,*[593] Lord Denning MR rejected the plaintiff's claim by holding that negligence and trespass needed to be differentiated. For the latter, intention is required. In this case, the plaintiff was sunbathing in a hotel car park and the defendant drove over her legs unintentionally, causing her injury. The plaintiff brought an action under trespass

589. *Corby Group Litigation Claimants v. Corby BC* [2008] EWCA Civ 463; [2009] QB 335.
590. Hong Kong Basic Law, Art. 28.
591. The Hong Kong Bill of Rights Ordinance (Cap 383).
592. [1959] 1 QB 426.
593. [1965] 1 QB 232 (CA).

to avoid the limitation period of three years for negligence, but, since the defendant did not injure her intentionally and three years was held to be a sufficient time, she lost her case. Trespass to the person is also applicable in cases of abuse of power by the police (e.g., wrongful arrest or detention);[594] the actions are unlawful in nature as they interfere with a person's civil liberties.

304. Consent, self-defence, legal authority, provocation and necessity are the available defences for this tort. In *Chatterton v. Gerson,*[595] the patient did not have to be informed of all the risks associated with that surgery for the consent to be effective; information on the general nature of the procedure was sufficient. If the doctor goes beyond the terms of consent, though, it becomes battery. For self-defence, it must be shown that the plaintiff's use of force was reasonable.[596] However, if the plaintiff is arrested lawfully under statutory authority, he cannot bring an action under battery.[597] In *Davidson v. Chief Constable of North Wales & Anor,*[598] the police arrested the plaintiff based on the information provided by a store detective. The court refused to hold the store detective liable for incitement of arrest, as the police exercised its own judgment in making the decision. A defendant can employ provocation as a defence, although it is not a full defence.[599] Necessity can be used as a limited one.[600]

305. Remedies for trespass to the person include damages for personal injury, death and damage to property. The amount of damages will vary based on the severity of injury. Exemplary damages could be awarded for: (1) oppressive, arbitrary or unconstitutional actions by any government agent; or (2) where it is necessary to punish the wrongdoer (for deterrence). Further, injunctions could be awarded where the defendant is required to refrain from doing certain acts in order to protect the plaintiff's interests.

1. Assault

306. Assault involves direct and intentional acts or conduct that put a person in reasonable apprehension of imminent harm, even if no actual physical contact takes place. Assault has no connection to how brave or scared the victim is; hence, the defendant cannot use that as a defence. As such, the requirements are: (1) the reasonable apprehension of direct and immediate harm; and (2) the act was intentional in nature. In *Stephen v. Myers,*[601] the defendant was held liable for assault when he approached the plaintiff with a clenched fist before he was obstructed by a third party. In contrast,

594. *Thompson and Hsu v. Commissioner of Police of Metropolis* [1998] QB 498 (Wrongful arrest); *R v. Governor of Brockhill Prison, ex p Evans (N0 2)* [2000] 4 All ER 15 (HL) (unlawful detention).
595. [1981] QB 432.
596. *Chen Yung Hui v. Lam Shing* [1988] HCA 7200 of 1985 (Self-defence).
597. The Criminal Procedure Ordinance (Cap 221), s. 101; *Re Tran Quoc Cuong & Anor* [1995] 5 HKPLR 208.
598. [1994] 2 All ER 597.
599. *Lane v. Holloway* [1968] 1 QB 379.
600. *F v. Berkshire Health Authority* [1981] QB 432 (Lord Goff – Reasonable doctor's actions in the best interests of the patient do not constitute battery).
601. [1830] 4 C & P 349.

in *Innes v. Wylie,*[602] a policeman prevented the defendant from entering the plaintiff's room, but it was not held to be an assault since the plaintiff was not in apprehension of immediate bodily harm. It is also not assault where the words used did not carry any intention of causing physical harm.[603] However, if threatening and foul language was used, it could constitute assault,[604] as it was held in *Wong Wai Hing v. Hui Wei Lee.*[605] Threats made over the telephone[606] and conditional threats also constitute assault.[607]

2. Battery

307. Battery is the infliction of unlawful force by the defendant to the plaintiff. The requirements are: (1) the act must involve force; and (2) the force must be intentional and direct. The contact need not be physical (e.g., flesh to flesh) to be direct, since hitting with an object also qualifies as direct. For example, in *Scott v. Shepherd,*[608] the defendant was held liable for battery when he threw a lit firework into a market place, which fell onto many stalls before hitting the plaintiff's, exploding in his face. For the first requirement, the act must be positive (e.g., kicking, handcuffing,[609] etc.), as opposed to mere omission resulting in actual physical contact with the plaintiff's body. The severity of the injury caused will affect the damages claimable by the plaintiff (e.g., nominal, aggravated and exemplary damages).[610]

308. The defendant's use of force must be intentional and voluntary, and it does not matter if a person accidentally hits the wrong person. Under the principle of transferred intention, the defendant would still be liable. In *Livingstone v. Ministry of Defence,*[611] the defendant was held liable for striking the wrong target. Hence, mistake cannot be used as a defence. In certain instances, if the person acted unintentionally at first, but then intended to apply force later, he would be liable. This is demonstrated in *Fagan v. Metropolitan Police Commissioner,*[612] where the defendant stopped his car on a policeman's foot. At the beginning, it was said no battery was committed, as the defendant did not know he rolled his car onto the policeman's foot, and thus it was unintentional. However, he purposely did not move even when the policeman shouted to release his foot, and at that point the intention was established and the infliction of force was considered as ongoing, and thus constituted battery.

309. Force is generally interpreted to include even trivial acts, including things what one would generally find acceptable in carrying out ordinary conduct in daily

602. (1844) 174 ER 800.
603. *Tuberville v. Savage* (1669) 91 ER 1072.
604. *Chang Ming Fang Jacqueline Alias Chang Hwai Ying Jacqueline v. Zhang Zi Qiang*, [2011] HKCU 318.
605. [2001] HKCU 488.
606. *Wong Kwai Fun v. Li Fung* [1994] 1 HKC 549, HC, 580 (Woo J).
607. *Police v. Greaves* [1964] NZLR 295.
608. [1773] 2 W Bl 892, [1558–1774] All ER Rep 295.
609. *William Alan Terence Crawley v. Attorney General* [1987] HKLR 379, HC (Hunter J).
610. *Rookes v. Barnard* [1964] AC 1129.
611. [1984] N. I 356 (N Ireland CA).
612. [1969] 1 QB 439.

life.[613] In *Cole v. Turner*, it was accepted that the slightest touch made in anger is a hostile act.[614] On that basis, the Court of Appeal in *Wilson v. Pringle*[615] held that battery must be committed with hostility. However, the problem with *Wilson* is it that it raises the question of what hostile intent means, which is subjective in nature. In *F v. Berkshire Health Authority,*[616] it was stated that use of force is best defined as what has been accepted generally in daily life. The House of Lords also held that an unlawful act is hostile, and the element of consent must be considered to determine the nature of force used and the intention of the defendant.[617]

3. False Imprisonment

310. False imprisonment is the unlawful and intentional constraint of "another's freedom of movement. Whether the defendant knew he did something wrong is not relevant to proving the offence. Where means of escape are available, it will not constitute false imprisonment. In *Bird v. Jones,*[618] the defendant wrongfully enclosed part of the footway, and the plaintiff insisted on passing along the enclosed part. This did not constitute false imprisonment, as other parts of the footway could still be accessed.

311. In *Murray v. Ministry of Defence,*[619] the court declared that it is *not* necessary for the plaintiff to know that his movement is restrained in order to establish false imprisonment. In that case, the plaintiff was suspected of being involved in certain illegal activities, so the defendant's officers went to her home, asked her to accompany them and arrested her later. The plaintiff sued the defendant for detaining her for thirty minutes while no lawful arrest was made. The court held that it was lawful for the announcement of the arrest to be delayed, but had to decide on the issue of whether or not it is possible for a person to be imprisoned without their knowledge as a matter of law. Lord Griffiths stated in his judgment that, *'[I]f a person is unaware that he has been falsely imprisoned and has suffered no harm, he can normally expect to recover no more than nominal damages ...* '[620] Based on that, it can be inferred that the plaintiff's knowledge is important for assessing the amount of damages, but not for establishing liability.

312. False imprisonment liability is there to protect people's freedom. For example, it is possible to falsely imprison a mentally sick person even if he is not aware of it.[621] Likewise in *R v. Governor of Brockhill Prison, ex parte Evans (No. 2),*[622] the court held the defendant liable for false imprisonment when he miscalculated when

---

613. *Collins v. Wilcock* [1984] 3 All ER 374 (Robert Goff. J).
614. *Cole v. Turner* (1704) 87 ER 907; *R v. Brown* [1993] 2 All ER 75 (the unlawful act is hostile).
615. [1987] QB 237 (CA).
616. [1981] QB 432 (Lord Goff).
617. *F v. Berkshire Health Authority* [1981] QB 432 (Lord Goff); *Chan Kin Bun v. Wong Sze Ming* [2006] 3 HKLRD 208.
618. (1845) 7 QB 742.
619. [1988] 2 All ER 521 (HL).
620. [1988] 2 All ER 521 (HL), 530.
621. *A-G v. Chan Yuen Lung & Others* [1989] 1 HKC 470, 473 (Bewley J).
622. [2001] 2 AC 19.

to release the plaintiff, who was originally lawfully imprisoned for some criminal offences. The action was successful, even if the defendant did not have any intention to hold the plaintiff in prison for longer than necessary. This case highlights the importance placed on protecting people's liberty. A plaintiff's lack of knowledge will, however, affect the amount of damages payable by the defendant.

B. Intentional Infliction of Physical Harm (Wilkinson Principle)

313. 'IIPH' is different from trespass to the person and, as such, the former is not actionable per se. For IIPH, liability is imposed for any intentional act or statement that indirectly causes physical harm to the plaintiff. In that sense, IIPH could be perceived as complimentary to trespass to person. This tortious liability was created in *Wilkinson v. Downton,*[623] where the defendant lied to the first plaintiff, telling her that her husband, the second plaintiff, was seriously injured in a road accident. The defendant's false statement caused the plaintiff to suffer sudden shock, which resulted in serious and dangerous physical and psychological reactions. The defendant claimed he was only playing a 'practical joke'. The plaintiffs sought to recover damages for false, fraudulent, and malicious representation causing mental anguish, injury to health, and out-of-pocket expenses. The plaintiffs were allowed to amend their claim after submission by adding the travel expenses incurred by the men sent to fetch the husband home through the railway, due to the false statement. The court held the defendant liable for making a false statement intended for the wife to act on, and found that it was a wilful and calculated act to cause physical harm to the plaintiffs.[624] Although this case concerned the infliction of physical harm by an untrue statement, it equally applies to harm caused by other indirect conduct.[625]

314. To succeed in an action of IIPH, it is important to prove that the defendant's conduct was: (1) an indirect but intentional act/statement; (2) meant to cause physical harm to the plaintiff; and (3) actually caused the plaintiff physical harm. In *Khorasandjian v. Bush,*[626] the plaintiff relied on private nuisance and the *Wilkinson* rule to claim protection from her former boyfriend's harassment, who constantly called her over the phone. On the *Wilkinson* principle part, a broad brush approach was taken, and Dillon LJ stated that there was *'an obvious risk that the cumulative effect of continued and unrestrained further harassment, such as she has undergone, would cause [psychiatric] illnesses'*.[627] Therefore, an injunction was awarded to prevent further harassment.

315. Prior to the Protection from the Harassment Act 1997 in the UK, and SDO in Hong Kong, courts seemed willing to extend the *Wilkinson* liability to cover mere distress, even if no physical or psychiatric harm was suffered by the plaintiff. However, after the enactments, harassment was to be dealt under legislation. As a result, courts in the UK are now unwilling to extend the *Wilkinson* liability to cover mere distress, which could be recovered for under the legislation instead, as evidenced by *Wainwright*

623. [1897] 2QB 57; [1895–1899] All ER Rep 267.
624. [1895–1899] All ER Rep 267, 270 (Wright J.).
625. *Wong v. Parkside Health NHS Trust* [2003] 3 All ER 932.
626. [1993] QB 727.
627. [1993] QB 727, 736.

v. Home Office.[628] The plaintiffs were subject to strip searches when they went to visit a family member in prison. The trial judge considered that the torts of battery and invasion of privacy, as forms of trespass to the person, were made out. The Court of Appeal struck out the invasion of privacy charge but retained the finding of battery. This was approved by the House of Lords. Lord Hoffman, in obiter, stated in relation to *Wilkinson*: *'It does not provide a remedy for distress which does not amount to recognized psychiatric injury and so far as there may a tort of intention under which such damage is recoverable, the necessary intention was not established. I am also in complete agreement with Buxton LJ, at [2002] QB 1334, 1355-1356, paras 67-72, that* Wilkinson v Downton *has nothing to do with trespass to the person.'*[629] Given the Protection from Harassment Act 1997 there is no need for the Wilkinson principle as the basis of a tort for intentional harassment that causes damage short of physical or psychiatric harm.[630]

316. The defendant's conduct (act or statement) must produce the injury (physical or mental) that was calculated to cause harm to the plaintiff. Thus, it is not necessary for the defendant to make a statement in the plaintiff's presence.[631] In *Wong Kwai Fun v. Li Fung,*[632] the lender repeatedly assaulted and intimidated the debtor, who was unable to repay his loan (which had a very high interest rate) on time. The threats of violence caused the plaintiff (debtor) to try to commit suicide twice. The plaintiff was allowed to be awarded damages, based on the *Wilkinson v. Downton*[633] principle.

317. However, the status of the *Wilkinson* principle is still uncertain, due to the tort of negligence (psychiatric injury). The reason is because this tort, IIPH, was created at a time when there was no remedy in trespass available for harm inflicted indirectly.

C. *Sexual Harassment/Discrimination*

318. Harassment is an intentional harm under common law, and liability is dealt with under a range of torts, including the *Wilkinson* principle,[634] breach of confidence,[635] nuisance[636] and trespass to the person.[637] All of them are discussed in the relevant parts of this text. These civil remedies have certain disadvantages when applied to sexual harassment, which undermines the efforts to curb it. For example, under the *Wilkinson* principle, the scope of harassment is limited to mental and physical torture by threats or intimidation only. Under breach of confidence, the plaintiff needs to prove an established relationship with the defendant. Under nuisance, the exclusive right to possession of the land where the nuisance occurred has to be proven by the plaintiff.

628. [2003] 3 All ER 932; [2004] 2 AC 406 (HL).
629. [2003] 3 All ER 932; [2004] 2 AC 406 (HL), para. 47 (Lord Hoffman).
630. *Janvier v. Sweeney* [1919] 2 KB 316 (CA); *Nickerson v. Hodges* [1920] 84 Sol Jo 37.
631. *Bielitski v. Obadiak* [1922] 65 DLR 627 (Canadian case).
632. [1994] 1 HKC 549.
633. [1897] 2QB 57; [1895–1899] All ER Rep 267.
634. *Wilkinson v. Downton* [1897] 2 QB 57; *Wong v. Parkside Health NHS Trust* [2003] 3 All ER 932; *Wong Kwai Fun v. Li Fung* [1994] 1 HKC 549.
635. *Duchess of Argyll v. Duke of Argyll* [1967] 1 Ch 302.
636. *Khorasandjian v. Bush* [1993] 137.
637. *Chang Ming Fang Jacqueline Alias Chang Hwai Ying Jacqueline v. Zhang Zi Qiang*, (CFI, HCA 2714/2006).

Hunter overruled *Khorasandjian v. Bush.*[638] In *Bush,* the plaintiff sought an injunction after her ex-boyfriend, the defendant, harassed her with phone calls to the family home. The court granted an injunction to the plaintiff even when she did not have a substantial link to the land, as her parents owned the land instead. In *Hunter v. Canary Wharf Ltd,*[639] *Khorasandjian* was criticized, and it was said that *'[What] the Court of Appeal appeared to have been doing was to exploit the law of private nuisance in order to create by back door a tort of harassment, which was only partially effective in that it was artificially limited to harassment which takes place in her home.'*[640] In the United Kingdom nowadays, harassment is dealt with under the Protection from Harassment Act 1997.

319. In Hong Kong, liability for gender discrimination is determined under the 'SDO'. The SDO was enacted in 1995 to *'render unlawful certain kinds of sex discrimination, discrimination on the ground of marital status or pregnancy, and sexual harassment; to provide for the establishment of a Commission with the functions of working towards the elimination of such discrimination and harassment and promoting equality of opportunity between men and women generally; and to provide for matters incidental thereto or connected therewith'.*[641] Thus, its objectives are to: (1) put an end to sexual harassment, and sex discrimination due to marital status or pregnancy; and (2) establish Equal Opportunities Commission (EOC) to eliminate all discrimination/ harassment in order to promote available opportunities for different men and women. Ultimately, the SDO provides a greater degree of protection against discrimination, including sexual harassment, in sexually hostile environments. The SDO is quite comprehensive, as it contains ninety-one sections with eight schedules on various aspects of discrimination against women,[642] men[643] and married persons.[644] The SDO also protects contract workers,[645] applicants and employees[646] in different circumstances.[647] In 2014–2015, the SDO was amended on a number of fronts. A key change was the extension of protection to workers who are sexually harassed by clients,[648] and the protection extends to vessels registered in Hong Kong even when they are physically outside Hong Kong.[649]

320. Part III of the SDO outlines direct and vicarious liability[650] for sexual harassment in the course of employment,[651] education[652] and in other forms.[653] These

---

638. [1993] QB 727.
639. [1997] AC 655 (HL).
640. [1997] AC 655, 692 (HL).
641. *See* Long Title of Sex Discrimination Ordinance (Cap 480), ER 1 of 2013, 25 Apr. 2013.
642. SDO, ss 5 and 8.
643. SDO, s. 6.
644. SDO, s. 7.
645. SDO, s. 13.
646. SDO, s. 11.
647. SDO, s. 28.
648. SDO, s. 40.
649. SDO, s. 41(7).
650. SDO, s. 46.
651. SDO, s. 23.
652. SDO, s. 39.
653. SDO, s. 40.

other forms include while: (1) providing service and goods;[654] (2) providing, obtaining or staying at premises;[655] (3) offering pupillage or tenancy at barristers' chambers;[656] and (4) giving, withholding or accepting instructions to barristers.[657] For harassment that occurs in chambers, the SDO offers protection to both current and prospective pupils. It should be noted that section 39 has undergone an amendment in 2008 to incorporate the prohibition of sexually hostile environments in educational settings, as that concept used to only apply to work environments. The SDO defines activities that constitute sexual harassment and exceptions to liability. It should be noted that special treatment for special needs people does not imply sex discrimination, and is simply construed as satisfying realistic needs. Part VI also provides exceptions for matters under part III to VI. Such matters include charities,[658] sport,[659] insurance,[660] communal accommodation,[661] discriminatory training by certain bodies,[662] other discriminatory training,[663] acts done for protecting women,[664] etc. However, complete though the SDO may seem to be, it still has loopholes in certain areas. First, it does not seem to explicitly address the problems of harassment committed against someone of the same sex as the defendant.[665] Second, it seems that one can only file a claim within the scope of the SDO, so harassment outside it may not be addressed.

321. Sexual harassment in the form of unwanted sexual attention is classified as a civil offence. Abusive physical, verbal or non-verbal behaviours can constitute sexual harassment. Examples of abusive physical behaviours includes violence, touching and unnecessarily close proximity; offensive verbal behaviour includes comments and questions about appearance, lifestyle and sexual orientation, and offensive phone calls; and applicable non-verbal behaviour includes whistling, sexually suggestive gestures and sexual material being displayed. Sexual harassment also includes intimidation of a claimant in a sexually hostile environment. Under the SDO, the plaintiff can sue for the offence even if the employer is not the perpetrator, if a co-worker or service provider is.

322. Sexual harassment may essentially take two forms. One is any unwelcome, offensive, humiliating or intimidating sexual behaviour or conduct; for example, imposing a condition onto the victim to engage in demanded sexual behaviour in exchange for a pay rise, promotion, or even continued employment. The conduct does not have to be a one-time thing; it can be carried out over time. Another form is a hostile working environment, in which the conduct creates intimidating or humiliating

---

654. SDO, s. 40(1).
655. SDO, s. 40(2).
656. SDO, s. 40(6).
657. SDO, s. 40(7).
658. SDO, s. 49.
659. SDO, s. 50.
660. SDO, s. 51.
661. SDO, s. 52.
662. SDO, s. 53.
663. SDO, s. 54.
664. SDO, s. 57.
665. D.K. Srivastava, '*Progress of Sexual Harassment Law in India, China and Hong Kong*', 51 Harv. ILJ Online, 179 (11 Aug. 2010).

conditions for the victim. Both forms are covered by the SDO.[666] It also defines *'conduct of a sexual nature' '(涉及性的行徑)',*[667] as making an oral or written statement of sexual nature to a woman, or in her presence but not to her. There is no exhaustive list describing all behaviours that might constitute such acts, but paragraph 6.1 of the Code of Practice on Employment under the SDO sheds some light on its meaning by providing examples of conduct that can constitute sexual harassment. Examples include lewd gestures, deliberately brushing up against another person, etc. In *Yuen Sha Sha v. Tse Chi Pan,*[668] the defendant was found to have covertly hidden a camcorder in the plaintiff's room to record the plaintiff while she slept, changed and undressed. Upon discovery of the recording device, the plaintiff had an immediate apprehension of fear that others were using and obtaining unlawful enjoyment from the recordings of her naked body. It was held that the defendant committed sexual harassment under section 39(3) of the SDO. In *Yuen Chi Man Daniel v. Cheng Pui Man,*[669] the plaintiff (a teaching assistant) brought an action against the defendant (an assistant principal), for his offensive acts that contravened the 'Preventing Sexual Harassment Policy' enacted by the school. The defendant was held liable and it was found that the defendant had committed similar offensive acts at his previous place of employment.

323. In *Bloomfield v. Quadrant Stationery,*[670] the plaintiff, a sales representative, brought a claim against her employer company as its sales manager had exposed his genitals to her many times. The plaintiff initially filed complaints with the sales director. However, instead of acting upon this complaint, the director condoned the manager's behaviour by exposing his own genitals to her. The plaintiff succeeded in her claim. In *Reed & Bull Information Systems v. Stedman,*[671] the plaintiff, a former company secretary, brought a claim against her former employer as its marketing manager kept making sexually provocative remarks to her many times during the course of her employment. Despite her protests against this behaviour, the manager continued. The company's management team was made aware of the matter by other colleagues communicating the information on behalf of the plaintiff but they took no timely and appropriate measures. It was found by the tribunal that the manager knew that his comments were unacceptable and amounted to sexual harassment. The question that the tribunal had to decide was whether the company was liable where no official complaint was filed. It was held that the company was liable, because the management team had knowledge of the ongoing harassment. By failing to taking prompt actions against the manager, the company thus became liable for their omission.

324. Sexual harassment in workplaces is covered by section 2(5)(b) of the SDO. What creates a sexually hostile or intimidating work environment? One example is posting obscene pictures. Paragraph 6.2 of the Code of Practice on Employment under the SDO sheds some light on what constitutes sexual harassment in the employment context. Paragraph 6.3 states that a series of incidents can constitute sexual harassment, but not necessarily for all cases. Paragraph 6.4 makes it clear that an employee may

666. SDO, s. 2(5).
667. SDO, s. 2(7), subs. 5.
668. [1999] 1 HKC 731.
669. [2015] HKCU 3025.
670. [1998] ET/3201144/97.
671. (1999) IRLR 299.

be the victim of a hostile work environment if all the single acts create a pattern when put together, but do not amount to harassment on their own. An example of how section 2(5)(b) of the SDO applies is the recent Hong Kong case of *A v. Chan Wai Tong,*[672] the defendant on one occasion put his head close to the plaintiff and said, 'Let me kiss!' On another occasion, the defendant stared at her breast and said, 'What big breasts!' The plaintiff subsequently reported the matter to her boss. The defendant harassed her more upon finding out about the complaint by suggesting having sexual intercourse with her. This was held to be sexual harassment.

325. To establish sexual harassment, the plaintiff has to satisfy two tests: one subjective and one objective. The subjective test determines whether the defendant's sexual conduct is offensive from the plaintiff's perspective, so it has a lower threshold. The objective test determines whether a reasonable person would find the defendant's conduct offensive; it is not concerned with the plaintiff's personal proclivities and idiosyncrasies. The objective test is likely to create problems for certain plaintiffs, such as disabled persons.[673] The plaintiff may fail the objective test for dressing provocatively, as a reasonable person may think she intends to provoke people.[674] The objective test will be hard to satisfy in cases with a plaintiff who does not resist, or a plaintiff who had previously consented to such acts.[675] If sexual harassment is reported at a later time, the plaintiff may be assumed to be biased and could be rejected, as evidenced by *Chen v. Taramus Rus and Another.*[676] If the plaintiff tolerates unwelcome sexual advances by a defendant over a period of time (e.g., several months), she may lose her claim. The importance of the temporal factor was illustrated in *Wong Kwok-mui v. Lee Yuen-tim,*[677] where the plaintiff alleged that the defendant *sifu* had caressed the plaintiff, and requested her to perform a number of sexual acts multiple times. The defendant even asked the plaintiff to be 'his woman' after telling her about his failing marriage. However, the claim ultimately failed, because the plaintiff took several months before bringing about an official complaint. The court also found her to be highly sensitive to physical contact.

326. Remedies are provided by the SDO,[678] which states that courts can award damages for sexual harassment under injury to feelings, exemplary damages, loss of earning, and equitable and other forms of relief. Section 76 compliments the common law damages that the plaintiff can claim, i.e., ordinary, aggravated, punitive and equitable damages. For example, in *L v. David Roy Burton,*[679] the defendant employer was sexually harassing his employee, and terminated her when she did not submit to his sexual advances. The court found the defendant liable to provide compensation

672. [2011] HKCU 2522; Equal Opportunities Commission, 'Significant cases: Hong Kong' http://www.eoc.org.hk/eoc/graphicsfolder/showcontent.aspx?content=significant%20court%20cases#sh_c6 (accessed on 10 Mar. 2016).
673. *Wong Kwok-mui v. Lee Yuen-tim* DCEO9/1999.
674. *Snowball v. Gardner Merchant Ltd* [1987] LRLR 397.
675. *Wong Kwok-mui v. Lee Yuen-tim* [2001] HKEC 249, DC,; *Chen v. Tamara Rus & Anor* [2002] 1 HKC 546.
676. DCEO2/1999 (5 Apr. 2000).
677. DCEO9/1999.
678. SDO, s. 76.
679. [2010] 5 HKLRD 397.

for: (1) injury to feelings at HKD 100,000; (2) exemplary damages at HKD 20,000; and (3) loss of earnings at HKD 77,039. Hence, the total amount was HKD 197,039. The court reviewed *Prison Service v. Johnson*[680] and *Vento v. Chief Constable of West Yorkshire Police*[681] to provide general guidelines for injury to feeling by clarifying that awards for injury to feelings should be: (1) compensatory to plaintiffs only; (2) not too low, as that would diminish respect for the anti-discrimination legislation policies; (3) bear some general similarity to the range of awards in personal injury cases; and (4) be reminded of the value in everyday life of the sum in mind by the tribunals, when exercising their discretion in assessing a sum. Furthermore, *'In general, the award of injury to feelings should not be below HKD$50,000.'*[682] The court also allowed the costs of getting the award to be included, after reviewing the District Court Ordinance (Cap 336). Section 73B(3) states that each party to the proceedings under the SDO should bear its own costs, unless the court rules otherwise on the ground that: (1) proceedings were brought maliciously or frivolously; or (2) special circumstances warranting an award of costs.

D. *Trespass to Land*

327. Trespass to land, like other trespasses, is actionable per se and refers to the direct, intentional and unwarranted interference with the plaintiff's immediate and exclusive possession or enjoyment of land. These laws aim to protect the plaintiff's fundamental rights to his property. Mistaken belief or honesty is no defence as it is not required for there to be the intention to trespass. There can be different kinds of interfering acts which amount to trespass to land, such entering without permission[683] or remaining on land after permission is revoked, directly putting or removing any physical objects to or from the land, etc. The act has to be direct or it will fall under nuisance. For example, an overhanging branch would be a nuisance but cutting and throwing them onto the plaintiff's land would be trespass. Hence, defendant's conduct must be to directly have an uninterrupted consequence of interfering with the plaintiff's land. The defendant's actions are presumed to be voluntary when intention is considered. In *Basely v. Clarkson,*[684] the defendant mistakenly cut the grass on another's land, believing that the land was owned by him. The court stated that, *'Upon this the plaintiff demurred, and had judgement; for it appears the fact was voluntary, and his intention and knowledge are not traversable; they cannot be known.'* Therefore, involuntary actions are presumed to be intentional unless the contrary is proven.

328. It may be difficult to establish intention when an animal is involved in trespass to land. Generally, the defendant could be held liable under negligence, the scienter rule or cattle trespass, etc. For trespass to land caused by animals, the defendant must have intended the animal to access the plaintiff's land or was negligent in preventing it from doing so. In *League Against Cruel Sports v. Scott,*[685] the defendant's

680. [1999] ICR 275.
681. [2003] ICR 318.
682. *L v. David Roy Burton* [2010] 5 HKLRD 397.
683. *McPhail v. Persons (Names Unknown)* [1973] Ch 447.
684. [1682] 3 Lev 37.
685. [1985] 2 All ER 489.

hound hunted on the plaintiff's land, which had a sanctuary for wild animals where hunting was prohibited. The court held the defendant liable as, no matter whether he intentionally caused his hound, or negligently failed to prevent his hound, from entering plaintiff's land, he should be vicariously liable for the hunt servants' or agents' conduct.

329. Trespass to land protects possession and ownership of land; therefore, the plaintiff must show that he has right to possess, or the legal or equitable interest in, the land. To bring an action under this tort, the plaintiff could be either someone who has a proprietary interest or someone who has exclusive occupation. The plaintiff must have possession, or the right to immediate possession, under the control test. However, gratuitous permission and license with interest must be distinguished (e.g., selling standing crop and letting buyers sever the crop implies the license that buyers can enter the land). The plaintiff can demonstrate his interest by showing possession of the land or legal and equitable interest in the land. Unlawful possession of land could protect the intruder from all but the true owner.

330. In *Lam Wing Ching & others v. Chow Kum Wing,*[686] the plaintiff rented out a hut and when she later went to the hut to collect rent, she discovered that instead of the tenant, a stranger had moved in. She brought a claim against the stranger for trespass to land. The court held that the respondent had shown that he had a sufficient degree of physical control over the hut to constitute possession and that a person in possession of land in the assumed character of an owner had a perfectly good title against the entire world but the rightful owner. Therefore, the defendant was liable. A person with legal or equitable interest in the land can also sue in this tort.[687] The plaintiff has a legal interest if he has a right or share in law, like legal title. An equitable interest is a beneficial interest in property and also thereby gives the holder a ground on which to claim, e.g., a trust beneficiary. Lessees who enjoy limited interests could also sue under trespass to land. In *Moreland Timber Co v. Reid*[688] the court held that an equitable interest would be sufficient with a right to extract minerals or cut timber.

331. Land is not just the place but also the surface, subsoil, airspace and property that is permanently attached to the land, such as houses. Trespass will include interference with all of these and some height above the land itself.[689] In *Anchor Brewhouse Developments v. Berkley House (Docklands) Development,*[690] the plaintiff applied for an injunction to stop the defendant from swinging cranes over the plaintiff's property, and the court held that the defendant's act was a trespass. Under certain statutes in Hong Kong, the height of buildings may be an issue in interference with airspace.[691]

332. Mining can also be trespass. In Hong Kong, under the Mining Ordinance (Cap 285), all minerals and oil underground belongs to the government.[692] Mining

686. [1985] 1 HKC 189.
687. Also *see* Conveyancing and Property Ordinance (Cap 219), s. 2.
688. [1946] VLR 237.
689. *Bernstein v. Skyviews & General Ltd* [1977] 2 All ER 962.
690. [1987] 38 Building Law Reports 82 (Invasion of airspace from structure).
691. Building Ordinance (Cap 123), s. 16(1)(g); Civil Aviation Ordinance (Cap 448) s. 8(1); Hong Kong Airport (Control of Obstructions) Ordinance (Cap 301) s. 3; Shipping and Port Control Ordinance (Cap 313), s. 9; Town Planning Ordinance (Cap 131), s. 4 and 4A.
692. The Mining Ordinance (Cap 285), s. 3.

rights can be delegated through mining licences in writing from the owner.[693] Likewise, in Hong Kong trespass to public spaces/places is a crime under the Summary Offences Ordinance (Cap 228).

333. Defences for trespass to land include consent (licence), legal authority, necessity, abatement and *jus tertii*. Therefore, if there is a licence there is no trespass but it would be trespass if such licence was revoked. In *Li Yuen Yi Irene v. Law Wai Chung & Another,*[694] the defendant used the excuse that he had an appointment with the plaintiff, but was liable in trespass for entering the plaintiff's space without authorization. The defence of legal authority is derived from statutes and the defendant has to prove that his entry was within the scope of legislative authority.[695]

334. Under necessity, a defendant can justify actions to stop potential and foreseeable hazards. In *Rigby v. Chief Constable of Northamptonshire,*[696] the defendant threw a gas canister into the plaintiff's property to catch a criminal, but it caused a fire. The defendants pleaded the defence of necessity and it was accepted. However, the plaintiffs pleaded negligence successfully because the fire service was not arranged for. Finally, the defendant can also plead *jus tertii*, meaning that the interference was on behalf of a superior right of the true owner.[697]

335. The remedies available are damages, injunction, ejectment, mesne profit and self-help. All trespasses are actionable per se and nominal damages can be claimed if no actual damage was caused.[698] Damages for trespass are usually pecuniary, which is to compensate for the loss and restore the plaintiff back to their pre-tort position. Further, mesne profits could be claimed when recovering the possession of land. An injunction will be granted with the court's discretion when monetary damages are not adequate. Further, the conduct of the parties will be considered in granting an injunction. In *Chan Woon Cheung v. Chan Yuk Ching and Another,*[699] the court considered the plaintiff's ex parte injunction application, assessing the adequacy of damages as compensation if the case succeeded and the financial burden on the plaintiff and defendant, and hence the injunction was granted.

336. The plaintiff could claim mesne profits, which is the actual loss suffered by the plaintiff for not being able to use the property; the rent would be measured in market value. In *Inverugie Investments Ltd v. Hackett,*[700] the plaintiff's claim for profits was accepted at the wholesale rate, considering the seasonal variation.

337. The plaintiff can also claim ejectment to repossess the land.[701] In *Zenuna Ltd v. Progress Year International Ltd & Others,*[702] the plaintiff as the landlord sued the defendants for possession after the defendant breached the lease agreement. The second defendants were trespassers and their possession was unlawful at its inception.

693. The Mining Ordinance (Cap 285), s. 25(c).
694. (2 May 2007, DCCJ2919/2004).
695. *Tse Soon Cheung v. William McIntyre Ross & Anor* [1965] HKLR 258.
696. [1985] 2 All ER 985.
697. *Lam Wing Ching & Ors v. Chow Kum Wing* [1985] 1 HKC 189.
698. *Armstrong v. Sheppard and Short Ltd* [1959] 2 QB 384.
699. [2001] HKCU 1266.
700. [1995] 1 WLR 713 (PC).
701. *McPhail v. Persons (Names Unknown)* [1973] Ch 447.
702. [2003] 2 HKLRD G5.

As such, they could not seek an order from the court staying proceedings for possession. Further, the first defendant was no longer in possession and it had not advanced any reason for the stay pertaining to itself.

338. In terms of self-help, the plaintiff could use reasonable force to resist trespassers but excessive force may amount to trespass to the person.

E. Wrongful Interference with Goods

339. Under the common law, wrongful interference with goods is broad and has three categories: trespass to goods; conversion; and detinue. The purpose of imposing liability under these torts is to protect the plaintiff's legitimate rights and interests in goods from all wrongful, direct and intentional interference. If the interference is unintentional, then a negligence case should be brought instead. Further, the plaintiff has to prove that he has possession or the right to immediate possession of the goods concerned in order to succeed in a trespass to goods case. Mostly, the interference may include an unlawful taking/removing/damaging of a personal good in a trespass to goods case. Conversion is a strict liability offence, and occurs when the defendant tries to exercise a right of ownership over the claimant's personal property without justification. Such interference includes selling, detaining, destroying, taking away or changing the quality of the chattel, etc. To ground an action in conversion, the act must be so serious that a compulsory sale would be granted with the full value of the chattel being returned. Detinue is where the defendant wrongfully detains and fails to return the goods upon lawful demand. In the UK the Tort (Interference with Goods) Act 1977 unified all kinds of trespass to goods, as well as abolishing law relating to detinue. In Hong Kong, the categorization under the common law is still used. In all wrongful interferences of goods, it is still important to consider the degree of intention and interference with possession (actual or constructive) of goods.

1. Trespass to Goods (Chattel)

340. Trespass to goods, where the plaintiff's personal chattel is unlawfully interfered with, is actionable per se in nature. In *Kirk v. Gregory*[703] the defendant took some jewellery away from plaintiff's testator, who was dead. The jewellery was subsequently stolen and the deceased's executor successfully claimed for nominal damages for defendant's asportation. For trespass to goods, accidental touching without damaging the chattel is insufficient. A direct and intentional interference is needed from the defendant to affect plaintiff's right to possession of the chattel.[704] Interference can be in various forms and there is no need for the defendant to take the goods away from the plaintiff's possession; unauthorized touching or handling museum exhibits may be sufficient. Other forms of interference include damaging, scratching and asportation of goods, etc.

341. Interference with the possession of the plaintiff's chattel must be both direct and intentional in trespass to goods cases. First, the plaintiff must have effective control of the goods, meaning that there must be actual possession or rights to the

703. [1876] 1 Ex D 55.
704. *Everitt v. Martin* [1953] NZLR 298.

immediate possession, like goods in bailment at the time of the trespass. Possession also means that there is presence of both power and intention to control the chattel. Therefore, it is not necessary to have immediate physical control, as power and intention to control are sufficient for both actual and constructive possession. In *Tsun Fat Finance Co Ltd v. Commissioner of Police*[705] the plaintiff's claim for trespass to goods failed because the plaintiff did not have the actual possession of the diamonds concerned, but only had the right to immediate possession, and as such would be insufficient for a trespass to goods case; the case was alternatively proved on conversion.

342. Second, we adopt the test of directness, which would be sufficient if it was the defendant's act which led to a series of events resulting in interference with plaintiff's possession of goods. In the case of *Hutchins v. Maughan,*[706] Herring CJ stated that laying poison on the plaintiff's land was an indirect interference and the death of the dog was hence not trespass. Finally, intentional conduct from the defendant is needed and accidents cannot suffice in trespass cases. Mistaken belief from the defendant that the goods belong to him is no defence and he would still be liable under trespass to goods. In *Wilson v. Lombank Ltd,*[707] the defendant mistakenly believed that the plaintiff's car belonged to him and he removed the car from the garage. The defendant had no defence in returning the car to the true owner and was liable for full value and cost of repair.

343. For trespass cases, the defences of consent, necessity and recovery of goods under lawful authority are available. Since trespass to goods is actionable per se, there is no need to prove actual damages caused; damages would be granted once the tort is proven. A further defence of *jus tertii* (right of a third party) could be pleaded if the defendant can prove that the legitimate title to the goods should be owned by a third party instead of the defendant. The defendant may plead *jus tertii* if the defendant is bringing an action on behalf of the lawful owner or he was committing trespass to chattel on behalf of the lawful owner. A *jus tertii* defence is difficult to plead and prove.

2. Conversion

344. Conversion is a strict liability tort[708] that occurs when the defendant tries to exercise ownership over the plaintiff's chattel in a wrongful manner without lawful justification. For example, conversion includes using others' chattel with the intention of exercising domination, its use and duration is not relevant. Interference may include selling,[709] detention, destroying or taking chattel, changing the quality of the chattel,[710] wrongful dispossession of goods by the defendant[711] and exercising domination over the plaintiff's goods,[712] withholding possession, etc. There are many instances that

705. [2002] 3HKC 232.
706. [1947] VLR 131.
707. [1963] 1 WLR 1294.
708. *OBG v. Allan* [2007] UKHL 21; [2008] 1 AC 1 (HL).
709. *Hollins v. Fowler* [1875] LR 7 HL 757; Sale of Goods Ordinance (Cap 26) s. 20 (rules for ascertaining intention), s. 24 (market overt) and s. 48 (how stoppage in transitu is effected).
710. *Penfolds Wines v. Elliott* (1946) 74 CLR 204 (Australia).
711. *Yien Yieh Commercial Bank Ltd v. Kwai Chung Cold Storage Co Ltd* [1988] 2 HKLR 569 (CA).
712. *Wilson v. New Brighton Panelbeaters* [1989] 1 NZLR 74 (Tipping J).

could constitute conversion, but it is generally where the defendant acts beyond detention of goods, which includes receiving, removing, withholding,[713] damaging and using goods. These instances constitute serious interferences with the plaintiff's right to possession and would amount to conversion.

345. In *Advance Equipment Services (Hong Kong) Ltd v. Tonge (Hong Kong) Ltd & Anor,*[714] it was stated that conversion relates to the plaintiff's possessory rights of the goods. Hence, conversion is an intentional interference with 'goods', depriving the possession or right to immediate possession of goods belonging to the plaintiff. Conversion is a common law tort in the UK that existed prior to the Torts (Interference with Goods) Act 1977. The criminal counterpart of conversion is theft, and has its genesis in the common law action of trover.

346. The subject matter of conversion could be both tangible and intangible. For conversion, the defendant's action must be intentional instead of negligent. In *Moorgate Mercantile Co Ltd v. Finch and Read,*[715] the defendant borrowed the plaintiff's car to carry contraband watches and the car was later confiscated because of that. The defendant was liable in conversion as he intentionally used the car to carry such contraband watches and a result like this could be foreseeable. Hence, using a chattel belonging to another person in a way that would likely deprive him from using such property amounts to conversion.[716] To ground an action in conversion, the plaintiff must either establish actual or constructive possession, or the immediate right to possession, of the chattel. There must also be denial of the possessory interest or title to the plaintiff's goods[717] and the defendant would exercise ownership rights over plaintiff's property in the absence of any lawful justification.

347. If the plaintiff is not the owner of the goods, then he must show his interest in the goods under his possession when suing in conversion. A finder of goods could have all the rights in the goods found if the true owner has not yet been discovered.[718] Further, bailors or bailees can sue in conversion, depending on which kind of bailment the goods are on. If the bailment has limited purposes, then the bailment would end and the bailor has the right to sue when the bailee acts inconsistently with the agreement.[719] If the bailment is at will or gratuitous, both the bailee (actual possession) and the bailor (right to immediate possession) can sue. However, the bailor can sue a third party under conversion for infringing his own right in some cases. In a bailment at term case, the bailee can sue the bailor for his wrongful acts during the bailment term, but the bailor does not have the right to launch a claim. If the bailment has a fixed period, the bailor cannot sue in conversion when the bailment is in force, unless such bailment is determined. The bailor may even be liable for interfering with the possession of the bailees.

713. *Fouldes v. Willoughby* [1841] 151 ER 1153.
714. [2009] HKCU 99.
715. [1962] 1 QB 701 CA.
716. *Tsun Fat Finance Co Ltd v. Commissioner of Police* [2002] 3 HKC 232 (CFI).
717. *Tai Ping Yeung Motors Ltd. v. Man Kan Heung and ors.*, (unrep.) DCCJ14620/2000, 27 Jul. 2001.
718. *Parker v. British Airways Board* [1982] QB 1004.
719. *Penfolds Wines v. Elliott* (1946) 74 CLR 204 (Australia).

348. Defences for trespass could also apply to conversion. Further defences are *jus tertii*,[720] buying the chattel though illegal means[721] and a special defence is available for bailiffs for seizure of chattel under the common law.[722] For conversion, damages are available, and the full amount can be granted when the goods are disposed of, and the plaintiff could claim any cost of repair, loss in profit and consequential loss (if it is not too remote) for damage to the goods. Further if the case is severe, aggravated and exemplary damages may be awarded. For actions in conversion, the goods are valued at the date of conversion. For a cheque, the plaintiff can recover its face value. Where the value of chattel increases after the date of conversion, the increase in value is not recoverable.[723]

3. Detinue

349. Detinue regulates acts that wrongfully detain the plaintiff's goods and the failure to return them upon lawful demand. In England, the action in detinue has been abolished by section 2 of the Torts (Interference with Goods) Act 1977. Detinue means the defendant intentionally detained the plaintiff's chattel without lawful justification after the plaintiff lawfully asked for its return; hence, merely keeping the plaintiff's property does not amount to detinue. Further, the plaintiff should have the right to immediate possession of the chattel to claim in this tort. There are two requirements to prove, namely, a demand and a refusal. The plaintiff must demand his goods to be specifically returned to somewhere and by someone.[724] In proving that there was a refusal or failure to return goods, the reasonableness of the period of time is a question of fact. Refusal may be express or implied; 'implied' could either be the defendant's ignorance of the plaintiff's request or the goods having been lost or destroyed.[725] Further, detinue can become evidence for conversion.[726]

350. The defences for detinue are *jus tertii*, where the defendant alleges that the possessor's title is illegitimate, and that the defendant bought chattel in a public market. Detinue allows for damages for the value of the chattel, as well as the return or recovery of the chattel concerned. In *General and Finance Facilities Ltd v. Cooks Cars (Romford) Ltd*,[727] it was held that remedies can be threefold; namely, return of the value of the chattel as at date of the judgment and monetary compensation for its detention; the return of the chattel or the value of the chattel recovered as at the date of judgment; and damages for detaining the chattel, returning the specific chattel and compensation for its detention.

720. *Jeffries v. Great Western Rly Co* (1856) 5 E & B 802.
721. *Thomas Brown & Sons Ltd v. Fazal Deen* (1962) 108 CLR 391.
722. *Fu Lok Man James v. Chief Bailiff of the High Court* [1998] 2 HKC 1.
723. *PBL Publication (Hong Kong) Ltd v. Marks Hundred Co Ltd* [1987] 2 HKC 157; *BBMB Finance (Hong Kong) Ltd v. Eda Holdings Ltd* [1990] 2 HKLR 74 (PC).
724. *Lloyd v. Osborne* [1899] 20 LR (NSW) 190.
725. *Tsun Fat Finance Co Ltd v. Commissioner of Police* [2002] 3 HKC 232 (CFI).
726. *Advance Equipment Services (Hong Kong) Ltd v. Tonge (Hong Kong) Ltd & Anor* [2009] HKCU 99, para. 22.
727. [1963] 2 All ER 314.

Part II. Liability for Acts of Others

Chapter 1. Vicarious Liability

351. Lord Hoffmann stated that under tort law, employer's liability is an aspect of general negligence.[728] There are three main sources of employer's liability: personal liability under negligence, vicarious liability and statutory liability. The statutes, such as the SDO or the Factories and Industrial Undertaking Ordinance (Cap 59), are formulated to provide protection to employees at the workplace. The breach of statutes render the employer liable as such, paving a way forward towards the protection of the employee's interests.

352. Under tort law, to claim against an employer, an employee must prove: (1) the existence of an employer-employee relationship; (2) that a tort has been committed; and (3) that the tort was committed during the course of employment. Employers may have personal liability in workplace accidents,[729] based on their negligence in fulfilling non-delegable duties.[730] According to the *maxim respondeat* superior, even the Employer appoints someone to discharge the duty, he still remains liable.[731] In other words, the law places a heavy burden on the employers, which is to take personal and non-delegable duty of care to reasonably ensure his employees' health and safety during the course of their employment. There are four facets of this duty of care: to employ competent employees,[732] to provide adequate material/maintain adequate plant and appliances,[733] to provide proper system of work (including effective supervision)[734] and to provide a safe place of work.[735] In addition, occupational health stress[736] is a developing area of law. The employer may be found liable by the court for employee's poor health conditions, such as psychiatric illness.[737]

728. *White v. Chief Constable of SYP* [1999] 2 AC 455.
729. *Chung Ping Wai v. Pedder Logistics Goodwn Ltd*, District Court DCPI 1770/2007.
730. *Wilsons & Clyde Co Ltd v. English* [1938] AC 57 (HL).
731. *Wilsons & Clyde Co Ltd v. English* [1938] AC 57 (HL) (Lord Thankerton).
732. *Hudson v. Ridge Manufacturing Co. Ltd* [1957] 2 QB 248.
733. *Fan Hung Shing v. Hang Fung Shipping Company Ltd* HCPI 1192/1995.
734. *Altaf Ahmed v. Innovative Network Engineering Company Ltd* [2010] HKCU 2792.
735. *Kristan Bowers Phillips v. The Hong Kong Philharmonic Society Limited & Ors* (1998) HKEC 1011 (CFI).
736. Occupational Safety and Health Ordinance (Cap 509).
737. *Walker v. Northumberland County Council* [1995] 1 All ER 737; *Hatton v. Sutherland* [2002] 2 All ER 1.

353. This liability is based on the employer-employee relationship.[738] The tort is committed by an employee towards a co-employee or a third party during the course of employment.[739] Under the rule of vicarious liability, an employer may be held liable for the wrongs committed by the employees, even if he himself did nothing wrong. Such liability is secondary in nature and is based on the special relationship between employer and employee. The reasons behind this principle include the fact that the employer benefits from the employee and it is fair to accept a burden for employees' wrong. Also the employer has insurance and better means to compensate the injury of the affected employee or a third party. The employer remains liable for some intentional/criminal conduct of employees, such as trespass[740] or theft[741] as well as fraudulent conduct[742] as long as it can be proven that it was closely connected with the employment.

354. In Hong Kong, apart from claiming under the common law (personal and vicarious liability), a person who gets injured during the course of employment can claim under the 'ECO', a scheme which is managed by the Employees Compensation Division of the Labour Department. The claim must be brought within two years. Under section 2(1) of the ECO, the employee must be engaged under a contract of service and must suffer injury during the course of employment (section 5) or suffer from an occupational disease (Schedule 2 of ECO). In accordance with section 15 of the ECO, the employer is under a duty to report workplace accidents. Section 40 of the ECO requires all employers (including contractors and sub-contractors) to have insurance policies to cover their liabilities both under the ordinance and at common law for injuries at work in respect of all their employees, irrespective of the length of employment contract or working hours, full-time or part-time, permanent or temporary employment.

§1. Vicarious Liability of the Employer

355. As stated above, the vicarious liability is based on a relationship. Therefore, the existence of this relationship as well as establishing that a tort was committed within the course of employment, are essential ingredients of this liability.

I. Employer-Employee Relationship

356. In order to establish vicarious liability, it is significant to prove that the tortfeasor was a part of the employer's business; otherwise the tortfeasor will be seen as an independent contractor for whose activities the employer is not usually liable. In other words, the employer is liable for those who have a 'contract of service' instead of 'contract for services' with him at the time of the commission of tort. In *Stevenson*

738. *Poon Chau Nam v. Yim Siu Cheung* [2007] 10 HKCFAR 156.
739. *Ming An Insurance Co (HK) Ltd v. Ritz- Carlton Ltd* [2002] 2 HKLRD 844 (CFA).
740. *Dyer v. Munday* [1895] 1 QB 742 (trespass to goods); *Chan Kwok Wai v. Secretary for Justice* [2000] HCPI 134 of 1999 (assault and battery).
741. *Morris v. CW Martin* [1966] 1 QB 716.
742. *Lloyd v. Grace, Smith & Co* [1912] AC 716; *Ronia Ltd v. William Clarke*, CFI, HCA 3972/2000.

Jordan & Harrison v. Macdonald & Evan,[743] Denning J differentiated between 'contracts of service' and 'contracts for service' by saying that under 'contracts of service', the work is done as an integral part of business, whereas under 'contracts for service', the work is only accessory to the employer's business.

357. Although this distinction is helpful, it is not a clear cut one. The nature of the employment relationship in practice is a mixed question of fact and law,[744] which has been further complicated by conventional employment practices. Sometimes, the employers categorize employees as independent workers in order to avoid paying taxes for their employees and avoiding taking out insurance. Because of this, judges have created a number of tests to determine the relationship by evaluating the factual circumstances in which the work was carried out. Hence, generally, the employment relationship cannot be dependent solely and conclusively on the construction of a written document.[745] This position has been accepted in Hong Kong by the CFA in *Poon Chau Nam v. Yim Siu Cheung*[746] where the court accepted that it is the court's duty to make sure that the label (contractor or employee) correctly represents the true relationship between the parties.

358. At common law various tests, such as the control test, enterprise or 'integral part of the business' test, mutuality of obligations test and multiple test or economic reality test, were created over the years to determine whether a person is an employee or not. For the control test, which does not apply to skilled workers, the court tries to find out what control the employer has over the employee and his work.[747] Other tests try to determine whether an employee was an integral part of the business and whether the employer was obliged to provide work to the employee. For instance in *Cheng Yuen v. Royal Hong Kong Golf Club,*[748] a caddie was trained, given a number, a locker and a uniform by the golf club, and worked only when he wished. Lord Slynn of the Privy Council reminded the court to not only focus on whether the relationship between the club and caddie was a 'contract of service', but also '*... to consider sufficiently ... as to whether the contract (if any) between the club and the claimant was of a different nature and whether, if there was a contract of employment (whether of service or to provide services), it was with individual golfers rather than with the club*'.[749] After considering all the relevant facts, the Privy Council concluded that:

The only reasonable view of the facts is that the arrangements between the club and the claimant went no further than to amount to a licence by the club to permit the claimant to offer himself as a caddie for individual golfers ... Thus he was required to wear a uniform, to behave well on the club premises and to charge a fee per round at a scale uniform for all caddies which was fixed and collected by the club and paid to the caddies. The club was not, however, obliged to give him work or to pay him other than the amount owed by the individual golfer for whom he caddied. Conversely he

743. [1952] 1 TLR 101.
744. *Lee Ting Sang v. Chung Chi Keung* [1990] 1 HKLR 764 (PC) (Lord Griffiths).
745. *Davies v. Presbyterian Church of Wales* [1986] 1 WLR 323.
746. [2007] 10 HKCFAR 156.
747. *Chan Ming v. Wayfine Investment Ltd* [2000] 2 HKLRD E12 (DC).
748. [1998] ICR 131.
749. *Cheng Yuen v. Royal Hong Kong Golf Club* [1998] ICR 131, 137.

was not obliged to work for the club and he had no obligation to the club to attend in order to act as a caddie for golfers playing on the club premises. He did not receive any of the sickness, pension or other benefits enjoyed by employees of the club nor indeed any pay over and above that resulting from particular rounds of golf for which the golfer was debited by the club even if as a matter of machinery the club handed the fee to the claimant.[750]

359. Nowadays the courts use a composite text called a multiple test, which is used to determine whether the worker was performing a task as a person in business on his own account, and the court enquires about the economic reality of the employer-employee relationship, and the profit enjoyment and risks of losses between them, which assists in determining whether there is a contract of service or not. In *Ready Mixed Concrete (South East) Ltd v. Minister of Pension and National Insurance,*[751] a written contract was made between a company and Mr Latimer declaring that the employee was an independent contractor. Under the contract, Mr Latimer would carry concrete for the company using his own car. He was not allowed to operate as a carrier of goods except under this contract and, *inter alia*, was asked to wear the company's uniform, comply with the company's rules, and to paint his car in the company's colours. It was held that this contract was not a contract of service, but a contract of carriage. The court stated that '*...an obligation to do work subject to the other party's control is a necessary, though not always a sufficient, condition of a contract of service. If the provisions of the contract as a whole are inconsistent with its being a contract of service, it will be some other kind of contract, and the person doing the work will not be a servant*'.[752] Mr Latimer enjoyed enough freedom as an independent contractor.

360. In *Poon Chau Nam v. Yim Siu Cheung,*[753] the appellant suffered a personal injury while welding a part in an air-conditioner. The appellant was free to take up work for others and had chosen to make his own Mandatory Provident Fund (MPF) arrangement as a self-employed person. He received a payment at the end of each job from the respondent, who also supplied most of the equipment for the appellant's work. The CFA held that the appellant was an employee, and stated that the following criteria must be reviewed to determine the employer-employee relationship: (1) the degree of control exercised by the employer; (2) whether the worker had any prospect of profit or risk of loss; (3) whether the worker was properly regarded as part of the employer's organization; (4) whether the worker was carrying on business on his own account or carrying on the business of the employer; (5) the provision of equipment; (6) the incidence of tax and national insurance; (7) the parties' own view of their relationship; and (8) the structure of the trade or profession concerned and the arrangements within it.

361. On 2 March 2016, the UK Supreme Court in the cases of *Cox v. Ministry of Justice*[754] (Mrs Cox, the catering manager of a prison, was injured by a prisoner

750. *Cheng Yuen v. Royal Hong Kong Golf Club* [1998] ICR 131, 138.
751. [1968] 2 QB 497.
752. *Ready Mixed Concrete (South East) Ltd v. Minister of Pension and National Insurance* [1968] 2 QB 497, 517.
753. [2007] 10 HKCFAR 156.
754. [2016] UKSC 10.

who was working in the kitchen under her supervision), and *Mohamud v. WM Morrison Supermarkets plc.*[755] (The claimant was attacked by a person who was hired by the respondent to look after the kiosk and whose employment had no close connection with his tortious conduct), extended the application of vicarious liability for cases which do not fit in the conventional employer-employee relationship. In *Cox v. Ministry of Justice*, prisoners who were required to work in the kitchen were recognized as employees of the prison. In *Mohamud v. WM Morrison Supermarkets plc,* the Supreme Court found a sufficient connection between the tortfeasor's duty and his wrongdoing, and thus ruled the employer liable.

362. In the case of a causal worker, the employer is not usually liable if he is employed for a purpose other than for the employer's trade/business, as they are not an employee. A casual worker who works for his employer's trade and business is an employee whether he is employed on a casual or regular basis. In *On Hang Chu v. Chan Ngun,*[756] a construction worker was employed by the respondent to work in Flat A, and after he finished his work, was sent to work in Flat B and got injured. The court held the respondent vicariously liable. Likewise, if the main employer lends an employee to a temporary employer, the general rule is that where the damage has been caused by an employee while he was working under the direction and control of the general employer, the general employer is liable. Where the damage has been caused by an employee of the main employer while working under the direction and control of the temporary employer, the temporary employer is liable.[757]

II. The Tort Must Occur in the Course of Employment

363. The employer can be vicariously liable for negligence,[758] wrongful intentional acts[759] or fraud[760] by an employee if they are committed during the course of employment. The wrongful act said to have been committed in the 'course of his employment' should be either: (i) a wrongful act authorized by the employer or (ii) a unauthorized mode of doing the act which is authorized by the employer[761] (Salmond test). This test was reinvented in *Lister v. Hesley Hall Ltd*[762] to a 'close connection test', which looks at whether the employee's tort is so closely connected with his employment that it would be fair and just to hold his employer vicariously liable. In *Lister v. Hesley Hall*, a residential warden sexually abused children and his acts were held to be connected to his employment. The House of Lords held the defendant liable. Lord Clyde stated that '*... In addition to the opportunity which access gave him, his position as warden and the close contact with the boys which that work involved created a sufficient connection between the acts of abuse which he committed and the work which he had*

755. [2016] UKSC 11.
756. [2003] HKCU 814.
757. *Mersey Docks & Harbour Board v. Coggins & Griffith (Liverpool) Ltd* [1947] AC 1.
758. *Ming An Insurance Co (HK) Ltd v. Ritz- Carlton Ltd* [2002] 2 HKLRD 844 (CFA).
759. *Morris v. CW Martin* [1966] 1 QB 716.
760. *Dubai Aluminium Co Ltd v. Salaam* [2002] UKHL 48.
761. *Century Insurance Co Ltd v. Northern Ireland Road Transport Board* [1942] AC 509.
762. [2002] 1 AC 215 (HL).

been employed to do... '[763] In recent times, the UK Supreme Court in cases such as *The Catholic Child Welfare Society and others (Appellants) v. Various Claimants (FC) and The Institute of the Brothers of the Christian Schools and others (Respondents),*[764] *Cox v. Ministry of Justice*[765] and *Mohamud v. WM Morrison Supermarkets plc*[766] have adopted a similar approach, and the close connection test is by no means confined to cases of intentional wrongdoing, but could be applied to cases of vicarious liability concerning fraud, theft, misfeasance in public office and negligence, etc.

364. In Hong Kong, the *Lister* approach was adopted by the CFA in *Ming An Insurance Co (HK) Ltd v. Ritz- Carlton Ltd,*[767] where the hotel employed a doorman who sometimes acted as a car jockey and parked cars for hotel customers. On the day of accident, the doorman drove the hotel's car to purchase food for him and other staff members and caused an accident injuring two pedestrians. The hotel argued that the act was outside the scope of employment. However, the CFA held the hotel liable because it allowed its staff to buy food outside, as its canteen facilities closed early in the evening. According to Bokhary PJ, the doorman's tort was so closely connected with his employment that it would be fair and just to hold the hotel company vicariously liable.

365. It is hence clear that an employer is liable for any conduct that is either expressly or by implication allowed by the employer, having regard to the fact that there is a risk from such conduct (class of acts) and the business provides an opportunity to an employee to commit the relevant wrongful act. In *Lloyd v. Grace, Smith and Co,*[768] a widow was cheated by a managing clerk of a law firm who conveyed her cottages and transferred her mortgage to himself. The law firm was held liable, and Earl Loreburn ruled that, '*If the agent commits the fraud purporting to act in the course of business such as he was authorized, or held out as authorized, to transact on account of his principal, then the latter may be held liable for it.*'[769]

366. Generally speaking, an employer is not liable when an employee ignores his instructions, but he could be vicariously liable if the act (conduct) of an employee is sufficiently connected with the employment because the instructions given by the employers are related more to the manner in which work is conducted instead of limiting the sphere of the employment.[770] In *Rose v. Plenty,*[771] the defendant, a driver of a milk delivery van, ignored the instructions of his employer and hired the plaintiff, who was 13-years-old, to help fulfil his duty. The plaintiff was injured, and the trial court did not hold the employer vicariously liable on the basis that the act was outside the course of employment. However, this judgment was reversed by Court of Appeal, and Lord Denning in his leading speech ruled that the defendant's behaviour was, although prohibited, within the course of the employment, and hence the employer

763. *Lister v. Hesley Hall* [2002] 1 AC 215 (HL) 237, para. 50.
764. [2012] UKSC 56.
765. [2016] UKSC 10.
766. [2016] UKSC 1.
767. [2002] 2 HKLRD 844 (CFA).
768. [1912] AC 716 (HL).
769. *Lloyd v. Grace, Smith and Co* [1912] AC 716 (HL), 725.
770. *Majrowski v. Guy's and St Thomas' NHS Trust* [2006] UKHL 34 (HL).
771. [1976] All ER 97.

was liable. This position is accepted in Hong Kong, as illustrated by *Dense Billion Ltd v. Hui Ting-Sung & Others and Lam Siu-Hung.*[772]

367. However, where an employee does something totally unconnected with his employment and goes on a frolic, the employer does not owe any responsibility to the victim. To determine whether an employee was on a frolic, the court focuses on whether the prohibition from the employer limits the sphere of employment or just limits the mode or conduct within the scope of employment, and may consider the degree of the employee's deviation, period of absence from the employment, and the purpose of the deviation, etc. Lord Clyde in *Lister* stated that caution should be exercised in '*cases where the court is engaged in an exercise of statutory construction...A particular statutory context may determine the extent of the application of the phrase and make the example an unsafe precedent to apply to vicarious liability... The first is that in considering the scope of the employment a broad approach should be adopted...*'[773].

368. Generally, an employer will not normally be liable for the criminal acts of employees. However, in some cases, liability will be imposed depending on whether the act was broadly connected to employment. The performance of a duty in a criminal manner can invite vicarious liability. In *Morris v. C W Martin & Sons Ltd,*[774] the employer was the bailee of a coat and asked the employee to clean the coat. The employer was held vicarious liability for the employee's theft. Diplock LJ stated that the employee was within the scope or course of his employment while he was stealing the coat, and the employer was hence responsible for his tortious act. Likewise the employer could be vicariously liable for trespass[775] if committed in the course of employment. Liability for assault is illustrated by *Dyer v. Munday,*[776] where a manager of a hire purchase furniture company assaulted the landlord's wife while collecting back some furniture. The court held the employer liable for he had placed his employee in a situation where the employer was aware of the possibility of personal violence.

§2. Vicarious Liability for the Conduct of Independent Contractors and Agents

369. Generally speaking, the employer is not liable for any tortious acts or omissions of independent contractors who are hired under 'contracts for services' as long as employers choose competent independent contractors.[777] However, where an employer owes a primary non-delegable duty to a victim, then delegating such a duty will not absolve the employer's liability. Hence, the employer could be held liable in two exceptional circumstances: where the employer is personally negligent or ratifies the work of an independent contractor; or where the employer's delegation is of his non-delegable duty.

772. [1996] 2 HKC 110 (CA).
773. *Lister v. Hesley Hall* [2002] 1 AC 215 (HL) para. 40 (Lord Clyde).
774. [1966] 1 QB 716 (CA).
775. *Kimmy Suen King-On v. AG* [1987] HKLR 331 – (False imprisonment by Police officer).
776. [1895] 1 QB 742.
777. *Yeung Shea Chun v. Director of Legal Aid* [2000] HCA 8439 of 1999.

370. Likewise, vicarious liability is not generally extended to principal-agent relationship. This is because the agent's work, even if done at the principal's request, is considered as the independent function of the agent.[778] However, in special circumstances, the principal may be vicariously liable for the acts of an agent who is not an employee. For instance, a vehicle owner is liable for the negligence of the vehicle driver as he owes a personal non-delegable duty to other road users,[779] and the principal is liable for the fraud of his agent acting within the scope of his authority.[780]

371. The employer is liable for the negligence of an independent contractor where he engages an incompetent contractor/or an insufficient number of men to carry out specific work/or interferes with the work of an independent contractor in a way that results in the plaintiff's injury. In *Shan He Electronics Components Co Ltd v. Skybo International Food Co Ltd & Anor,*[781] the court did not hold the first defendant liable and stated that, '*Generally the rule is that the employer of an independent contractor is not responsible for a tort committed by the contractor or his employees during the course of his work.* '[782]

372. However, if an employer is under a non-delegable duty of care, he cannot get rid of his responsibility by delegating the performance of such a duty to an independent contractor.[783] Hence where an employer has statutory liability or strict liability, and the employee is involved in hazardous activities[784] or is involved in administering medical treatment, the employer remains liable. Providing proper system of work or safe place of work will not help the employer to evade their statutory duties.[785] As an occupier of premises, the employer owes a duty to take reasonable care in the selection of a competent contractor and make sure that the work is properly done. He is liable for dangers arising from *'the faulty execution of any work of construction, maintenance or repair by an independent contractor'*, for instance, construction work adjacent to the highway.[786] Hospitals have a non-delegable primary duty to make sure reasonable care is provided to patients and that liability cannot be avoided by delegation to surgeons or doctors.[787]

---

778. *Wong Wai Hing and Anor v. Hui Wei Lee* [2001] 2 HKLRD 736 (CA); *Ronia Ltd v. William Clarke* [2005] HKCU 261.
779. *Ormrod v. Crosville Moter Service Ltd* [1953] 1 WLR 1120; Motor Vehicles Insurance (Third Party Risks) Ordinance (Cap 272) s. 4.
780. *Colonial Mutual Life Insurance Society Ltd v. Producers and Citizens Co-Operative Assurance Co of Australia Ltd* [1931] 46 CLR 41.
781. (2002) HKCU 212.
782. *Shan He Electronics Components Co Ltd v. Skybo International Food Co Ltd & Anor* (2002) HKCU 212, para. 25.
783. *Wah Hung Choi v. Cheng Kam Shui & Others* (1990) HCA 9450 of 1983.
784. *Rogers v. Night Riders* [1983] RTR 324.
785. Factories & Industrial Undertakings Regulations (Cap 59 A); The Occupiers Liability Ordinance (Cap 314) –S. 3(4) (b).
786. *Holliday v. National Telephone Co* [1899] 2 QB 392 (CA).
787. *Cassidy v. Ministry of Health* [1951] 1 All ER 574; *Wilsher v. Essex Area Health Authority* [1986] 3 All ER 801.

§3. Liability of Legal Entities for Acts of Their Organs (and for Acts of Persons Entrusted with the Power to Act Without Being an Organ)

373. In common law systems, a legal entity such as a corporation is liable for the tortious actions of its organs and employees. There is no distinction made in relation to the tortious liability of an employee and an organ. Hence, there is little practical importance in demarcating this liability from vicarious liability. As such, similar rules are operative in both instances.[788]

788. *Ready Mixed Concrete, Ltd v. Minister of Pensions* [1968] 2 WLR 775 (QB).

Chapter 2. Liability of Parents, Teachers, Instructors and Others for the Conduct of Children, Minors and Students

374. In the UK and in Hong Kong parents, teachers and instructors are not vicariously liable for the acts of children, minors or students based on their relationship. The general principle is that parents and children must exercise reasonable care to safeguard against the potential injuries that may be caused by children under their control. Obviously more care must be exercised where the child has a propensity for viciousness. This duty to control is based on the neighbour principle and the standard of care is objective in nature. The court will expect a child to conform to the standard of care required of an ordinary child of his age and maturity, which will be lower than the standard of care required of an adult. The liability of a parent arises out of their responsibility to prevent harm caused by their child to others. The parents are under a duty to warn their child about the dangers of any devices when using them. In *Phipps v. Rochester Corp*,[789] where a 5-year-old child fell into a trench and got injured, the occupier was not held liable because '*reasonable parents will not permit their children to be sent into danger without protection*'.[790] In *Newton v. Edgerley*,[791] the plaintiff was injured by the defendant's 12 years old son by a shotgun. Given the fact that the defendant instructed his son on how to use the gun but not on how to handle the gun when others were present, the defendant was found negligent: '*He should either have forbidden the use of the gun at all, or else have ensured, by giving him very careful instructions as to the use of the weapon if others were present, that if the boy succumbed to temptation and went out he would not be a danger to others.*'[792]

375. In *Carmarthenshire County Council v. Lewis*,[793] the court held a school liable when a 4-year-old child left the school premises and wandered onto the highway, resulting in an accident when a driver tried to prevent an injury to a child and it resulted in the driver's death. In contrast, in *Chan Kin Bun v. Wong Sze Ming*,[794] a pupil was injured in schoolyard horseplay. Given the fact that the school had a sufficient system of supervision, the court found the school discharged its duty of care. Also, the court went further and stated, 'T*he evidence does not establish that had a teacher been on patrol in the playground, the incident would necessarily not have occurred*',[795] thus no causation was established. In contrast, in *Jolley v. Sutton London Borough Council*,[796] the council was held liable and the court stated that it was foreseeable that children playing of a boat might suffer injury. From all these cases it is clear that the court imposes liability on councils or schools on the basis of whether reasonable care was

789. [1955] 1 ALL ER 129.
790. *Phipps v. Rochester Corp* [1955] 1 ALL ER 129,143.
791. [1959] 1 WLR 1031.
792. *Newton v. Edgerley* [1959] 1 WLR 1031, 1031.
793. [1955] UKHL 2.
794. [2006] 3 HKLRD 208.
795. *Chan Kin Bun v. Wong Sze Ming* [2006] 3 HKLRD 208, 219.
796. [2000] 1 WLR 1082.

taken or not and liability is not based on the relationship. In *Mullins v. Richards,*[797] 15-year-old girls (the plaintiff and defendant) were playing with a plastic ruler when it snapped, injuring and blinding the plaintiff in one eye. The defendant school was not held liable as the risk of injury was not foreseeable.

376. Likewise in *Chan Wai Nga v. Tam Chi Wai,*[798] the 8-year-old boy turned a turntable and toppled a jug of hot tea onto the 2-year-old plaintiff. At the time of the incident, all the parents were sitting around another table. The court in paragraph 24 quoted *Clerk & Lindsell On Torts.*[799] at paragraph 8-173, that '*There is no general duty arising simply from parenthood to prevent a child from causing damage to third parties and a parent is not vicariously liable for his child. Rather, any duty must be based on the particular responsibility of the parent for the kind of damage caused by the child.* ... ', and found the defendant not negligent, based on the fact that the defendant's son was '*well-behaved and had no aggressive temperament; there was no evidence that the defendants could have foreseen any danger or special circumstances*'.[800] In the Australian case of *McHale v. Watson,*[801] a girl's eye was injured when a 12-year-old boy threw a metal object, injuring her. The High Court of Australia held that the boy's actions must be judged according to the prudence of an ordinary 12 year old.

797. [1998] 1 WLR 1304.
798. [2006] HKCU 1097.
799. (19th edn, Sweet and Maxwell 2005).
800. *Chan Wai Nga v. Tam Chi Wai* [2006] HKCU 1097, para. 45.
801. (1966) 115 CLR 199.

Chapter 3. Liability for Things and Animals

377. A defendant could be held liable for damages caused by animals based on: (1) any tortious liability (e.g., negligence, occupier's liability, trespass to person/land, nuisance, defamation and trespass to person/goods); (2) breach of a statutory duty; (3) strict liability under the scienter rule; and (4) liability for cattle trespass. Contributory negligence and *volenti non fit injuria* can be used as defences, depending on which tort the plaintiff is bringing a claim under. In the UK, animal liability is outlined in the Animals Act 1971, which replaces the common law principles under the scienter rule.[802] In Hong Kong, there is no specific legislation that deals with animal liability, although the Rabies Ordinance (Cap 421),[803] Dogs and Cats Ordinance (Cap 167),[804] and Dangerous Dogs Regulation (Cap 167D)[805] are significant. Although these ordinances do not give rise to a civil remedy for breaching them, they create criminal offences instead.

378. An animal can be seen as an agent, so that its owner or keeper may be held accountable for some types of tortious liability. In *Amrol v. Rivera,*[806] the Court of Appeal held the defendant to negligent for failing to exercise reasonable care to control her dog in an open public area on a public holiday. As a result of throwing a ball for her dog to retrieve into an area where children were playing, it resulted in a 4-year-old boy getting injured. In *Birch v. Mills,*[807] the defendant was held liable when cows that were known for chasing dogs injured the plaintiff while she walked her dog. The court held that the injury to the plaintiff was foreseeable.

379. Defendants may also be held liable for nuisance in situations that impede onto the landowner's freedom to enjoy his land. In *Wheeler v. JJ Saunders Ltd,*[808] the defendant was held liable for the smell that emanated from the pigpen near the plaintiff's property. In *Manton v. Brocklebank,*[809] the defendant was held liable for trespass to goods when his dog stole some golf balls, which his owner taught him to do. In *Paul v. Summerhayes*[810] the court held the defendant liable for trespass for going onto the plaintiff's land for the purpose of fox hunting, despite being told he was prohibited many times before.

380. Strict liability for cattle trespass and under the scienter rule are governed by specific principles particularly made for cases where injuries are caused by animals. Under cattle trespass, liability is imposed for straying livestock. In the UK, liability for cattle trespass is retained under section 4 of the Animal Act 1971, and the owner

---

802. Section 1(a) replaces the rules of the common law imposing strict liability in tort for damage done by an animal. Section 2 provides for liability done for damage caused by dangerous animals.
803. Rabies Ordinance (Cap 421) ss 2 & 24, 25 & 26.
804. Dogs and Cats Ordinance (Cap 167) s. 5.
805. Dangerous Dogs Regulation (Cap 167D) reg 9.
806. [2008] HKLRD 110.
807. [1995] 9 CL 354.
808. [1996] Ch 19.
809. [1923] 2KB 212.
810. [1878] 4 QBD 9.

could be held liable. Cattle trespass applies in situations where the animals stray and cause damage to another person's property. Similarly, under the common law, the cattle owner/keeper incurs strict liability for their straying cattle causing damage to other landowners' property. Damages may be awarded for damage to land, property on the land and personal injury. Under section 4(1)(b) of Animal Act 1971, damages may also cover any expenses incurred by others in managing the livestock that cannot be restored to the owner.

381. To succeed under the scienter rule for injuries caused by animals, the plaintiff needs to prove the following: (1) the animal either belonged to a species which is classified as: (a) dangerous ('wild, untamed, undomesticated', e.g., lion), in which case a mischievous propensity is presumed; or (b) tame ('domesticated' e.g., pet cat) with a mischievous propensity of which the owner/keeper had knowledge; and (2) injury was caused by its known vicious propensity. It is important to understand that both cattle trespass and the scienter rule are closely related to the *Rylands* rule, as they are governed by the natural or direct consequence test for the remoteness principle. However, as we know in the contemporary times, *Rylands* is governed by the same causation and remoteness principles of reasonable foreseeability in negligence.[811] For animal liability, the direct consequence test is outlined under the UK Animal Act 1971.[812]

382. The scienter rule is adopted under Hong Kong's common law. In *Mujiati v. Chong Wai Kwan,*[813] the owner was held strictly liable under the scienter rule. The plaintiff was a housemaid who was severely injured on two occasions by the defendant's dogs in his home. It was proven that the defendant knew the dogs could be vicious. Where a dangerous animal is involved, there is a presumption that the defendant has knowledge of its dangerous propensity. For instance, in *Behrens v. Bertram Mills Circus Ltd,*[814] the defendant was automatically liable for the plaintiff's injuries during a circus act involving elephants, as they are classified as a dangerous species.

811. *Cambridge Water Co v. Eastern Counties Leather Plc* [1994] 2 AC 264 (HL).
812. UK Animal Act 1971, s. 2(1).
813. [2004] HKCU 1226.
814. [1957] 2 QB 1.

Part III. Forms of Strict Liability

383. A 'strict liability' tort action imposes a responsibility on the defendant to compensate the plaintiff even if the defendant was not intentional or negligent in causing the plaintiff's loss. Strict liability is not based on fault, carelessness or the intention of the tortfeasor. Strict liability torts have been created by legislation in some common law jurisdictions for defective products, premises and damage caused by animals. Hong Kong has not done so. However, like other common law jurisdictions, Hong Kong adopts a general strict liability tort action approach for: (1) the breach of statutory duty, where the interpretation of the statute implies that the duty includes preventing individual harm (examples include preventing injury to employees,[815] or occupancy under Occupiers Liability Ordinance (Cap 314) (OLO) and damages due for sex discrimination imposed by SDO); (2) injury to the plaintiff's land caused by the defendant's non-natural use of land (bringing and storing dangerous substances on his land that eventually escape onto the land of the plaintiff causing him harm); and (3) injury caused by dangerous animals[816] under the scienter rule. All of these topics are discussed at appropriate places in this text as they also form specific cases of liability. This section will discuss some specific strict liability regimes in Hong Kong.

815. Factories and Industrial Undertakings (Guarding and Operation of Machinery) Regulations (Cap 590), reg 4; *see also World Wide Stationery Manufacturing Co Ltd v. Fong Chi Leung* [1994] 2 HKC 449 (CA).

816. *Halsbury's Laws of Hong Kong* (2nd edn, Lexis Nexis 2012) vol. 2, para. 20.146.

Chapter 1. Road and Traffic Accidents

384. The tort of negligence in relation to motor accidents cases has been significantly encroached on by the insurance system in Hong Kong. In Hong Kong, the Motor Vehicles Insurance (Third Party Risks) Ordinance (Cap 272) and Motor Insurers' Bureau of Hong Kong ('MIB'), together form a compulsory motor vehicle insurance system in Hong Kong. Section 4 of the Motor Vehicles Insurance (Third Party Risks) Ordinance (Cap 272) requires motor vehicle users to set up provisions in order to protect thirds parties from the risk that they may pose to them.[817] In 1980, the MIB was incorporated as a company requiring all insurance companies that are authorized by the Government to insure motor vehicles in Hong Kong to be members of the Bureau.[818] The principal objective of the MIB is *'to secure the satisfaction of claims made by the injured or his/her dependents in respect of liability for death or bodily injury which arises from the use of motor vehicles on the road, when the use of the vehicle is required to be covered by the Motor Vehicles Insurance (Third Party Risks) Ordinance'*.[819] This covers instances where the accident victim is not able to recover damages from the owner or driver of a motor vehicle due to: (1) the lack of valid insurance; (2) breach of the policy conditions allowing the insurer to repudiate his liability; and (3) failures of some insurers to meet their obligations under their policies due to insolvency.

817. Fozia Nazir Lone, *Hong Kong Tort Law: Texts, Cases and Ordinances* (Lexis Nexis, October 2014) Chapter 5 & 6.
818. Motor Insurers Bureau, 'About Us' (Motor Insurers Bureau) http://www.mibhk.com.hk/eng/aboutus_MIB.php (accessed on 1 Jun. 2016).
819. Motor Insurers Bureau, 'About Us' (Motor Insurers Bureau) http://www.mibhk.com.hk/eng/aboutus_MIB.php (accessed on 1 Jun. 2016).

Chapter 2. Environmental Liability

385. Environmental law, which consists of legislation and self-regulatory codes, has replaced tort law as the primary means to address ecological concerns. In Hong Kong, environmental legislation covers noise, water and air pollution, waste disposal, protection of the marine environment, the ozone layer, trees, animals, country parks, conservation areas, and so on.[820] This legislation includes the Environmental Impact Assessment Ordinance (Cap 499), the Air Pollution Control Ordinance (Cap 311), the Water Pollution Control Ordinance (Cap 358), the Noise Control Ordinance (Cap 400), and the Waste Disposal Ordinance (Cap 354), the Animals and Plants (Protection of Endangered Species) Ordinance (Cap 187), the Fisheries Protection Ordinance (Cap 171), and the Country Parks Ordinance (Cap 208). These types of legislation provide a more effective alternative to tort litigation and their emphasis is to adhere to environmental standards and ensure compliance.

386. However, there are three torts (private nuisance, the rule in *Rylands v. Fletcher* and negligence) that are pertinent to environmental protection. Especially significant are the tort of private nuisance and *Rylands* liability, which deal with balancing the interests of the landowners, based on the reasonable use and non-natural use of land. For these torts, liability is based on unreasonable interference with the comfort and convenience of the plaintiff's use of land, which qualifies as a form of unreasonable or unnatural use of his land. Most tort litigation concerning environmental harm deals with air or sound pollution due to industrial or construction sites. For instance in *Hunter v. Canary Wharf Ltd,*[821] the claimants, apart from bringing an action for an interference with the television reception at their homes, also claimed damages under negligence, nuisance and the *Rylands v. Fletcher* rule from London Docklands Development Corporation for the excessive amounts of dust created by the construction process.

387. The tort in *Rylands v. Fletcher*[822] was created in the nineteenth century for situations involving a single escape of dangerous substances from the defendant's land into the neighbouring land caused by the defendant's non-natural use of their land. Nowadays, *Rylands* is regarded as an extension of the law of nuisance to isolated escapes from land. The requirements to prove the Rylands liability have since been modified pursuant to the House of Lords case of *Cambridge Water Co v. Eastern Counties Leather Plc,*[823] including the addition of foreseeable damage of the relevant type. Lord Goff stated that '*...those responsible at E.C.L. could not at the relevant time reasonably have foreseen that the damage in question might occur, the claim of C.W.C. for damages under the rule in Rylands v Fletcher must fail'.*[824]

820. Professor Anthony Cooray, '*Environmental Torts*', in *Tort Law & Practice in Hong Kong* (Justice Kemal Bokhary, N. Sarony & D.K. Srivastava eds, 3rd edn, Sweet & Maxwell 2014), Chapter 14 at 14.005.
821. [1997] UKHL 14; AC 655 (HL).
822. *Rylands v. Fletcher* (1866) LR 3 HL 330.
823. [1994] 2 AC 264 (HL).
824. [1994] 2 AC 264 (HL), 306–307.

Chapter 3. Others (Breach of Statutory Duty)

388. In all common law jurisdictions, including Hong Kong, legislatures create numerous statutes/ordinances for regulating and controlling different activities (e.g., occupier's liability, rights of unborn children, etc.) and restrict the undesirable effects of such actions on others by setting statutory standards, conferring powers, proving rights and creating civil liability for breaching duties. Certain statutes directly confer a private law cause of action to the claimant for damages.[825] Other ordinances expressly prohibit a civil action for breach of statutory duty.[826] On the contrary, ordinances that confer powers, as opposed to imposing duties, on public authorities do not create civil liability for breaches of a statutory duty.

389. Breach of a statutory duty ('*simpliciter*') is a separate tort and may apply in situations where the statute is silent on the creation of civil liability. In these situations, based on how the statute is constructed, and how the court interprets it, the court creates a civil liability for its breach if it finds the duty to be strict. This category, as per Lord Browne Wilkinson in *X (Minors) v. Bedfordshire Council,*[827] is comprised of such cases '*where the statement of claim alleges simply (a) the statutory duty, (b) a breach of that duty, causing (c) damage to the plaintiff. The cause of action depends neither on proof of any breach of the plaintiffs "common law rights nor on any allegation of carelessness by the defendant'.*[828]

390. There is a presumption that the statutes themselves strictly define the standard of private civil liability. The courts would be reluctant to find such a duty if the statute does not categorically provide for it. However, there are exceptions: (1) if a duty was implied by the legislature upon construction of a statute to be imposed for the benefit of a class of the public, and as such the class of the public is allowed to bring a private action; (2) if it can be proven by the claimant that a legislative intention existed in favour of creating a civil cause of action,[829] based on the statutory context, pre-existing law and current circumstances;[830] (3) if the remedy (fine or imprisonment) is classified as inadequate, since no civil action for breach of statutory duty can arise generally for statutes that already provide one for breach of its provisions;[831] or (4) if the situation involves workplace safety, as the legislation was enacted to protect workers.[832]

391. In *X (Minors) v. Bedfordshire Council,*[833] the House of Lords held the council liable for a breach of statutory duty in a parental neglect and abuse case. The

825. Occupier's Liability Ordinance (Cap 314), the Banking Ordinance (Cap 155) and Sex Discrimination Ordinance (Cap 480), etc.
826. Fire Services Ordinance (Cap 95) s. 22 etc.
827. [1995] 2 AC 633 (Lord Browne-Wilkinson).
828. [1995] 2 AC 633 (Lord Browne-Wilkinson) Page 4.
829. *Ex parte Island Records Ltd* [1978] 3 All ER 795 (CA) (Lord Denning MR).
830. [1949] AC 398–407 (Lord Simonds); *R v. Deputy Governor of Parkhurst Prison ex parte Hague* [1992] 1 AC 58.
831. *Groves v. Lord Wimborne* [1898] 2 QB 402.
832. *Latimer v. AEC Ltd* [1953] AC 643.
833. [1995] 2 AC 633 (Lord Browne-Wilkinson).

court held that a breach of statutory duty does not by itself give rise to any private law cause of action, unless no remedy is provided under the statute. It only works if the plaintiff can prove that a statutory duty for the protection of a specific class of the public is imposed, and that Parliament approved of it, as a matter of construction of the statute. In *Cutler v. Wandsworth Stadium Ltd,*[834] it was stated that if the statute provides some other means of enforcing the duty that would logically indicate that the statutory right was intended to be enforceable by those means only. In *Lonrho Ltd. V. Shell Petroleum Co. Ltd. (No. 2),*[835] it was stated where a statute prescribes some remedies/penalties, it indicates that such a statute would not give rise to a civil action, unless it was enacted for the benefit of a particular class of the public for them to assert their rights. In *R v. Deputy Governor of Parkhurst Prison ex parte Hague,*[836] the claimant brought a civil action for breach of the Prison Act 1952 for his segregation from other prisoners. The House of Lords rejected his claim on the ground that rules under the statute are to guide prisons in regulating themselves, not to protect injured prisoners.

392. To determine the existence of a breach of a statutory duty, the court must determine whether the benefits to a class of the public are in accordance with the legislative intention to confer a private right of action to an identified member of that class.[837] In *Atkinson v. Newcastle Waterworks Co,*[838] the claimant was not found entitled to bring a civil action after his house burned down due to lack of water to fight the fire. The defendants were in breach of their statutory duty to maintain water pressure in their pipes, but the court insisted that the statutory intention was to protect the public as a whole, not just certain households like the claimant's. A breach of statute *'must, to a great extent, depend on the purview of the legislature in the particular statute, and the language which they have employed.'*[839] In contrast, in *Read v. Croydon Corporation,*[840] Stable J held that a failure in the duty to provide pure water was actionable.[841] In *Ex parte Island Records Ltd,*[842] it was stated that an injunction could be awarded to any person who could show that a private right/interest was interfered with through a criminal act. As per Lord Denning MR, whether to grant or reject a civil claim is oftentimes not clear and '*may as well be decided by the toss of a coin*'.[843] As evidenced by different outcomes in cases involving the same statutory duty, legislative intention is not easily identifiable.

393. In *Mohammed Yaqub Khan v. Attorney General,*[844] the trial judge rejected the civil claim for the breach of statutory duty,[845] which makes it a criminal offence to disclose to any person who is the subject of an investigation any details, but was

834. [1949] AC 398–407 (Lord Simonds).
835. [1982] AC 173 (Lord Diplock).
836. [1992] 1 AC 58 (Lord Jauncey).
837. *X (Minors) v. Bedfordshire Council* [1995] 2 AC 633 (Lord Browne-Wilkinson).
838. [1877] LR 2 Ex D 441.
839. [1877] LR 2 Ex D 441, 448 (Lord Cairns LC).
840. [1938] 4 All ER 631.
841. Waterworks Clauses Act 1875, s. 35.
842. [1978] 3 All ER 795 (CA).
843. Ex parte Island Records Ltd [1978] 1 Ch 122, 134–135.
844. [1987] HKLR 145 (Fuad JA); [1990] HKCU 0269.
845. Prevention of Bribery Ordinance (Cap 201) s. 30.

overturned on appeal. The Court of Appeal also held the defendant liable for negligence in *Amrol v. Rivera.*[846] However, it was noted that a statutory regulation[847] created under Dogs and Cats Ordinance (Cap 167) does not give rise to civil actions for breached of statutory duty, since the legislation aims to protect the general public, and was not created for the benefit of a particular class.

394. This tort is most clearly demonstrated in the context of workplace safety legislation if the court finds the penalty prescribed to be inadequate. The presence of statutory remedies is clearly not definitive, as it is possible to demonstrate that upon the true construction of the statute, the protected class was intended by the legislature to have a private remedy in such cases. In *Groves v. Lord Wimborne,*[848] it was held that the specific duties imposed on employers in relation to factory premises are enforceable by an action for damages, irrespective of the fact that the statute provided for the remedy. However, if the common law remedy provided is seen to be adequate, the courts will be inclined to reject the claim for a civil action for a breach of statutory duty. In *Phillips v. Britannia Hygienic Laundry Co Ltd,*[849] the court found no legislative intention to allow for creating a breach of statutory duty under the Motor Cars (Use and Construction) Orders 1904, since such liability was well covered under the common law. A breach of statutory duty that causes psychiatric injury to a co-employee as a secondary victim, such as witnessing an explosion and the loss of the life of a worker, does not give rise to a civil action.[850]

395. In Hong Kong, Regulation 31 of the Construction Sites (Safety) Regulations (Cap 591, Sub. Leg)[851] is silent on the accessibility of civil causes of action, but it is allowed since these enactments are not merely for regulating the activity, but also for benefitting a class of the public, even if a common law remedy under negligence may be available. In *Rainfield Design & Associates Ltd v. Siu Chi Moon,*[852] the CFA stated that the breach of statutory duty which led to the construction workers getting injured also allowed the plaintiff to bring a civil cause of action. In *Yeung Yu v. Wong Yung,*[853] the court found for the plaintiff in his claim for breach of statutory duty under the Shipping and Port Control Ordinance (Cap 313). The plaintiff was injured due to the mishandling of cargo resulting in the collapse of the lifting gear onto his truck. Upon construction of the statute, the court held that there was legislative intention to create a private right of action, as the court found that the ordinance provided protection against accidents to persons employed for cargo handling.

846. [2008] HKLRD 110.
847. Dangerous Dogs Regulations (Cap 167 D) reg 9(1).
848. [1898] 2 QB 402.
849. [1923] 1 KB 539 (Lord Atkin).
850. *Hunter v. British Coal* [1999] QB 140.
851. Created under the Factories and Industrial Undertaking Ordinance (Cap 59).
852. [2000] 3 HKCFAR 134.
853. [1986] HKC 5.

Part IV. Defences and Exception Clauses

396. The burden of proof shifts to the defendant if the claimant successfully pleads his case. The defendant will be liable in full if no defence is successfully pleaded. In Hong Kong, under the LO, there are different limitation periods for various torts. At common law, certain defences are common to different types of tort. The general defences for negligence are contributory negligence, *volenti non fit injuria* (voluntary assumption of risk) and *ex turpi causa non oritur actio* (illegality). The common defence for nuisance is statutory authority,[854] prescription,[855] act of God[856] and contributory negligence.[857] As for trespass to the person, goods or land, the general defences/ justifications are consent,[858] license,[859] legal authority,[860] self-help,[861] self-defence[862] and necessity,[863] etc. In this text, specific defences are discussed in the relevant section for each tort and we will focus on general defences for the time being.

854. *Lam Yuk Fong and Another v. AG and Another* [1987] HKLR 263.
855. *Chu Chung Shing Investment Co Ltd v. Lam Chung & others* [2015] HKCU 2918.
856. *On Park Property Management Ltd v. The Incorporated Owners Of Kwan Yick Building Phase II* [2014] HKCU 221.
857. *The Pool Co Ltd v. Sino Rise Realty Ltd & Anor.* [2014] HKCU 2266.
858. *Kau Chun Wing v. Main Shine Development Ltd* [2010] HKEC 216.
859. *Westlands Estates Ltd & Another v. Swilynn (HK) Ltd* [1985] HKLY 1005.
860. *Li Wai Ying & Another v. West Global Ltd & Others* (2001) HCA 1810/2000.
861. *Macnab v. Richardson* [2008] EWCA Civ 1631.
862. *Ng Ching Ying v. Lee Siu Yeung & Another* [2001] HKLRD (Yrbk) 646.
863. *Incorporated Owners of Fu Fai Court, Tin Hau Temple Road v. Henble Ltd* [2003] HKEC 1254.

Chapter 1. Limitation of Action/Statutory Defences

397. The Limitation Ordinance sets deadlines for bringing civil actions in Hong Kong. The limitation period differs based on the tort involved. For breaching a commercial contract[864] and defamation,[865] claims should be brought within six years counting from the day that the breach or the defamation occurred. The same limitation applies to nuisance and trespass cases. For personal injuries claims, the limitation period is three years,[866] '*except where subsection (5) applies, the said period is 3 years from– (a) the date on which the cause of action accrued; or (b) the date (if later) of the plaintiff's knowledge. (5) If the person injured dies before the expiration of the period in subsection (4), the period as respects the cause of action surviving for the benefit of the estate of the deceased by virtue of section 20 of the Law Amendment and Reform (Consolidation) Ordinance (Cap 23) shall be 3 years from– (a) the date of death; or (b) the date of the personal representative's knowledge, whichever is the later*'. Likewise, the LO also provides time limits which bar death claims.[867] For any action for "employees' compensation and work-related injuries, the claim should be instituted within two years from the date of the accident.[868]

398. The court can only extend the time limits in exceptional circumstances;[869] such as if the plaintiff suffers from mental illness for certain period or the plaintiff's action was delayed due to the defendant's fraud. Then the court would count the limitation period from the time when the plaintiff recovered from the disability or discovered the fraud. The general principle is that the courts have a discretionary power to override the limitation period on a case-by-case basis. In *Mok Lai Fong v. Ng Po Sui,*[870] the plaintiff's right shoulder was dislocated after she underwent stretching treatment administered by the second defendant in first defendant's clinic. After several dealings with a law firm, the plaintiff went to the Legal Aid Department and found that her claim was time barred. The plaintiff pleaded that the period delayed was caused by the law firm not processing her case. The court overrode the time limit under section 30 of the LO and held that, after considering the six factors listed in the statue, the balance of prejudice was tilted in favour of the plaintiff. On the other hand, in *Liu Tsz Wah v. Lui Kwok Fai,*[871] the plaintiff's claim was struck out due to the LO.

864. Limitation Ordinance (Cap. 347) s. 4(1)(a).
865. Limitation Ordinance s. 4(1).
866. Limitation Ordinance s. 27(4).
867. Limitation Ordinance s. 28.
868. Limitation Ordinance s. 14(1).
869. Limitation Ordinance s. 30.
870. [2011] 3 HKLRD 67.
871. [2015] 1 HKLRD 566.

Chapter 2. Contributory Negligence

399. The claimant is contributory negligent in common law if their conduct partly causes his own injury. This is a partial defence[872] and the plaintiff can still recover damages from the defendant, but damages are reduced by the amount that the court thinks 'just and equitable'. Under section 21 (apportionment of liability in case of contributory negligence) of the Law Amendment and Reform (Consolidation) Ordinance (Cap 23) ('LARCO')[873] it is stated that:

> Where any person suffers damage as the result partly of his own fault and partly of the fault of any other person or persons, a claim in respect of that damage shall not be defeated by reason of the fault of the person suffering the damage, but the damages recoverable in respect thereof shall be reduced to such extent as the court thinks just and equitable having regard to the "claimant's share in the responsibility for the damage. Provided that: (a)this subsection shall not operate to defeat any defence arising under a contract; (b) where any contract or enactment providing for the limitation of liability is applicable to the claim, the amount of damages recoverable by the claimant by virtue of this subsection shall not exceed the maximum limit so applicable.

400. Generally speaking, contributory negligence includes both the claimant's deliberate as well as careless actions. In *Reeves v. Metropolitan Police Commissioner,*[874] the court rejected the defendant's argument that the prisoner broke the chain of causation by the intentional act of committing suicide but accepted that the deceased was responsible for his own life. The defendant still had duty of care towards the deceased. The court reduced damages by 50% under the Law Reform (Contributory Negligence) Act 1945. In this case, Lord Hope stated:

> This problem did not emerge until after the reform which was introduced by the Act of 1945. Until that Act introduced a new approach to the question of contributory negligence, the fact that the plaintiff"s own act contributed to the damage was always a complete defence to the claim. It made no difference to the result whether his act was a negligent or a deliberate one. There was no need for the question to be explored, because there was no opportunity in either case for an apportionment of the liability in damages. But at least it can be said that no authority was cited from the law as it existed before the Act of 1945 which would make it impossible for us to say that a person was negligent, in the sense of failing to take reasonable care for his own safety, where he acted deliberately by inflicting harm on himself. That would lead to what I would regard as the proper result, which is that he should accept a share of the responsibility for the consequences.

---

872. *Butterfield v. Forrester* (1809) 103 ER 926 (Old position the court was of the opinion that the defendant has a complete defence to an action in negligence cases where the plaintiff was contributory negligent).
873. LARCO is based on the Law Reform (Contributory Negligence) Act 1945. Also *see Davies v. Mann* (1842) 10 M & W 546.
874. [2000] 1 AC 360.

401. The burden of proof for contributory negligence is on the defendant to prove that the plaintiff's negligence contributed to or aggravated the damage he suffered. The test for the plaintiff's conduct is a reasonable person test, outlined by Lord Denning in *Jones v. Livox Quarries Ltd,*[875] expressed as follows: *'A person is guilty of contributory negligence if he ought reasonably to have foreseen that, if he did not act as a reasonable, prudent man, he might be hurt himself; and in his reckonings he must take into account the possibility of others being careless.'* In *Froom v. Butcher,*[876] the plaintiff suffered from head and chest injuries after a collision due to the defendant's negligent driving. The injury would likely have been prevented by the plaintiff wearing a seat belt. The court reduced the damages by 20% and considered what had caused the damage to the plaintiff. Where injuries would have been altogether prevented by the wearing of a seat belt, the damages should be reduced by 25%; where injuries would have been 'a good deal less severe' the reduction should be 15%. Likewise, in the Hong Kong case of *Ho Wing Cheung v. Liu Sin Fun & Another,*[877] the court followed the *Froom* case and held that the first claimant's damages should be reduced by 20% for his contributory negligence in not wearing a seatbelt.

402. The standard of care would vary; a child would be held to a less stringent than an adult and a professional would be held to a higher standard than normal person. A child will be assessed on the standard of care expected form his age group and would only be found guilty of contributory negligence if he would be expected to take precautions for his safety at his age.[878] In *Ho Kwai-Loy v. Leung Tin-Hong & Another,*[879] the plaintiff was a 6-year-old boy who ran into the path of an oncoming vehicle after a call from his sister who had crossed the road already. In the lower courts, the boy was held to be contributory negligent, but, on appeal, the court held that though the boy had the capability to be contributory negligent, he was no't in this case as it was natural for a child at that age to consider his elder sister's call to be an indication that the road was clear. The standard of care for a professional is based on the standard of skill expected from a reasonable person in that profession. This can be illustrated by *Chan King Wan & Anor v. Honest Scaffold General Contractor Co Ltd & Anor (No 2),*[880] where the two scaffolders died after they climbed on a partly constructed scaffold which was detached. The deceased plaintiffs were not wearing safety belts or harnesses though there was also no place for them to wear or put safety equipment on. The court held that the plaintiffs were liable for 40% for their contributory negligence. The court stated that the danger the plaintiffs were facing was obvious and they were mature and well-experienced men who ought to have asked the defendant to erect life lines. The second defendant was liable for the remaining 60%.

403. In some cases, the court must assess if the defendant created an emergency situation[881] that obliged or compelled the plaintiff to rescue him. The court will also

875. [1952] 2 QB 608, [1952] 1 TLR 1377 (CA).
876. [1976] QB 286 (CA).
877. [1980] HKLR 300.
878. *Yachuk v. Oliver Blais Co Ltd* [1949] AC 386 (PC).
879. [1978] HKLR 72.
880. [2000] 1 HKLRD 751.
881. *Baker v. TE Hopkins & Son Ltd* [1959] 1 WLR 966 (CA).

consider whether the plaintiff was an employee acting in the course of employment (the employer owed him a duty of care), the plaintiff's own skill, whether the employer put pressure on the employee to maintain or increase output without considering the risk, and whether the employee was familiar with the potential injuries involved in the activity. Further, the court may take a stricter approach if the employer breaches his statutory duty. In *Chan Yu Chau v. Fong On Construction & Engineering Co Ltd & Others,*[882] the plaintiff was using a circular saw to cut some wooden board. He used the hammer as a push stick to push the board when there were 2 to 3 inches left. At the time of the incident, there was around 6 inches left and he slipped forward and his right hand came into contact with the blade. The court held that there was causation between the first defendant's breach of statutory duty (the Factories and Industrial Undertakings (Woodworking Machines) Regulations) and the injury. The court, however, allocated 15% of the injury as contributory negligence of the plaintiff for failing to sweep away the tube ends and the wood chips, which caused him to fall.

404. Causation has to be proven to hold plaintiff contributory negligent. Under section 21 of LARCO, damages should be reduced by a 'just and equitable' amount by the court. In *World Wide Stationary Manufacturing Co Ltd v. Fong Chi Leung,*[883] the plaintiff suffered a crush injury to his hand at work while he was cleaning a dangerous part of a power press from which he had removed the fixed guards. It was the duty of the employer to guard the dangerous part of the machine and the plaintiff did not operate the emergency stop switch for the machine before he cleaned it. The court held that the defendant breached his statutory duty, as well as that the plaintiff did not take reasonable care of himself in exposing himself to a foreseeable risk of injury. Therefore, they were both 50% liable for the plaintiff's injury.

405. A defendant can recover some damages from other tortfeasor's. In Hong Kong, under the Civil Liability (Contribution) Ordinance (Cap 377), there is a provision for contributions from persons who are jointly or severally liable.

882. [2002] HKCU 678, [2002] 2 HKLRD F14.
883. [1994] 2 HKC 449.

Chapter 3. Volenti Non Fit Injuria (Voluntary Assumption of Risk) and Exemption Clauses

406. Under this complete defence, the defendant has no liability if the plaintiff ran the risk voluntarily and thereby waived the right to claim any damages suffered. Where the waiver is express, it becomes an exclusion clause or disclaimer to defendant's liability. The exclusion clause can be operative if there was no coercion, fraud or duress in making the contract. In Hong Kong, the 'CECO' controls such exemptions. The purpose of CECO is to limit the extent of civil liability for breach of contract, negligence or other duties. Generally exemption notices only limit liability in certain circumstances. Its application cannot extend to personal injury caused by negligence.[884] The exemption notices or contract terms have to satisfy the reasonableness[885] test. In *Wong Wai-chun, Administratrix of the Estate of Cheung Chung Wai Deceased v. the China Navigation Co Ltd,*[886] the plaintiff was the widow and administratrix of the deceased, who was killed when travelling as a passenger on board the "defendants' ship, when the deceased slipped while stepping on the hatches in progress. The company relied on a clause stating that *'the acceptance of a ticket was conclusive evidence that the passenger had no right of action in respect of any injury, whether fatal or otherwise and however caused'*. The court upheld the trial finding and stated that the company did not give adequate warning and, hence, the clause could not exempt the company from liability.

407. The defence of *volenti* relies on proving that the plaintiff had knowledge of the risk and its extent, and agreed to accept the risk voluntarily. In *Morris v. Murray,*[887] after drinking alcohol during the whole of the afternoon, the plaintiff and the defendant decided to go on a flight in the defendant's light aircraft. The plaintiff drove the car which took them to the airfield and he helped to start and refuel the aircraft, which was piloted by defendant. Shortly after taking off, the aircraft crashed, killing the defendant and severely injuring the plaintiff. The court dismissed the *volenti non fit injuria* defence but allowed the claim in contributory negligence. The court found that the plaintiff willingly embarked upon the flight, knowing that the pilot was so drunk as to be incapable of discharging a normal duty of care; that the danger in embarking upon the flight was both obvious and great; and that the plaintiff was not so drunk as to be incapable of appreciating the nature and extent of the risk involved.

408. Hence, mere knowledge of risk is not sufficient; the defendant must show that the plaintiff consented to waive his rights before the negligence occurred. In *Nettleship v. Weston,*[888] the plaintiff gave the defendant driving lessons, knowing that the car was insured to cover injury to passengers. The defendant failed to straighten out after turning left, and struck a lamp, causing the plaintiff's kneecap to break. The defendant did not waive any rights by checking the insurance and the duty of a learner driver was the same as every driver; hence, being a learner was no defence. Besides,

884. Control of Exemption Clauses Ordinance (Cap 71) s. 7.
885. Control of Exemption Clauses Ordinance (Cap 71) s. 3.
886. [1969] HKLR 471.
887. [1990] 3 All ER 801 (CA).
888. [1971] 2 QB 691.

there are special rules that are applicable for passengers of motor vehicles. The Motor Vehicle Insurance (Third Party Risks) Ordinance (Cap 272) provides that the defence of *volenti non fit injuria* will not succeed for passengers in motor vehicles. It also prohibits the use of motor vehicles that are not insured for the protection of third parties.[889] Allowing *volenti* as a defence in motor accidents claims may defeat the purpose of the Motor Vehicle Insurance (Third Party Risks) Ordinance (Cap 272). In relation to sporting activities, any risks that occur in normal games are deemed to be accepted by the players and spectators. However, *volenti* would not be successful if injuries are caused due to poor sporting facilities[890] or occur beyond the rules of the game.[891]

409. The plaintiff must also run the risk voluntarily. In *Smith v. Charles Baker & Sons,*[892] the plaintiff was employed by railway contractors to drill holes in a rock near a crane worked by men in the employ of the contractors. The crane lifted stones and at times swung them over the "plaintiff's head without warning. The plaintiff was fully aware of the danger to which he was exposed by working near the crane. However, the House of Lords rejected the *volenti* argument and stated that the mere fact that the plaintiff knew and understand the danger and continued working did not waive his right to recover damages. The plaintiff would have had to make a voluntary choice.

889. Motor Vehicle Insurance (Third Party Risks) Ordinance (Cap 272) s. 4(1).
890. *Watson v. British Boxing Board Control* [2001] QB 1134.
891. *Simms v. Leigh Rugby Football Club Ltd* (1969) 2 All ER 923.
892. [1891] AC 325 (HL).

Chapter 4. Illegality

410. The defence of illegality or *ex turpi causa non oritur actio* (no cause of action should arise from an illegal or flagrantly immoral act) is a complete defence which prevents any plaintiffs from claiming damages arising from their illegal conduct. The doctrine of illegality comes from contract law, wherein contracts are voided for illegality. In tort law, allowing the plaintiff to recover would be an affront to the public conscience if he was involved in any breach of common law or statues. The landmark case of *Pitts v. Hunt,*[893] the plaintiff was passenger on a motorcycle driven by the deceased Mr Hunt (the case was brought against his representatives), who was driving dangerously and was encouraged by the plaintiff. The pair was hit by another vehicle while they were on the wrong side of the road, killing Hunt and leaving the plaintiff disabled. Rejecting the plaintiff's appeal, Lord Justice Beldam stated that the plaintiff was playing an active role and he would have been responsible for manslaughter if the deceased was someone other than the defendant. He further stated that it was an affront to the public to compensate the plaintiff for his criminal conduct. On the other hand, in *Tinsley v. Milligan*[894] the court did not accept the illegality defence. In this case, the plaintiff and defendant bought a property which was registered using the plaintiff's name in order to defraud the government. The defendant failed to use illegality as a defence as the plaintiff had sufficient interest in the house, regardless of the illegality (per Lord Browne-Wilkinson). The Hong Kong court used a similar approach in *Lau Kwai Kiu v. Bian Xintian and Another.*[895]

411. From these cases it can be seen that the court considers whether the claim would be an affront to the public conscience and whether the illegal act was linked to defendant's tort before allowing the defence. Hence, the courts are not willing to set a standard of care for parties engaged in joint criminal enterprises. In *Kirkham v. Chief Constable of Greater Manchester,*[896] the court had to determine whether it would affront the public conscience to allow recovery for damages from the defendant, the police, for not warning prison services of the deceased's suicidal tendencies. The defence of illegality failed and damages were awarded for defendant's failure to report the condition of the deceased. Likewise, the claim can still succeed if the conduct of the plaintiff is trivial and unrelated to the defendant's tort. This is illustrated by *Lau Kwai Kiu v. Bian Xintian and Another.*[897] The plaintiff paid HKD 100,000 as an additional premium, along with construction costs, to the deceased for a house on a lot and an agreement to transfer the property to the plaintiff five years later. The defendant, the deceased's wife, failed to plead illegality as the effect was procedural, and the plaintiff could still establish her interest in the property through the cost she paid, and the act did not show any breach of public policy. Likewise in *Chung Man Yau & Anor v. Sihon Co Ltd,*[898] the plaintiff was injured while illegally hawking, and the court rejected the illegality

893. [1991] 1 QB 24 (CA).
894. [1994] 1 AC 340 (HL).
895. [2012] 2 HKLRD 954, [2012] 4 HKC 313, [2012] HKCA 169 (CA).
896. [1990] 2 QB 283 CA.
897. [2012] 2 HKLRD 954, [2012] 4 HKC 313, [2012] HKCA 169 (CA).
898. [1997] 1 HKLRD 1221, [1997] 3 HKC 197 (CA).

argument based on the fact that there was no connection between the illegal act and the injury.[899]

899. Also *see Leung Tsang v. Tse Yin Piu* [2004] HKCU 515 (unreported, HCPI 595/2002, 12 May 2004).

Part V. Causation and Remoteness (Negligence)

412. Causation plays a significant part in proving a tort action. Specific causation principles for different torts are discussed in the relevant parts of this text. In this part, the aim is to discuss the third element for establishing negligent tortious liability, which is relevant to Chapter 1 (Part I) of this text, where the tort of negligence is discussed.

413. To establish causation, the plaintiff needs to show that the defendant's act was responsible for the plaintiff's injuries. This proves that the defendant's breach of duty was the material cause of the plaintiff's injury, and that determines whether the injury was factually caused by defendant's act. If only a single cause is involved, the 'but for' test is used. In multiple cause cases, following need to be considered: existence of the chain of causation; the ***novus actus interveniens*** principle; involvement of multiple independent causes; and the significance of simultaneous and consecutive events. Legal causation has to be proven after factual causation in order to hold the defendant liable for reasonably foreseeable damages. Damages that are not sufficiently foreseeable are considered too remote to be compensated. The reasonable foreseeability test is used to determine this. The remoteness tests consider foreseeability of the kind of damage, the manner in which the damage was caused and the extent of damage (along with the thin or eggshell skull rule). The overall assessment on causation and remoteness helps to establish whether and to what extent the defendant should be held liable for the plaintiff's injury.

Chapter 1. Causation in Fact (Factual Cause)

414. In single cause cases, the plaintiff has to use the 'but for' test, showing that his injury would not have been caused but for the defendant's conduct or breach. This test is to see if defendant's conduct has induced plaintiff's injury and the test would not suffice if the injury would occur anyway, and this helps to filter out unlikely claims. In *Barnett v. Chelsea Hospital Management Committee,*[900] the plaintiff's husband went to the hospital suffering from a serious stomach ache and vomiting. The hospital doctor advised him to go back home and consult his personal doctor later. He died five hours after leaving the hospital due to arsenic poisoning. The court had to consider whether there was any negligence on the part of the hospital. It was held that even if the husband had been treated and examined at that time, there was no chance to issue an antinode in time to cure him and prevent his death. After applying the 'but for' test, the defendant's conduct could not be said to be the cause of the plaintiff's death and hence no liability was imposed. In the Hong Kong case of *Cheng Kin Ping & Anor v. Woo Cho Wing & Cheung Ming Wo (third Party),*[901] the plaintiff and the third party's car wherein a collision and both stopped to inspect the damage to the cars. The defendant suddenly saw the third party and broke sharply, hitting plaintiff's car and injuring him. The trial judge held that the defendant's conduct was the operative cause of the collision and that the third party was also liable. On appeal, the court held that the 'but for' test would apply to evidence whether the defendant would have applied the footbrakes and still lost control of the car despite seeing the third party's car.

415. In cases involving the failure to perform duty, the 'but for' test must be considered to compare how the outcome would have differed if the defendant had performed their duty. In *McWilliams v. Sir William Arrol & Co Ltd,*[902] an employee fell and died while working at a height in a construction site without a safety belt being provided by his employer. However, the court did not hold the employer liable as Lord Devlin applied the 'but for' test to deduce that, even if the employer had provided a safety belt, the deceased would not have worn it anyway. In comparison, in *Young v. Dr Ho Chun Kit Peter,*[903] the court held that the defendant was negligent and liable for the injury of the plaintiff. The court was of the view that the operation would not have been performed but for the negligent advice of the defendant. However, in *Bolitho v. City & Hackney Health Authority,*[904] the doctor was not liable as the intubation would not have been performed even if the doctor had arrived on time.

416. If there is more than one cause (apart from defendant's conduct), then the 'but for' test is not applied. There are several ways to assess cases in which there are multiple causes for the harm suffered by the plaintiff: firstly, where there are multiple defendants (the court has to apportion their liability for the plaintiff's injuries); secondly, where there are simultaneous or consecutive events occurring; and thirdly, where an

900. [1969] 1 QB 428.
901. [2000] 3 HKLRD 743 (CFA).
902. [1962] 1 WLR 295 (HL).
903. [2012] 3 HKC 146.
904. [1998] AC 232.

intervening event breaks the chain of causation. This in turn will affect the type of liability the defendants owes to the plaintiff such as joint (liable to pay full amount jointly) or several (proportionate) liabilities. This is discussed under Part IV (Remedies) of this text.

417. In such situations the plaintiff has to show that defendant's negligent conduct was the material and operative reason for the plaintiff's injury and they can do that by proving either that the defendant's conduct materially contributed to or increased the risk of the plaintiff's injury. In the case of *Gregg v. Scott,*[905] the plaintiff was suffering from cancer and his prospects were uncertain. However, due to the negligent diagnosis from the defendant, the treatment was delayed for several months, which reduced the probability of recovery drastically. The court had to ascertain the amount of loss suffered by the plaintiff, which Lord Nicholls considered:

> Thus, assessed at the date of trial the appellant would have had a 72% chance of survival had he received appropriate treatment. On the expert evidence that chance was reduced by the negligent delay: it had been 10%-15% assessed at the date treatment should have been given but had increased to 20%-30% as at the date of trial. Thus, if (as the judge did) one takes the mid-way point the appellant's lost chance assessed at the date of trial was 72% – 25% = 47%. In those circumstances the correct approach was to have awarded the appellant damages on the basis of a 47% loss of the chance of survival.[906]

418. When there are competing acts in a multiple cause cases, the court decides on the most appropriate approach for determining the causation of the plaintiff's injury. In assessing whether there was a material contribution by the defendant, the court tries to see if the defendant's conduct was the material cause of plaintiff's injury and whether the cause is a consecutive or simultaneous cause. In *Bonnington Castings Ltd v. Wardlaw,*[907] the plaintiff was working at the defendant's factory, and, due to poor ventilation and a dusty working environment, the plaintiff contracted a lung disease from inhaling silicon dust. The court held that the onus of proof lay on him to show, by the ordinary standard of proof in civil actions, that on a balance of probabilities the breach caused or materially contributed to the injury, and not merely that it was possible that the injury might have been so caused.

419. If there is not enough knowledge or evidence to show the material cause, then the court may apply the material increase of risk approach. This approach is mostly applied in medical negligence cases. It can be used if there are difficulties in producing evidence to deduce the main cause of plaintiff's injury and, once the test is satisfied, the defendant is held liable. In *McGhee v. National Coal Board,*[908] the plaintiff worked in a brick kiln, and the working environment was dusty and hot. As a result, the plaintiff suffered from dermatitis. The trial judge held that the defendant was not liable for plaintiff's injury as the plaintiff did not prove that the absence of showers materially caused the plaintiff's injury. However, on appeal, the court considered that

905. [2005] 4 All ER 812.
906. [2005] 4 All ER 812, 851.
907. [1956] AC 613 (HL).
908. [1973] 1 WLR 1.

the defendant would be liable if the breach of duty had materially increased the risk of injury. The causation test could be met even if there were two concurrent potential causes, if the defendant breached his duty and increased the risk of injury. Even if the plaintiff had taken a journey home that further increased the risk of injury, the defendant would still be liable.

420. In *Wilsher v. Essex Area Health Authority,*[909] a case was brought on behalf of a prematurely born baby who contracted an incurable condition of the retina (RLF) due to excess oxygen being given and was consequently blinded. The plaintiff sued the defendant for allowing excess oxygen to be given and causing the injury. The House of Lords held that the defendant was not liable as the plaintiff could not establish that the cause of the injury was the excess of oxygen; as stated by medical evidence, excess oxygen was just one of the causes of RLF. *Wilsher* shows that the defendant's negligent conduct must materially contribute to the injury and merely showing the increase of risk of injury without proving the actual contribution to the injury is insufficient.

421. In the later decision of *Fairchild (suing on her own behalf) etc v. Glenhaven Funeral Services Ltd and Others etc*[910] the House of Lords adopted the *McGhee* and *Wilsher* approach that the plaintiff must prove on balance of probabilities that the defendant's conduct materially increased the risk of injury and thereby caused a material contribution to the plaintiff's injury. In that case, Mr Fairchild was an employee working in the factory that built packing cases lined with asbestos, used for the transportation of industrial ovens. He inhaled a substantial amount of asbestos dust, which induced a mesothelioma of the pleura, and he died subsequently from that. In *Barker v. Corus,*[911] *Fairchild* was considered. The plaintiff was exposed to asbestos while working for two different employers (a company that became insolvent and another company which inherited the liability of the first company) and when he was self-employed. Lord Hoffman held that liability would be split depending on the probability of being harmed during the course of each employment.[912]

909. [1988] 2 WLR 557 (HL).
910. [2002] UKHL 22.
911. [2006] 2 WLR 1027 (HL).
912. [2006] 2 WLR 1027 (HL), 1042.

Chapter 2. Concurrent Causes and Consecutive Events

422. It may be difficult to determine the cause of the plaintiff's injury if two or more events happened concurrently and injured the plaintiff (concurrent causes) or some unconnected events happened consecutively, in a way that they all could be the sole cause of plaintiff's injury (consecutive causes or events). In these cases, the cause(s) that materially contributed to the injury are difficult to determine. Generally, the court would hold each defendant fully liable for concurrent events and apportion the liability on the actual attribution of responsibility for consecutive events. Sometimes the court may deduce a single cause as being the operative cause of injury by using the *McGhee*, *Wilsher* and *Fairchild* decisions.

423. In the case of *Hale v. Hants & Dorset Motor Services Ltd & Anor,*[913] the plaintiff was a passenger on a bus driven by an employee of the first defendant and was blinded in one eye by a branch on a tree planted beside the highway by the second defendant. The court held both defendants liable as they contributed to the injury; the Poole Cooperation, responsible for planting the tree, were held two thirds liable and the bus company were one third liable. In *Fitzgerald v. Lane,*[914] the plaintiff was a pedestrian and the first driver's car hit him and subsequently injured another driver. The court adopted the *McGhee* reasoning and held that both defendants were fully and equally liable, as both acts were the operative cause of injury.

424. In a case involving consecutive causes, *Lai Ping Wah v. China Insurance Co Ltd & Anor,*[915] the deceased suffered serious injuries after a collision, and was later given a contaminated tetanus toxoid injection, which later led to his death. The court held that the defendants were responsible as there was a connection between the accident, the injection and deceased's death. In *Baker v. Willoughby,*[916] the plaintiff's leg was injured due to the first defendant's driving and it affected the mobility of the plaintiff; the second defendant shot the plaintiff's leg while the first case was still pending for trial, and the plaintiff amputated the leg as a result. The court held that the first defendant would be fully liable for their act, as the damage they caused was not obviated by the shooting. The court utilized the principle that the tortfeasor takes the victim as he finds him. In the subsequent case of *Jobling v. Associated Dairies Ltd,*[917] the plaintiff hurt his back at his workplace due to his employer's negligence reducing his work capacity by 50%. Before the trial he developed a spinal illness, not related to the accident, which completely disabled him. The House of Lords, dismissing the appeal and taking into account the 'vicissitudes of life' principle, held that damages would be limited to the period before the disease was discovered, or at least reduced while taking into account the previous incapacitation.

---

913. [1947] 2 All ER 628.
914. [1987] QB 781 (CA).
915. [1999] HKCU 1371 (unreported, HCPI 874/97, 25 Nov. 1999).
916. [1970] AC 467 (HL).
917. [1982] AC 794.

425 – 428

Chapter 3. New Intervening Causes (*Novus Actus Interveniens*

425. The principle of *novus actus interveniens* may relieve the defendant's liability if an intervening act breaks the chain of causation. However, the event must be the responsibility of the plaintiff or a third party, not natural forces,[918] and such acts should substantially damage the plaintiff. Generally, the defendant can use this to defend himself, with the argument that the intervening act broke the chain of causation and obviated any damage caused by them. The court would evaluate whether defendant's negligence or the intervening act has caused plaintiff's injury.

426. Different approaches are used depending on whether the intervening act is an unforeseeable negligent act, an intentional act or the claimant's own negligent act. In cases involving unforeseeable negligent intervening acts, the courts will examine the degree of negligence, foreseeability and substantiality to see of the chain of causation was broken. In *Corr v. IBC Vehicles,*[919] the plaintiff's husband was struck by a machine. He became disfigured after the reconstructive surgery and suffered from PTSD. He committed suicide six years after the incident. The court held that the PTSD was not an intervening act as it was a usual and foreseeable consequence after such accident, and that the suicide was involuntary and did not break the chain of causation. In *Attorney General v. Yiu Yun,*[920] the defendant left a swab in the plaintiff's body during surgery and later another doctor did not discover the problem; the court held that the second doctor's negligence broke the chain of causation as he did not conform to the standard of a reasonable doctor.

427. A third party's intentional act can also break the chain of causation. In *Lamb v. Camden LBC,*[921] the defendant council damaged the foundation of the plaintiff's house while mending a water pipe. The house was further damaged by squatters later on. The court dismissed the claim for damages to the property as the council had no duty to control third parties and the plaintiff was insured against the damage. In comparison, in *Home Office v. Dorset Yacht,*[922] the defendant was liable for the intentional damage to the plaintiff's yacht by the borstal boys as it was seen as a foreseeable consequence from the defendant's breach of duty.

428. The plaintiff's own negligent conduct can either break the chain of causation or, alternatively, be pleaded as contributory negligence. In *Cheang Kam Ian v. Hong Kong Prime Printing Company,*[923] the plaintiff used the toilet in defendant's factory and stepped into a container which caused his right trousers leg and shoe to be soaked in a flammable liquid. The plaintiff went out of the factory to light a cigarette and his trouser leg caught fire and his legs were burned. The plaintiff sued for damages and

---

918. *Scott v. Shepherd* [1773] 2 Wm. Bl. 892; natural causes should be distinguished from the instinctive reaction/intervention.
919. [2008] UKHL 13 (HL).
920. [1990] 2 HKC 238 (CA).
921. [1981] QB 625 (CA).
922. [1970] 2 All ER 294.
923. [2000] HCPI 143 of 1998.

defendant argued that he had asked the plaintiff to clean the liquid off with water, and that there was a poster on the wall stating the risk. The court held that the later act of the defendant was unreasonable and broke the chain of causation. In the case of *Armsden v. Kent Police,*[924] the defendant was only found 40% liable for plaintiff's death after considering the contributory negligence of the plaintiff failing to notice the police flashing light.

924. [2009] RTR 387 (CA), 269.

Chapter 4. Causation in Law (Remoteness)

429. The concept of remoteness of damage limits the unforeseeable damages claims to the consequences of defendant's breach. The current test for remoteness is the reasonable foreseeability test from *Wagon Mound (No. 1)*,[925] which overruled the old direct consequences test created by the Court of Appeal in *Re an Arbitration between Polemis and Furness, Withy & Co Ltd*,[926] under which the defendant would be liable for all damages from the direct consequences regardless of foreseeability. In the *Wagon Mound (No. 1)*, the defendant's vessel negligently leaked furnace oil into the harbour, which spread to the claimant's vessel. The defendant made assurances that the oil would not be ignited but it was subsequently ignited by sparks from welders, and caused damage to plaintiff's wharf and equipment. The claimant brought an action and succeeded in an Australian court under the direct consequence test, but failed in the Privy Council since such damage was not foreseeable. Viscount Simonds stated:

> Who knows or can be assumed to know all the processes of nature? But if it would be wrong that a man should be held liable for damage unpredictable by a reasonable man because it was 'direct' or 'natural', equally it would be wrong that he should escape liability, however 'indirect' the damage, if he foresaw or could reasonably foresee the intervening events which led to its being done: cf. Woods v Duncan. Thus foreseeability becomes the effective test.[927]

430. In *Leung Sin Fai v. Perfect World Co Ltd & Ors*,[928] the plaintiff was an employee at the defendant's factory. The plaintiff spent his lunch hour at the place which used to be the ladies toilet and the defendant was aware of that. The area was dim and the plaintiff attempted to create some light, which induced an explosion due to the flammable liquid in the toilet dumped by a third party. The court held that, although there was a breach of duty in allowing plaintiff to use the premises, the third party leaving such flammable liquid was unforeseeable and it broke the chain of causation.

431. The courts consider various factors when looking at the classification of foreseeable kinds of damages during the application of the reasonable foreseeability test. In *Hughes (Russell McDonald) v. Lord Advocate*,[929] a manhole was opened under statutory powers for the purpose of maintaining underground telephone equipment. It was covered with a tent and, in the evening, left by the workmen unguarded but surrounded by warning paraffin lamps. An 8-year-old boy entered the tent and knocked or lowered one of the lamps into the hole. An explosion occurred, causing him to fall

---

925. *Overseas Tankship (U.K.) Ltd. v. The Miler Steamship Co. and anor (The Wagon Mound No. 1)* [1961] AC 388 (PC).
926. [1921] All ER 40.
927. *Overseas Tankship (U.K.) Ltd. v. The Miler Steamship Co. and anor (The Wagon Mound No. 1)* [1961] AC 388 (PC), 436 (Viscount Simonds).
928. [1998] 2 HKLRD 115.
929. [1963] AC 837(HL).

into the hole and become severely burned. The court held the defendant liable as the lamp could be reasonably foreseen to pose danger. Lord Pearce in this case stated that:

> The allurement in this case was the combination of a red paraffin lamp, a ladder, a partially closed tent, and a cavernous hole within it, a setting well fitted to inspire some juvenile adventure that might end in calamity. The obvious risks were burning and conflagration and a fall. All these in fact occurred, but unexpectedly the mishandled lamp instead of causing an ordinary conflagration produced a violent explosion. Did the explosion create an accident and damage of a different type from the misadventure and damage that could be foreseen? In my judgment it did not. The accident was but a variant of the foreseeable.[930]

Clearly, the courts adopt a wider approach to the kinds of damage in personal injury cases, as there are countless aspects of accidents.

432. In *T v. Kan Ki Leung & Anor,*[931] a teacher was held liable for imposing unreasonable punishments, such making the plaintiff complete work in the entrance hall and letting students tease the plaintiff, which caused the plaintiff, a Form 6 student, to develop schizophrenia. The court held that it was foreseeable by a reasonable teacher that recurrent humiliation might cause mental illness.

433. Foreseeability of the manner in which damage occurred is significant but it must fall under the scope of the foreseeable risk created and that is determined on a case-by-case basis. This could be illustrated by *Jolley v. Sutton London Borough Council,*[932] where the plaintiff was rendered paraplegic when he attempted to repair an abandoned boat, which should have been dealt with by the defendant. The House of Lords held that the child's act was not unforeseeable and was the mimicry of adult behaviour. The defendant was hence held liable. A more flexible interpretation of foreseeable risk was adopted in *Doughty v. Turner Manufacturing Ltd.*[933]

434. In relation to the foreseeability of the 'extent of the damage' (the thin or eggshell skull rule)[934] principle, the extent of damage would increase where the claimant had a pre-existing physical or psychiatric disease, but the defendant would be liable so long as damage to the plaintiff was foreseeable. Hence, the extent of damage may be unforeseeable and depends on the exacerbation of plaintiff's situation, but the courts' position is that the defendant takes the plaintiff and his property as he finds it. Hence, the defendant needs to compensate for all the aggravated harm suffered by the plaintiff if it is reasonably foreseeable. In *Smith v. Leech Brain & Co,*[935] molten metal caused a burn to the workman's lip during work. The burn was the promoting agent of a cancer in tissue which already had a pre-malignant condition, which in three years killed the plaintiff's husband. The court held that the injury was foreseeable and that the defendant was liable for damages under the eggshell skull rule. Lord Parker decided in favour of the claimant. The court in Hong Kong still applies and considers the thin or eggshell

930. [1963] AC 837(HL), 858.
931. [2002] 1 HKLRD 29 (CFI).
932. [2000] 1 WLR 1082.
933. [1964] 1 QB 518.
934. *Smith v. Leech Brain & Co* [1962] 2 QB 405.
935. [1962] 2 QB 405.

skull rule. In *Hung Sau Fung v. Lai Ping Wai*,[936] the court considered the thin skull rule, though they distinguished its application in that case as there was no direct link between the plaintiff's injury and the sickness. A similar approach is adopted when a plaintiff can recover for the psychiatric shock suffered and all damages relating to that, if foreseeable. A similar test of reasonable foreseeability as to economic state applies to the plaintiff's physical susceptibility.[937]

936. [2016] 1 HKLRD 106.
937. *Lagden v. O'Connor* [2004] 1 All ER 277.

Part VI. Remedies

Chapter 1. General Principles

435. In tort actions, the major remedies are damages and injunctions. The equitable remedy of injunction is available in cases of trespass, defamation and nuisance, to either prevent the possible occurrence or continuance of a tort, or to undertake some positive action. This part of the text will broadly discuss the commonly sought tort remedy of damages, which are awarded to the plaintiff (or his dependants in case of death) for his injuries, such as personal injury, pecuniary loss, non-pecuniary loss, provisional awards and damage to property and damages for death (sought by the dependants of the deceased). Damages are also awarded when the claimant's legal rights have been interfered with, like in a trespass situation or in cases where the plaintiff suffered additional distress; the court may then award punitive damages.

436. In Hong Kong, under the Civil Liability (Contribution) Ordinance (Cap 377), statutory provision is made for entitlement to contribution (section 3) between persons who are jointly or severally, or both jointly and severally, liable for the same damages or debt and, in certain other similar cases, where two or more persons have paid or may be required to pay compensation for the same damage or debt. By virtue of section 4(1), recoverable contributions shall be such as may be found by the court to be just and equitable, having regard to the extent of that "person's responsibility for the damage in question. Further, section 4(3) states that, where the amount of the damages was subject to any limit imposed by law or by any agreement made before the damage occurred or to any reduction by virtue of section 21 of the Law Amendment and Reform (Consolidation) Ordinance (Cap 23), or any other limit or reduction under the law of a place outside Hong Kong, the person from whom the contribution is sought shall not be required to pay a greater amount than the amount of those damages as so limited or reduced.

437. Under the common law rules, the assessment of compensatory damages for personal injury, death, damage to property, etc. is a technical and intricate process and courts have to consider numerous factors, such as pecuniary and non-pecuniary losses, pure economic loss, actual/future damage (lost profits such as reduced earning capacity, future loss of earnings, medical expenses, etc.), mitigation of damages, joint and several liability, the impact of insurance/social security on damages, preventing unjust enrichment and punitive damages, etc. This text aims at covering the most important issues and policies concerning claims of damages, and consulting specialized texts is recommended to facilitate further understanding.[938]

438. At this point, it should be mentioned that a remedy can also be sought through a non-statutory mechanism called the Criminal and Law Enforcement Injuries Compensation Scheme. A claimant (or his dependents in case of death) can seek financial assistance, which is given to persons who are injured as a result of a crime of violence, or by a law enforcement officer using a weapon in the execution of his duty. This is not tort remedy but it does supplement tort damages in some cases where the criminal injuries sustained by the claimant may fall under intentional torts such as assault, battery or false imprisonment. The scheme is non-contributory and non-means-tested. Payments under the scheme come from public funds and for that reason this ex gratia compensation is not deducted from the common law tort action, which the claimant may commence. This scheme consists of criminal injuries compensation and law enforcement injuries compensation, administered by the Criminal Injuries Compensation Board and the Law Enforcement Injuries Compensation Board respectively. The Board awards compensation if the victim satisfies the conditions under this scheme, such as if they can produce the record of hospitalization/sick leave certificate. The circumstances of injury must be reported to police without unreasonable delay or have been the subject of criminal proceedings. The victim should have a right to stay in Hong Kong.

439. Further, a claimant who is a victim of intentional torts that are also crimes, such as trespass to the person, apart from pursuing a claim for damages under a tort law action can be entitled to receive limited compensation through the criminal law under the Magistrates Ordinance (Cap 227). A magistrate under section 98 (power to award compensation) of this ordinance has the jurisdiction to order the convicted person to pay compensation not exceeding HKD 100,000 to the aggrieved person if he sustained: (a) personal injury; (b) loss of or damage to property; or (c) both. To avoid over compensation of the victim and to be fair to the convicted person, any damages that are paid by him under the conviction order are deducted from any common law tort action that the victim may commence. Similarly, under section 73 of the Criminal Procedure Ordinance (Cap 221), the District Court and the Court of First Instance have similar powers to award compensation and order the convicted person to pay compensation, which is deducted from the award of damages under any subsequent tort action.[939]

938. Harvey McGregor QC, *McGregor on Damages* (19th edn, Sweet and Maxwell 2015); P. Cane, *Atiyah's Accidents Compensation and the Law* (7th edn, CUP 2006).

939. *Pang Kwai Wah v. Tsang Kwong Wing* [1988] HKLY 411.

Chapter 2. Kinds of Damages

440. The primary purpose of damages is to compensate the victim through financial means. The ideal remedy would of course be to restore the plaintiff to how they were before the wrongful act was committed (*restitutio in integrum*). It is not always possible to achieve this aim, especially in situations where a claimant may have lost a limb. The court in such a case is unable to fully restore the claimant's pre-tort position through monetary damages. Nonetheless the courts can award both pecuniary (such as for personal injury, loss of earnings and loss of profit) as well as non-pecuniary (pain and suffering) damages to compensate the claimant in so far as money can achieve. There are various kinds of damages, such as individual and collective damage, direct and indirect, pecuniary and non-pecuniary losses, pure economic loss, lost profits, costs in obtaining judicial or extra judicial payment. The court will also take into account any mitigation of damages.

441. Under the common law, tort law damages remain the main arsenal to compensate the losses of victims and damages are broadly divided into four types: (1) compensatory or actual damages; (2) nominal damages; (3) aggravated damages; and (4) exemplary (punitive) damages. For the tort of negligence, the compensatory damages awardable are of two types: pecuniary damages (or special damages) and non-pecuniary damages (or general damages). At this point, it should be noted that nominal, aggravated and exemplary damages are usually provided for harm caused by trespass and is not available for harm caused by the tort of negligence, including occupier's liability and breach of statutory duty.

§1. Individual and Collective Damages

442. The claimant's damages in tort law are calculated on an individual basis and epitomize the individualized justice tradition. This is the case even if the defendant may have injured more than one person, such as in accident, product liability or psychiatric injury cases. That said, in class action cases, the court may categorize the plaintiffs into various classes based on similarity of their injuries. For instance, in *Hunter v. Canary Wharf Ltd,*[940] hundreds of claimants brought tort actions under negligence, nuisance and the rule in *Rylands v. Fletcher*. The court categorized the plaintiffs, who consisted of a substantial group of local people, into two actions: interference with television signals (690 plaintiffs) and excessive dust (513 plaintiffs). In any case, under this case-by-case adjudication system it is completely acceptable that two different claimants who may have suffered similar personal injuries will be entitled to different financial damages due to their particular circumstances, such as earnings capacity, age, dependency and causal connection of the plaintiff's injury to the defendant's conduct.[941]

443. Collective liability is an important feature of tort law as it allows spreading the cost of liability and a wrongdoer then contributes to collective compensation based

940. [1997] UKHL 14; AC 655 (HL).
941. *H West & Son Ltd v. Shepherd* [1964] AC 326.

on his share of the liability. However, claims for collective damages are rare in tort law litigation and may be possibly awarded in some cases involving violations of civil rights, such as discrimination. During the US civil rights movement in 1960s, collective damages were awarded against many school districts for racial discrimination against people of African descent. In the US, collective liability can be imposed in multiple ways: if the division of fault among the defendants is impossible for the plaintiff to know, the doctrine of 'alternative' liability can be utilized; 'enterprise liability' can make manufacturers collectively liable; and joint liability can also be imposed on defendants who conspire to engage in tortious activities.[942]

§2. Direct and Indirect

444. The distinction between direct and indirect damages is a matter of causal connection between the injury and the tortious conduct of the defendant. For direct damages, the defendant's tortious conduct is a direct cause of the plaintiff's injury. For indirect damages, the defendant's misconduct is a consequent cause. Indirect damages, also called as consequential damages or special damages, are relatively difficult to establish (e.g., loss of future earnings), and the plaintiff is required to provide evidence of his losses and that damages are not too remote. If damages are too remote and not consequent upon[943] any physical injury to the plaintiff or loss of his property, then it is not recoverable.

§3. Pecuniary and Non-pecuniary Losses

445. Generally, pecuniary (special damages) and non-pecuniary damages (general damages) at common law are types of compensatory or actual damages. Pecuniary damages include all financial losses, such as loss of earnings (including loss of actual and future earning capacity), property damage and expenses (including medical expenses). Non-pecuniary damages are non-financial in nature and include pain, suffering and loss of amenities (PSLA)[944] and emotional distress. Different rules are applied in assessing pecuniary and non-pecuniary losses, which will be discussed at relevant places in this text.

§4. Pure Economic Loss

446. The damages for pure economic loss are mainly recoverable under contract law and not tort law. However, under specific circumstances (which are discussed in Part I, §3 (IV) of this text), it may be recoverable under tort law. Calculating damages for pure economic loss caused by negligent activities/statements is a very complex

942. Allen Rostron, '*Beyond Market Share Liability: A Theory of Proportional Share Liability for Non-fungible Products*', 52 UCLA L. Rev. 151 (2004).

943. *Spartan Steel And Alloys Ltd v. Martin & Co (Contractors) Ltd* [1973] QB 27.

944. *H West & Son Co Ltd v. Shepherd* [1964] AC 326.

matter and is awarded by the courts on a case-by-case basis. Courts in such situations strictly consider the remoteness of damage principle, which in turn assists the court in assessing the damages in each case. The reader should also consult specialized texts for further understanding.[945]

§5. Actual and Future Damages (Lost Profits)

447. Actual damages are compensatory in nature and are accumulated as pre-trial financial losses or special damages, such as medical expenses or lost income that the claimant has suffered directly due to the tortious conduct of the defendant. Actual damages can be claimed after the plaintiff produces evidence to that effect. The pre-trial loss of income or loss of business profits is calculated based on the plaintiff's actual income on the date of accident. In some cases the court accepts the evidence of probable increase of income between the accident and trial, such as pay rise or promotion.[946]

448. The future lost profit is an indirect result of the accident and includes post-trial pecuniary loss, such as future medical expenses, future loss of earnings,[947] loss of earning capacity and all non-financial losses (e.g., pain, suffering, loss of amenities). Calculating these consequential damages is more difficult and it is subjected to more strict proof at trial.

§6. Other Costs

449. For civil proceedings in Hong Kong, the court in contentious proceedings may order the losing party to pay 'legal costs,' which include fees, charges, disbursements, expenses and remuneration, to the winning party to compensate him/her for the incurred expense in litigation. Order 62 of the Rules of the High Court (Cap 4A) allows costs to be awarded on an indemnity basis, subject to the court's discretion. The winning party can recover up to 60%–70% of their legal costs and the rest has to be incurred by the claimant personally.

450. In relation to the sex discrimination claims, section 73B(3) of the District Court Ordinance (Cap 336) states that each party to proceedings under the Sex Discrimination Ordinance should bear its own costs unless the court otherwise orders on the ground that: (1) the proceedings were brought maliciously or frivolously; or (2) there are special circumstances which warrant an award of costs. In *L v. David Roy Burton*,[948] the court allowed the award of costs against the defendant based on the existence of special circumstances.

945. Harvey McGregor QC, *McGregor on Damages* (19th edn, Sweet and Maxwell 2015).
946. *Lai Hing Wan v. Kowloon Canton Railway Corp* (HCA No. 4338 of 1984).
947. *Chan Pui Ki v. Leung On* [1995] 3 HKC 732.
948. [2010] HKCU 2270.

§7. Mitigation of Damages

451. Mitigation of damages refers to the injured party taking reasonable actions to prevent additional injury or loss. A failure on the part of the plaintiff to take reasonable steps to mitigate his losses, such as by seeking timely medical treatment where possible, can reduce his future damages for loss of earnings or damage to property. For instance, in *Kowloon Bus Co (1933) v. KK Cargo Systems (HK) Ltd,*[949] the court reduced the plaintiff's claimed period of repair from 153 days to 74 days on the basis that it was unreasonable. Likewise, a failure to mitigate will also apply in cases where a plaintiff fails to take up employment where he is capable to do so[950] or failing to accept an apology in a defamation case.

949. [2002] HKLRD (Yrbk) 386.
950. *Choy Wai Chung v. Chun Wo Construction & Engineering Co Ltd* [2005] HKEC 1077.

Chapter 3. Assessment and Compensation of Damages

§1. Objective Versus Subjective

452. While assessing damages, the courts in Hong Kong do not make any distinction between objective and subjective damages. However, as we shall discuss under the methods of assessing damages in a later section, clearly certain assessments are objective in nature, in the sense that they are based on the actual loss of the claimant, whereas other damages are subjective, in the sense that they involve the courts making assumptions as to the loss of future earnings, which, although they are based on concrete formulas, are nonetheless a reflection of prospective earnings.

§2. Concrete Versus Abstract

453. In common law countries, including in Hong Kong, the courts do not describe calculation of damages based on 'concrete' and 'abstract' loss. However, within the framework of methods to calculate damages, such a test of remoteness of damages and the multiplicand/multiplier method, etc., the notion of concrete/abstract damages is very much extant.

§3. Methods of Assessing Damages

454. The overarching principle for calculation of compensation is to restore the plaintiff to the position they would have been in had the injury not occurred.[951] Generally, the test of remoteness of damages will apply in negligence cases, whereas in cases of trespassory torts,[952] the assessment will be based on directness of injury. For the purposes of consistency in personal injuries litigation, the court in Hong Kong adopted the multiplier approach until 2014, based on *Chan Pui Ki (an infant) v. Leung On & Others,*[953] which adopted the House of Lords decision of *Cookson v. Knowles.*[954] Under this method, calculations were made by considering net annual loss after paying tax and national insurance (multiplicand) which is then multiplied by the number of years the loss will continue (multiplier). The product of multiplicand and multiplier provided the final lump sum award that represented the loss of future earnings.

455. In assessing the multiplicand, the court took into account promotion prospects, increments as well as the contract renewals.[955] To find the total loss, the multiplicand was multiplied with the multiplier that represented the total number of

951. *Lo Ping Kin v. Yuen Tsz Shing* [2016] HKEC 941, 71.
952. *Wilson v. Pringle* [1987] QB 237.
953. [1996] 2 HKC 565; 1995] 3 HKC 732.
954. [1979] AC 556; [1978] 2 All ER 604 (HL).
955. *CMY v. Tam Siu Wing* [2008] 4 HKLRD 604.

years for which income was lost. Hence, the multiplier was the total number of working years of the plaintiff, calculated from the date of trial. In practice, however, the multiplier was reduced and adjusted to a lower figure for two main reasons: firstly, the court took into account the contingencies of life (vicissitudes of life) and the possibility that the claimant would not have worked until retirement age due to some unforeseen events or redundancy, etc.; secondly, the court reduced the multiplier because damages are paid in a lump sum, which has significant investment returns over a period of time.

456. To predict future loss of earnings, the position was based on the *Cookson v. Knowles,*[956] where the court assumed the net return was 4.5% above inflation. In *Chan Pui Ki (an infant) v. Leung On & Others,*[957] the court attempted to change the position in calculating the damages. At trial, Cheung J attempted to vary from the conventional *Cookson v. Knowles* approach. The learned judge accepted that a 1.2% discount rate should be recognized and that the multiplier would vary from conventional approach, but this was subsequently rejected by Court of Appeal. The Court of Appeal found that the evidence from economists and actuaries in assessing the future economic environment and was unnecessary and inappropriate. In the Court of Appeal decision, Litton VP stated that, '*Now that all outstanding issues have been resolved by this judgment, there should be no need in the future for non-medical expert evidence of that kind to be adduced ... Occasions for opinion evidence from experts on economic matters should be rare indeed.*'[958]

457. In the subsequent case of *Ta Xuong v. Incorporated Owners of Sun Hing Building,*[959] where the plaintiff required continued medical care for their whole lifetime, the court adopted the multiplier/multiplicand approach. The court considered the number of years the plaintiff was likely to be disabled and the difference between the age of the plaintiff at the time of accident and at the date of retirement from employment. Based on this assessment, the plaintiff was awarded about HKD 17 million for his disabilities, home care expenses and the expenses to alter his home for his disabilities. This case clearly demonstrates that assessing pecuniary damages can be multifaceted and difficult.

458. In 2014, however, the Court of Appeal in *Chan Wai Ming v. Leung Shing Wah,*[960] overruled the *Cookson v. Knowles* approach and adopted a new method. This change was not sudden. There had been a lot of debates and discussions on whether Hong Kong courts should continue to follow the *Cookson v. Knowles* approach in choosing multipliers in personal injury litigation,[961] despite the fact that in the UK the House of Lords had already rejected this approach in *Wells v. Wells.*[962] *Wells* set the discounted rate of 3% after tax and inflation for lump sum compensation for future loss. The court also recognized the Index Linked Government Securities index for

956. [1979] AC 556, [1978] 2 All ER 604 (HL).
957. [1996] 2 HKC 565; [1995] 3 HKC 732.
958. [1996] 2 HKC 565.
959. [1997] 4 HKC 171.
960. [2014] 4 HKLRD 669.
961. Felix W.H. Chan & Wai-Sum Chan, '*Actuarial Assessment of Damages in Personal Injury Litigation: The Hong Kong Position and the Comparative International Aspects*', 30 Hong Kong L.J. 272 [2000].
962. [1999] AC 345.

reasonable investments of the lump sum, rejecting the conventional 4%–5% return on investments, on the assumption that the claimant would invest his/her lump sum damages in equities. The court believed that, since the payment was made in lump sum and if it is invested prudently, it will produce an income equivalent to the loss of income suffered by the claimant. The House of Lords held that the Ogden Tables, which are actuarial tables based on the population mortality of the UK, should be used as the starting point rather than a check. Such evidence was admissible under the Civil Evidence Act 1985 for the purposes of assessing damages in personal injury and fatal accident cases. The court also warned against any departure from the use of actuarial tables on impressionistic grounds or by reference to the range of conventional multipliers.[963]

459. Previously, in 2012, the *Cookson v. Knowles*[964] assumption was challenged in the Court of First Instance by Bharwaney J, in *Chan Pak Ting v. Chan Chi Kuen and Another*,[965] when he questioned '*[w]hether, having regard to economic developments from 1995 up to the present time, the Cookson v Knowles assumption of a net rate of return of 4.5% remains valid in Hong Kong and, if not, what is the net rate of return based upon which multipliers ought to be assessed and awarded*'.[966] Justice Bharwaney allowed evidence from experts in relation to the multiplier on the basis that there had been substantial change in the economic landscape in Hong Kong since the *Chan Pui Ki v. Leung On*[967] decision and economic indicators suggested that low interest rates would continue for some time. On the assessment of future economic losses, he also reviewed the significant UK cases[968] and decided that the *Cookson v. Knowles* assumption under, which a net rate of return of 4.5% per annum was allowed, was no longer valid in Hong Kong, which was accepted by the defendants. Instead, he stated that instead of using the multiplier approach, a new discount rate for plaintiffs with future needs would be adopted as follows: (1) not exceeding five years, minus 0.5%; (2) not exceeding ten years, 1%; and (3) exceeding ten years, 2.5%. The judge was of the view even though the discount rates are lower than that of 4.5% as prescribed by the *Cookson v. Knowles* assumption, the multiplier could be adjusted to a higher number, which would then result in a higher award of damages that could fully and fairly, compensate the victim. Since then, many other Court of First Instance decisions have used this approach.[969]

460. Finally, in 2014, the Court of Appeal in *Chan Wai Ming v. Leung Shing Wah*,[970] formally adopted the new approach suggested by *Chan Pak Ting* and overruled

963. [1999] AC 345, p. 379F-G (Lord Lloyd of Berwick).
964. [1979] AC 556, [1978] 2 All ER 604 (HL).
965. *Chan Pak Ting v. Chan Chi Kuen and Another* [2012] HKCU 2083; *Chan Pak Ting v. Chan Chi Kuen* [2013] 1 HKLRD 634 and *Chan Pak Ting v. Chan Chi Kuen* (No 2) [2013] 2 HKLRD 1.
966. *Chan Pak Ting v. Chan Chi Kuen and Another* [2012] HKCU 2083 (Hon Bharwaney J).
967. *Chan Pui Ki v. Leung On* [1996] 2 HKLR 401 (CA).
968. *Wells v. Wells* [1997] 1 WLR 652 (CA), [1999] 1 AC 345 (HL) as well as *Simon v. Helmot* [2012] Med LR 394 (PC).
969. *Lam Chan Hung v. Hang Yue Engineering Ltd* [2013] 3 HKLRD420; *Lo Wai Shing v. Lik Sang Engineering Co Ltd* [2013] HKEC 1755; and *Mohammad Amjad v. John M Pickavant & Co* [2013] HKEC 1824.
970. [2014] 4 HKLRD 669.

the approach in *Chan Pui Ki v. Leung On*. The court, rejecting the conventional multiplier system which is based on the discount rate of 4.5%–5%, held that instead the multiplier should consider the net rate of return, actuarial tables and the new discount rates. The court held:

> 5.5 The parties now agreed that based on Table 11 of the Personal Injury Tables Hong Kong 2013 (Contributors: Professor Chan Wai Sum and Dr Felix Chan, General Editor: Mr Neville Sarony SC), the appropriate multiplier based on the 1% discount should be 9.13 for a man of 60 years of age with a working life of another 10 years.

461. Allowing the cross-appeal Yeung V-P, Cheung JA stated:

> 8.3 In my view it is not satisfactory that for a topic as important as this one which has a huge impact on the personal injury practice should be left to be decided in the future in a case where the parties chose to adduce expert evidence at trial and have the financial resources to take the matter to appeal. The parties in Chan Pak Ting who had the benefit of representation by leading specialist counsel from England and Hong Kong and the financial ability to call expert evidence had chosen not to appeal. Uncertainty will ensure if this Court chooses not to seize the opportunity and decide on this issue. With the benefit of the statèment of principles by the House of Lords in Wells v Wells and the Privy Council in Simon v Helmot together with clear expert evidence so ably summarised by Bharwaney J, this Court is in as good a position to address this topic.
>
> 8.4 It is recognised that great caution must be exercised before this Court departs from Chan Pui Ki v Leung On, a precedent which has been followed for nearly 20 years since its decision in 1996. But since that time, Hong Kong has undergone great change in its economic landscape.
>
> 8.5 In my view to hold on to the conventional multiplier approach which is based on the discount rate of 4.5-5% fails to provide full compensation to the victim because this notional return does not accord with the economic reality of present day Hong Kong. For my part, I would respectfully depart from Chan Pui Ki v Leung On and adopt the new approach.
>
> 8.6 Accordingly, I would allow the cross-appeal and adjust the multiplier so that the future loss of earnings will become: $193,366.20 x 9.13 = $1,765,433

462. Yeung V-P, Cheung JA further proposed that legislative changes should be introduced in Hong Kong to more easily identify return rates. In the UK, the award of damages is administered under the Damages Act 1996, which allows partial payment of instead of a lump sum, thereby enabling the use of different discount rates for subsequent payments. Section 1 of the Damages Act 1996 states that the court has to take into account *'such rates of return as may from time to time be prescribed by an order made by the Lord Chancellor'*. In 2001, and after the *Wells* decision, the Lord Chancellor prescribed the rate at 2.5%. It was noted:

6.14 The review now moves to Guernsey, a British Crown dependency in the English Channel which adopts the English common law in tort actions. Like Hong Kong, it does not have legislation on damage awards. It faces the same problem of determining the appropriate multiplier due to the low rate of return. The Privy Council hearing an appeal from Guernsey in Simon v Helmot reviewed the authorities and decided that the conventional multiplier approach decided in cases like Cookson v Knowles had served its purpose and accepted the Guernsey Court of "Appeal's approach in ascertaining the net rate of return by reference to expert evidence. The Court adopted a discount rate of minus 1.5% for earning related loss and 0.5% for other losses. …

9.1 Hong Kong does not have ILGS upon which the return rate may be more easily identified. In the long term, the only solution to the problem now faced by this Court which is bound to resurface time and again, is to introduce legislation similar to the United Kingdom Damages Act 1996 which allows the authority to prescribe a rate of return from time to time in order to meet changes in the economic condition. This is a call urged upon Guernsey by the Privy Council and I will repeat a similar call that the legislation should be introduced in Hong Kong without further delay.

9.2 Pending legislative change, Lord Clarke in Simon v Helmot suggested that the parties should resort more to structured settlements by way of periodical payment orders. This will ensure different net rate of returns to be taken into account at different times. He observed that structured settlements in fact were commonly used in the United Kingdom before the Damages Act 1996. In my view this is a matter worth looking into by personal injury practitioners.[971]

463. From this review of Hong Kong cases, it appears that the multiplier approach does not bind the court in all cases, such as in the calculation of loss of income in the form of lost business profits, where it is rather difficult to quantify sums in uncertain and fluctuating economic times, as such making multiplier/multiplicand method less suitable. In such cases, considering the remoteness of damages is more significant, along with the evidence of the plaintiff, to demonstrate that his losses are not speculative. Further, in terms of loss of future earnings, the court in Hong Kong awards a loss of MPF at the rate of 5%.[972]

§4. Equitable Limitation of Damages

464. In Hong Kong, the LO prescribes the limitation period for the commencement of various tort actions. If a claimant fails to bring an action without any reasonable justification within the statutory prescribed period his action may be defeated. The statutory limitation period for various tort actions in Hong Kong has been discussed in detail in Part IV of this text.

971. [2014] 4 HKLRD 669.
972. *Fung Wai Han v. Hui Chik Keung* [2006] 4 HKLRD 549.

§5. Methods of Payment

I. Lump Sum

465. In Hong Kong, the actions for personal injury suffered in a single tort, the court awards a lump sum, which is the total amount payable for both pecuniary and non-pecuniary loss incurred, and the claimant cannot claim for further awards later. However, in rare cases, a statutory provision under the section 56A of High Court Ordinance (Cap 4) allows a provisional award where the defendant develops some disease or where the situation is worsened.[973]

II. Annuities

466. Under statutory regimes in certain common law jurisdictions, such as Australia, Canada, England and the United States, periodic payments can be made instead of one of lump sum payment to settle personal injury claims. These periodic payment plans make it possible to avoid taxation through the creation of an annuity or trust arrangement,[974] which then guarantees the future payments.

467. In Hong Kong, there is no such statutory arrangement. However, in *Chan Wai Ming v. Leung Shing Wah*[975] Yeung VP and Cheung JA called for such a legislative intervention.

973. *Chui Wing Lai v. Chung Dok Restaurant Ltd* (unrep. HCA 3177/1989, 2 Mar. 1995).
974. Marcus L. Plant, '*Periodic Payment of Damages for Personal Injury*', 44 La. L. Rev. 1327 at 1330 (1984).
975. [2014] 4 HKLRD 669.

Chapter 4. Personal Injury and Death (Pecuniary and Non-Pecuniary Losses)

§1. Personal Injury

468. Personal injury remedies aim to restore, as far as possible, the pre-tort position of the claimant. Pecuniary as well as non-pecuniary damages can be awarded. Calculating pecuniary loss for personal injuries is rather difficult as issues such as loss of earnings and earning capacity (future earning capacity and prospect of future career opportunity, etc.), and expenses (medical expenses and future health care, increased living costs due to injury, etc.) need to be considered. It is to be noted that in Hong Kong the claimant is entitled to claim expenses for traditional Chinese medical treatment such as bone setting,[976] tonic foods,[977] etc. at both the pre-trial as well as the post-trial stage. These extra medical expenses are awarded alongside those for the necessary conventional western medical treatment.

469. In relation to non-pecuniary damages, the court will ascertain a single amount for the 'PSLA' incurred by the victim[978] following the injury, which technically is actual physical pain and inability to pursue recreational activities. It is provided where a person survives subsequent to injury, including if they are permanently unconscious or only conscious for a short while.[979] When awarding PSLA the Hong Kong courts consider a set of guidelines to decipher the severity of the injury and take inflation into account. The PSLA is categorized for serious injury, leaving the plaintiff with reasonable mobility despite, for example, the loss of a limb (HKD 400,000–HKD 540,000), substantial injury, involving prolonged treatment or significantly reduced mobility (HKD 540,000–HKD 660,000); gross disability, such as highly restricted mobility (HKD 660,000–HKD 1,000,000) and disastrous, such as the need for constant care for the rest of the victim's life (HKD 1,000,000 upwards).[980] To maintain consistency, the court usually allows set awards under each category, but do consider the special circumstances of each plaintiff, which may result in some variations.

470. Personal injury damages are of the following types; compensatory, nominal, aggravated and exemplary. Each type of damage is awarded after considering the kind of tort that may have occurred, such as negligence, trespass, etc.

---

976. *Lo Ping Kin v. Yuen Tsz Shing* [2016] HKEC 941, 96 and 97.
977. *Lo Ping Kin v. Yuen Tsz Shing* [2016] HKEC 941, 100.
978. *H West & Son Co Ltd v. Shepherd* [1964] AC 326 (Lord Pearce).
979. *Wise v. Kaye* [1962] 1 QB 638.
980. *Lau Che Ping v. Hoi Kong Ironwares Godown Co Ltd* [1988] 2 HKLR 650 (Cons ACJ).

I. Compensatory Damages

471. Compensatory damages apply to all types of tort actions where the victims seeks compensation for the harm he/she has suffered. The award of damages tries to put the victim in a pre-tort situation as much as the money can. In personal injury cases courts are often put in the rather difficult position of calculating indeterminate loss, such as for losing a limb, or to calculating the future financial status of a claimant while considering his promotion chances, salary increase, etc. To be as fair as possible to claimant, the common law judges consider both pecuniary loss and non-pecuniary loss. Pecuniary loss is a large part of compensation and includes loss of earnings, loss of earning capacity, medical expenses, increased living and care costs, etc. on the other hand, non-pecuniary loss includes PSLA, disfigurement, loss of enjoyment of life, etc.

II. Nominal Damages

472. Nominal damages are most often allowed where there is direct and intentional interference with a plaintiff's legal right to possession through trespass to lands or goods, or the plaintiff themselves, through trespass to the person, or even his reputation, such as in libel cases. The infringement of legal rights/civil liberties (trespassory action or libel) is actionable per se and the claimant does not need to prove that damages were suffered. It is easier for the plaintiff to prove his case but the court finds it difficult to award damages other than nominal ones. For example, in the nineteenth century case of *Stephen v. Myers,*[981] the plaintiff received nominal damages of one shilling (around GBP 2.50 today) after being threatened by the defendant. In a more modern case, *Constantine v. Imperial Hotels Ltd,*[982] the plaintiff received nominal damages of 5 guineas (around GBP 100 today) for being rejected from being given accommodation.

473. The position may best be summarized by the following quote in *McGregor on Damages*, 18th edition, pp 8-001 to 8-002, as cited by Harris J in *Effiscient Ltd v. Lehmanbrown Ltd:*[983]

A claimant claiming damages must prove his case. To justify an award of substantial damages he must satisfy the court both as to the fact of damage and as to its amount. If he satisfies the court on neither, his action will fail, or at the most he will be awarded nominal damages where a right has been infringed. If the fact of damage is shown but no evidence is given as to its amount so that it is virtually impossible to assess damages, this will generally permit only an award of nominal damages; this situation is illustrated by the old cases of Dixon v Deveridge (1825) 2 C & P 109 and Twyman v Knowles (1853) 13 CB 222. [emphasis added]

474. In most cases, it is difficult for a plaintiff to sue the defendant if they suffer no damage. The costs consequences should be taken into account and should be

981. (1830) 4 C & P 349.
982. [1944] 1 KB 693.
983. [2012] HKCU 2428.

considered before initiating any litigation. Nominal damages can be potentially useful, such as when suing law enforcement agencies for false imprisonment.[984]

III. Aggravated Damages

475. Aggravated damages can be granted in intentional tort cases like libel and trespass,[985] but not on all tortious claim. For example, in negligence cases the plaintiff cannot claim aggravated damages. In *Kralj v. McGrath,*[986] Woolf J (as he then was) explained that that it would be inappropriate to award aggravated damages for breach of contract and negligence as in these cases damages are awarded by the courts to address the plaintiff's actual suffering.

476. It is not very easy to define the term 'aggravated damages'. It has no precise meaning, although it is accepted that it could mean awarding a higher amount of damages due to the defendant's malicious or high-handed conduct causing additional mental distress to the plaintiff. It is certain that aggravated damages are above and beyond the pecuniary losses that can be specifically proved. Lord Devlin provided an authoritative analysis through the case of *Rookes v. Barnard.*[987] In his Lordship's opinion, aggravated damages are aimed to compensate for the defendant's acts that could warrant additional compensation, rather than to punish the defendant.

477. An award of aggravated damages is preceded by two conditions: (1) Exceptional or contumelious conduct or intention on the part of the defendant ('Exceptional Conduct'); and (2) as a result, mental distress being caused to the plaintiff.

478. In a recent Hong Kong case of *Chang Ming Fang Jacqueline v. Zhang Zi Qiang,*[988] the court provided damages of HKD 200,000 with no exemplary or aggravated damages as the court was of the view that such damage was sufficient. The court at paragraph 86 further explained the difference between aggravated and exemplary damages, taking into account the principles set out in *Barton v. Armstrong.*[989] The court stated: '*It cannot be doubted that in an action for assault, in certain circumstances, the damages may be aggravated by the manner in which the assault is committed. It is, I think, also clear that exemplary damages may be awarded where the facts show that the "defendant's conduct in committing the wrong exhibited a contumelious disregard of the plaintiff"s rights, see Uren v John Fairfax & Sons Pty Ltd [1967] ALR 25; 117 CLR 118. The distinction between aggravated damages and exemplary*

---

984. Courts in Hong Kong do not view false imprisonment lightly as it is infringement of claimants civil liberty, and judges are willing to award more than nominal damages in such cases: *see Ghulam Rbani v. Secretary for Justice for and on behalf of Director of Immigration* [2012] HKCU 364 (unreported, DCCJ 531/2010, 16 Feb. 2012); *Saeed Muhammad otherwise known as Mohammed Said v. Secretary for Justice sued for and on behalf of Director of Immigration* [2012] HKCU 2036 (unreported, DCCJ 1717/2010, 21 Oct. 2011).

985. *Ballard v. MPC* (1983) 133 NLJ 1133; *W v. Meah* [1986] 1 All ER 935; *Smith v. MPC* [1982] CLY 899; *Thompson v. MPC* [1997] 3 WLR 403 (CA); *Thompson v. MPC* [1997] 3 WLR 403; *McCarey v. Associated Newspapers Ltd (No 2)* [1965] 2 QB 86, 107D (CA).

986. [1986] 1 All ER 54.

987. [1964] AC 1129 (HL).

988. [2009] HKCFI 768.

989. [1969] 2 NSWR 451.

damages is pointed out in that case. The former are given by way of compensation for injury to the plaintiff; they are frequently intangible, resulting from the circumstances and manner of the "defendant's wrongdoing.' On the other hand exemplary damages are awarded, as Lord Devlin says in Rookes v Barnard, "to punish and deter the "wrongdoer', though in many cases the same set of circumstances might well justify either an award of exemplary or aggravated damages', per Taylor J.

479. In *Rookes v. Barnard,*[990] Lord Devlin considered that aggravated damage shall be awarded for acts which humiliate or insult the plaintiff and cause distress or pain to the plaintiff. These are categorized as exceptional conduct, like harassment, abuse, police misconduct, etc.[991] In *Sin Cho Chiu v. Tin Tin Publication Development Ltd,*[992] the learned judge took into account the defendant's malicious intention, his failure to remedy the harm, and accordingly awarded aggravated damages of HKD 1,000,000 to the plaintiff.

IV. Punitive/Exemplary Damages

480. Exemplary damages aim to punish/deter the defendant for his conduct and are awarded in limited circumstances. In *Kuddus (AP) v. Chief Constable of Leicestershire Constabulary,*[993] Lord Nicholls clarified that punishment is not normally the purpose for tortious liability but such damages should serve *'as a remedy of last resort, fill what otherwise would be a regrettable lacuna'.* The leading English case of *Rookes v. Barnard,*[994] which is equally applicable in Hong Kong,[995] explained in what circumstances the exemplary damages will be awarded. Lord Devlin restricted exemplary damages to three categories only: (1) where government servants act oppressively, arbitrarily or unconstitutionally; (2) where the "defendant's conduct made a larger profit for himself which exceeds the damages payable to the plaintiff; (3) where it is expressly authorized by statute.

481. For example, in *Hsu v. Commissioner of Police for the Metropolis,*[996] Lord Woolf awarded both aggravated as well as exemplary damages in a case where police acted oppressively and caused distress to the plaintiff. In *Yuen Sha Sha v. Tse Chi Pan,*[997] which is a sexual harassment case, the victim was awarded both aggravated and punitive damages for the defendant's unrepentant behaviour and the violation of the plaintiff's dignity. In *L v. David Roy Burton,*[998] an employee was awarded exemplary damages for sexual harassment. In assessing exemplary damages the court considered

990. [1964] AC 1129 (HL).
991. *See Thompson v. MPC* [1997] 3 WLR 403 (CA).
992. [2002] HKCU 127 (unreported, HCA 6662/1997, 11 Jan. 2002).
993. [2001] UKHL 29 (HL).
994. [1964] AC 1129 (HL).
995. *A v. Director of Immigration* [2009] 2 HKC 452; *Lee Ting-lam v. Leung Kam-ming* [1980] HKLR 657 (CA); *Chan Wai-tong v. Li Ping-sum* [1985] HKLR 176 (PC); *Chan Pui-ki v. Leung On* [1966] 2 HKLR 401 (CA).
996. [1998] QB 498.
997. [1999] 1 HKC 731 (DC).
998. [2010] 5 HKLRD 397, [2010] 6 HKC 463.

that the defendant's outrageous conduct had exploited the employee under an imbalance of power situation.

482. It is to be noted that some commonwealth jurisdictions do not follow (or do not strictly follow) the rules set by *Rookes v. Barnard.* For example, New Zealand has a more liberal test for exemplary damages. Over the years, Hong Kong courts have sometimes exercised their discretion to award exemplary damages. For example, in the cases of *Li Wei v. Brightec Ltd*[999] and *Choy Bing Wing v. Ng Yat Chi*[1000] the court awarded exemplary damages without referencing *Rookes v. Barnard.*

§2. Damages for Death

483. When the victim dies due to the tort (negligence, wrongful act or default) of the defendant, his estate or dependants can bring a claim for damages, either together or independently. Survivors can bring an action for the benefit of the estate under section 20 of the Law Amendment and Reform (Consolidation) Ordinance ('LARCO'). It also allows the estate administrator to recover debts claimed by creditors of the deceased.[1001] The estate can also claim from the defendant the losses of the money that the deceased could have accumulated over the year (section 20(2)(iii) of LARCO). This amount is calculated after considering the income and expenses of the deceased. Where the deceased does not die immediately, the estate, under section 20(2)(b) of LARCO, can claim for the pain and suffering that the deceased suffered. Further claims for medical and other expenses can be made by the estate during the time deceased lived (section 20(1) LARCO).

484. Further, under the Fatal Accidents Ordinance (Cap 22), under section 3, dependants have a right to sue persons for actions causing the victim's death. Under section 4, bereavement damages are a fixed sum of HKD 150,000.[1002] Under section 6(1), dependency claims[1003] could be made if the damages are based on the proportion of individual injuries contributing to the death of deceased. The court also uses a multiplier/multiplicand approach to consider both the age of deceased as well as of dependants in dependency claims. Seagroatt J in *Tsang Mei Ying v. Lam Pak Chiu*[1004] explained in some detail what Hong Kong courts adhere to in assessing the dependency claim (paragraphs 3–5). Further, under section 6(5), reasonable funeral expenses can be awarded. Finally under section 21(4) of LARCO a dependency award will be reduced if the deceased was contributory negligent.

999. [2001] HKCU 96, 1 HKLRD A18.
1000. [1992] 1 HKC 508.
1001. *Tse Fung Sin v. Tung Wah Group of Hospitals* [2007] HKEC 1899.
1002. *Wong Kam v. Shum Yuk Fong* [2001] HKEC 1220.
1003. *Chavez v. Fong Ka Yiu* [2001] 3 HKLRD 1.
1004. [1999] 2 HKLRD 807.

Chapter 5. Various Damages (Property)

485. The recovery standard in relation to property damage is *restitutio in integrum* which is same as is applicable to personal harm. The aim is to restore the plaintiff to their pre-tort position.[1005] Unlike personal injuries, remedying property damage is more objective than subjective in its assessment and, in most cases, the plaintiff can be successfully restored to the pre-accident state. However, there is an exception to this rule in cases of rare goods or artwork, etc.

486. In general, the damage to property is calculated in terms of the repair costs, reasonable costs of temporary replacement of goods (rental costs)[1006] and the depreciation of value of property from the time of the damage being incurred. Further diminution in value is usually calculated on the day of property damage. In cases where there is a total destruction of property, like in conversion cases, damages are payable on the basis of the market value of property on the day of its destruction. It includes any business profits if damaged goods were to be used commercially. For example, in *Maxson Transportation Ltd v. Poon Wai Hang*,[1007] where the plaintiff's light bus was completely damaged, he was awarded loss of profits for more than three weeks spent waiting.

487. The principle of mitigation also applies to property damages cases, under which a person who has suffered an injury is expected to take reasonable action in order to avoid additional injury during the period of repair. It should be noted that where goods are insured and insurance premiums are paid by the plaintiff under the insurance policy, no deductions from the compensation award are allowed by the court. It is because the plaintiff is entitled to such payments under their contract and do not receive such sum of money because of the accident.[1008]

1005. *Hong Kong Construction Co Ltd v. Ng Fuk Choi* [2004] HKEC 777.

1006. *Pateco Ltd Chan Cheuk Lam* [2006] HKEC 2350.

1007. [2007] HKEC 133.

1008. *Bradburn v. Great Western Railway Co* (1874–1875) LR 10 Ex 1 (Piggott B); *Yip Kwan Cheung v. Chim Hong Wing* [2007] HKEC 356.

Chapter 6. Interference with Collateral Benefits

488. In calculating the damages of the plaintiff the court is mindful of avoiding over-compensation. The aim is not to penalize the defendant. However, at some occasions the issue of over-compensation of plaintiff may arise such as where the claimant may have received payments subsequent to the accident, such as insurance, *ex-gratia* payments, sick pay, social security payments, etc. In such cases the court will have to decide whether to deduct such payments from the award.

§1. Insurance

489. The insurance system has now become an integral part of providing compensation in tort law cases. Insurance covers most of the defendant's liability for damages, like third-party motor vehicles insurance, employers' compulsory compensation, and occupier's insurance policy. Generally, insurance premiums are not deducted from the tort law damages payable to the claimant, mainly because a claimant cannot be penalized for his foresight.[1009] However, in cases of indemnity insurance, such as property damage, which is put in place to compensate policy beneficiaries, the insurer, after paying the claimant, can exercise its right to subrogation for the recovery of the paid money from the defendant. However in cases of personal injury which is not indemnity insurance, is not generally recoverable by the insurer and hence the claimant can recover proceeds of policy as well as the have damages from the court.[1010]

490. However, it should be remembered that any payments received by the claimant under any no-fault statutory schemes, such as the ECO, that the defendant has paid will be deducted from the award of damages made by the court. Likewise, sick pay is deducted from the damages and is not treated as insurance.[1011] However, a pension is seen as a kind of insurance and is not deduced from the damages for the loss of earnings. This is because the claimant makes compulsory pension contributions while in employment, and it is not taken into consideration while assessing the future loss of earnings.[1012]

§2. Social Security

491. Social security benefits are not considered in calculating damages. Any money payable from the public funds is not deducted. In Hong Kong, the backbone of the social security system is the Comprehensive Social Security Assistance Scheme and the Social Security Allowance Scheme, which provides the financial assistance to needy individuals or families up to a prescribed level to meet their basic needs, and includes Old Age Allowance, Normal Disability Allowance, Higher Disability Allowance

1009. *Bradburn v. Great Western Rail* (1874) LR 10 Ex 1.
1010. P. Cane, *Atiyah's Accidents Compensation and the Law* (7ed CUP, 2006) at 15.4.3.
1011. *Hussain v. New Taplow Paper Mills Ltd* [1988] AC 514.
1012. *Parry v. Cleaver* [1970] AC 1, 21.

and Old Age Living Allowance. To claim the assistance needy individuals need to satisfy the set eligibility criteria, including the residence requirements. In the judicial review case of *Kong Yunming (孔允明) v. The Director of Social Welfare,*[1013] the court held that the government's policy, which came into effect on 1 January 2004, requiring all recipients of Comprehensive Social Security Assistance to have been a Hong Kong resident for at least seven years, is not constitutional and is inconsistent with Articles 25, 36 and 145 of the Basic Law, as well as Article 22 of the Hong Kong Bill of Rights.

§3. OTHERS

492. Charitable payments are not deducted from the damages; they are to benefit the claimant and not the wrongdoer. Any monetary assistance given by friends in the post-accident period are not taken into account while assessing the damages.[1014] Funds received by the plaintiff under a government scheme like the Traffic Accident Victims (Assistance Fund) (Cap 229) to assist traffic accident victims and their dependants for post-accident needs are not deducted by the court. However, when the claimant receives the damages from the court that are more than the fund payment, then he is required to repay the amount of money paid from the fund.

493. The voluntary payments given by the defendant, in the absence of explicit evidence from the defendant that it should be disregarded in the calculation of damages, will be deducted from the award of damages.[1015]

1013. Final Appeal No. 2 of 2013 (Civil) (On Appeal from CACV No. 185 of 2009).
1014. *Chu Wo Heung v. Wong Pun Wai* [2001] HKEC 790.
1015. *Gaca v. Pirelli General Plc* [2004] EWCA Civ 373.

Chapter 7. Other Remedies

§1. Restitution (for Unjust Enrichment)

494. The law of unjust enrichment in Hong Kong remains the traditional common law 'unjust factors' approach. Mistake and failure of consideration form its foundations.[1016] Restitution is a remedy that can be sought for unjust enrichment, which is a part of the law of obligations, along with the law of contract, tort, and trusts. Restitution is a personal rather than a proprietary remedy.[1017] Under this remedy, the claimant can recover from the defendant the amount by which the defendant was enriched or benefited at the expense of the claimant in 'unjust' circumstances.

§2. Injunctive Relief

495. Equitable remedies such as injunctions, restraining orders, apology, re-employment, etc. are available under the court's discretion if the court believes that monetary damages may not restore the victim to their pre-tort position. All specific equitable remedies are discussed in this text under the respective torts.

496. Generally, in nuisance and trespass cases, the court may allow temporary or permanent injunctions to stop the defendant's acts or order the defendant to take affirmative steps. In *Chang Ming Fang Jacqueline v. Zhang Zi Qiang,*[1018] the defendant was found liable for assault, intimidation and the plaintiff's psychiatric injury for 'the series of acts carried out by the defendant against her from 23 December 2005 to 20 October 2006'. In this case, Anthony Chan SC awarded a permanent injunction prohibiting the defendant from going to the plaintiff's workplace. The court may also allow an interlocutory injunction after considering principles under *Turbo Top Ltd v. Lee Cheuk Yan,*[1019] (per Godfrey Lam J), namely: (1) whether there are serious issues to be tried; (2) whether damages would be adequate; and (3) where the balance of convenience lies in whether an interlocutory injunction is granted. These guidelines were first laid down by Lord Diplock in *American Cyanamid Co v. Ethicon Ltd.*[1020]

§3. Punitive Damages

497. This has been discussed in Chapter 4 under §1 Personal Injury, above.

1016. *Shanghai Tongji Science and Technology Industrial Company Ltd v. Casil Clearing Ltd* (2004) 7 HKCFAR 79 at p. 104D-J, §§66–68 (Ribeiro PJ); *Takahashi v. Cheng Zhen Shu* (2011) 14 HKCFAR 558.

1017. *Foskett v. McKeown* [2001] 1 AC 102.

1018. [2009] HKCFI 768.

1019. [2013] 3 HKLRD 41, para. 14.

1020. [1975] AC 396.

Selected Bibliography

Books

Clerk and Lindsell on Torts, 20th edn, Sweet & Maxwell Ltd 2010.

Fozia Nazir Lone, *Hong Kong Tort Law: Texts, Cases and Ordinances.* Lexis Nexis, October 2014.

Carty, H. *An Analysis of the Economic Torts,* 2nd edn, OUP 2010.

Halsbury's Laws of Hong Kong, 2nd edn, Lexis Nexis 2012.

Michael Ramsden & Dr Hsiao-Pen Chang. 'Misfeasance In Public Office'. 'In *Tort Law & Practice in Hong Kong, edited by* Justice Kemal Bokhary, N. Sarony & D.K. Srivastava, 3rd edn, Sweet & Maxwell 2014.

Cane, P. *Tort Law and Economic Interests,* 2nd edn, Clarendon Press 1996.

Cane, P. *Atiyah's Accidents Compensation and the Law,* 7th edn, CUP 2006.

Post-Traumatic Stress Disorder. In *Diagnostic and Statistical Manual of Mental Disorders*, 4th edn, American Psychiatric Association, 1994.

Rick Glofcheski, *Tort Law in Hong Kong,* 2nd edn, Sweet & Maxwell, 2012.

Singh, S.P. *Law of Tort,* 5th edn, Universal Law Publishing, 2010.

Harpwood, V.H. *Modern Tort Law,* 7th edn, Routledge- Cavendish, 2009.

Articles

Srivastava, D.K. 'Progress of Sexual Harassment Law in India, China and Hong Kong'. Harvard ILJ Online 51 (11 August 2010): 179.

Equal Opportunities Commission, 'Significant Cases: Hong Kong' <http://www.eoc.org.hk/eoc/graphicsfolder/showcontent.aspx?content=significant%20court%20cases#sh_c6>.

Carty, H. 'The Economic Torts in the Twenty First Century'. Law Quarterly Review 124 (2008): 641.

Jose Antonio Maurellet & Adrian Lai, 'The Minibond Saga: Caveat Emptor or Financial Adviser Beware?', Hong Kong Lawyer (2008 December).

Marcus L. Plant, 'Periodic Payment of Damages for Personal Injury'. Louisiana Law Review 44 (1984): 1327 at 1330.

Deakin S. & J. Randall, 'Rethinking the Economic Torts'. Modern Law Review 72 (2009): 519.

Allen Rostron, 'Beyond Market Share Liability: A Theory of Proportional Share Liability for Non-fungible Products'. UCLA Law Review 52 (2004): 151.

Table of Cases

A v. Director of Immigration [2009] 2 HKC 452.

Abdul Razzak Yaqoob and Ors v. Asia Times Online Ltd and Anor [2008] HKCU 679.

Abid Saeed v. Secretary for Justice [2015] 2 HKC 187.

ACL Electronics (HK) Ltd v. Bulmer Ltd [1992] 1 HKC 133 (CA).

Advance Equipment Services (Hong Kong) Ltd v. Tonge (Hong Kong) Ltd & Anor [2009] HKCU 99.

A-G v. Chan Yuen Lung & Others [1989] 1 HKC 470.

Alan Tam Wing Lun & Others v. Tam Kwok Hung [1991] HKLY 417.

Alcock v. Chief Constable of the South Yorkshire Police [1991] UKHL 5

Allen v. Flood [1898] AC 1.

Allen v. Gulf Oil Refining Ltd [1981] 1All ER 353.

Allsop v. Allsop [1865] 5 H & N 534.

Altaf Ahmed v. Innovative Network Engineering Company Ltd [2010] HKCU 2792.

American Cyanamid v. Ethicon Ltd [1975] AC 396.

Amrol v. Rivera [2008] HKLRD 110.

Anchor Brewhouse Developments v. Berkley House (Docklands) Development [1987] 38 Building Law Reports 82.

Andrews v. Hopkinson [1956] 2 All ER 422.

Anns v. Merton London Borough Council [1978] AC 728 (HL).

Armsden v. Kent Police [2009] RTR 387 (CA).

Armstrong v. Sheppard and Short Ltd [1959] 2 QB 384.

Atkinson v. Newcastle Waterworks Co [1877] LR 2 Ex D 441.

Attorney General v. Chaudry [1971] 1 WLR 1614 (CA).

Attorney General v. Yiu Yun [1990] 2 HKC 238, (CA).

Attorney General v. PYA Quarries [1957] 2 QB 169.

Au Yee Ming Ivan v. Ng Fei Tip (District Court, DCCJ 4595/2008).

Axa China Region Insurance Company Limited v. Lin Kwai Ying Katie [2012] HKCU 853

Baker v. TE Hopkins & Son Ltd Baker [1959] 1 WLR 966.

Baker v. Willoughby (HL).

Ballard v. MPC (1983) 133 NLJ 1133.

Bamford v. Turnley [1860] 3 B & S 62.

Barker v. Corus [2006] 2 WLR 1027 (HL).

Barkway v. S. Wales Transport Co. [1950] AC 185.

Barnett v. Chelsea Hospital Management Committee [1969] 1 QB 428.

Barnett v. H&J Packer & Co Ltd [1940] 3 All ER 575.

Barton v. Armstrong [1969] 2 NSWR 451.

Basely v. Clarkson [1682] 3 Lev 37.

BBMB Finance (Hong Kong) Ltd v. Eda Holdings Ltd [1990] 2 HKLR 74 (PC).

Behrens v. Bertram Mills Circus Ltd [1957] 2 QB 1.

Berkoff v. Burchill [1996] 4 All ER 1008 (CA).

Bernstein v. Skyviews & General Ltd [1977] 2 All ER 962.

Bhana, Angela Mary v. Ocean Apex Trading Limited (DCPI 1732/2009).

Bielitski v. Obadiak [1922] 65 DLR 627.

Billion Star Development Ltd v. Wong Tak Chue [2012] 2 HKC 369.

Birch v. Mills [1995] 9 CL 354.

Bird v. Jones (1845) 7 QB 742; [1845] 115 ER 668.

Bliss v. Hall (1838) 4 Bing. N.C. 183.

Bloomfield v. Quadrant Stationery [1998] ET/3201144/97.

Blyth v. Birmingham Waterworks Co (1856) 11 Exch 781, (1856) 156 ER 1047.

Bolam v. Friern Hospital Management Committee [1957] 2 All ER 118; [1957] 1 WLR 582.

Bolitho v. Hackney Health Authority (1998) AC 232 (HL).

Bolton v. Stone [1951] AC 850.

Bonnington Castings Ltd v. Wardlaw [1956] AC 613 (HL).

Bourhill v. Young [1943] AC 92.

Bradford Corporation v. Pickles [1895] AC 587.

Bradford Third Equitable Benefit Building Society v. Borders [1941] 2 All ER 205.

British Railways v. Herrington [1972] AC 877.

Bunt v. Tilley [2007] 1 WLR 1243.

Burnie Port Authority v. General Jones Pty Ltd (1994) 179 CLR 520.

Burton v. Winters [1993] 3 All ER 847 (CA).

Butterfield v. Forrester (1809) 103 ER 926

Byrne v. Deane [1937] 1 KB 818 (CA).

C Y Foundation Group Ltd Anor v. Best Max Holdings Ltd & Ors [2013] HKCU 1273.

Cambridge Water Co v. Eastern Counties Leather Plc [1994] 2 AC 264 (HL); [1994] 1 All ER 53.

Campbell v. MGN Ltd [2003] EMLR 39.

Caparo Industries plc v. Dickman [1990] 2 AC 605; [1990] 1 All ER 568.

Capital Prosperous Ltd & Anor v. Sheen Cho Kwong [1999] 1 HKLRD 633 (CFI).

Carmarthenshire County Council v. Lewis [1955] UKHL 2.

Cassidy v. Daily Mirror Newspapers, Limited [1929] 2 KB 331(CA).

Cassidy v. Ministry of Health [1951] 1 All ER 574.

Cathay Pacific Airways Ltd v. Wong Sau Lai [2006] 2 HKLRD 586 (CFA).

Cattle v. Stockton Waterworks Co (1875) LR 10 QB 453.

Century Insurance Co Ltd v. Northern Ireland Road Transport Board [1942] AC 509.

Chadwick v. British Railway Board [1967] 1 WLR 912.

Chan Kin Bun v. Wong Sze Ming [2006] 3 HKLRD 208.

Chan King Wan & Anor v. Honest Scaffold General Contractor Co Ltd & Anor (No 2) [2000] 1 HKLRD 751.

Chan Kwai Ngor v. Leung Fat Hang (t/a Fu Restaurant) [1992] 1 HKC 408.

Chan Kwok Wai v. Secretary for Justice [2000] HCPI 134 of 1999.

Chan Ming v. Wayfine Investment Ltd [2000] 2 HKLRD E12 (DC).

Chan Pak Ting v. Chan Chi Kuen and Another [2012] HKCU 2083.

Chan Pui Ki v. Leung On [1995] 3 HKC 732; [1996] 2 HKC 565 (CA).

Chan Wai Ming v. Leung Shing Wah [2014] 4 HKLRD 669.

Chan Wai Nga v. Tam Chi Wai [2006] HKCU 1097.

Chan Woon Cheung v. Chan Yuk Ching and Another [2001] HKCU 1266.

Chan Yan Nam v. Hui Ka Ming & Others [2003] 1 HKC 341 (CA).

Chan Ying Wah v. Bachy Soletanche Group Ltd [2004] HKEC 1483.

Chan Yu Chau v. Fong On Construction & Engineering Co Ltd & Others [2002] HKCU 678, [2002] 2 HKLRD F14.

Chang Ming Fang Jacqueline Alias Chang Hwai Ying Jacqueline v. Zhang Zi Qiang, [2011] HKCU 318.

Charles Sin Cho Chiu v. Tin Tin Publication Development Ltd [2002] HKCU 127.

Charleston v. News Group Newspapers Ltd [1995] 2 AC 65 (HL).

Chau Fung Yee v. Lee Chi Ming [2000] 2 HKLRD 690.

Chaudhry v. Prabhakar [1988] 3 All ER 718.

Chavez v. Fong Ka Yiu [2001] 3 HKLRD 1.

Cheang Kam Ian v. Hong Kong Prime Printing Company [2000] HCPI 143 of 1998.

Chen v. Tamara Rus & Anor [2002] 1 HKC 546.

Chen v. Taramus Rus and Another (DCEO2/1999).

Chen Yung Hui v. Lam Shing [1988] HCA 7200 of 1985.

Cheng Kin Ping & Anor v. Woo Cho Wing & Cheung Ming Wo (third Party) [2000] 3HKLRD 743 (CFA).

Cheng Yuen v. Royal Hong Kong Golf Club [1998] ICR 131.

Cheung Ping v. Siu Chung-yee & Another and American United General Insurance Ltd and Scotland Insurance Co Ltd [1984] HKCU 32.

Chiang Lily v. Secretary for Justice [2010] HKCU 698 (CFA).

China Light & Power Co Ltd and Anor v. Michael Edward Ashton Ford [1996] 1 HKLRD 57, (CA).

Chiu Luen Public Light Bus Co Ltd (潮聯公共小型巴士有限公司) v. Persons Unlawfully Occupying Or Remaining On The Public Highway Namely, The Westbound Carriageway Of Argyle Street Between The Junction Of Tung Choi Street And Portland Street And/Or Other Persons Hindering Or Preventing The Passing Or Repassing Of Argyle Street [2014] HKCU 2435 (CFI).

Choy Bing Wing v. Ng Yat Chi [1992] 1 HKC 508.

Christie v. Davey [1983] 1 Ch 316.

Chu Chung Shing Investment Co Ltd v. Lam Chung & Others [2015] HKCU 2918.

Chu Siu Kuk Yuen v. Apple Daily Ltd and Others [2001] 1 HKLRD 1.

Chung Loi v. MTR Corporation Ltd & Another (2005) HCPI 939 of 2002.

Chung Man Yau & Anor v. Sihon Co Ltd [1996] HKLY 668; [1997] 1 HKLRD 1221; [1997] 3 HKC 197 (CA).

Chung Ping Wai v. Pedder Logistics Goodwn Ltd, District Court DCPI 1770/2007.

Clark Fixing Ltd v. Dudley Metropolitan Borough Council [2001] EWCA Civ 1898.

Club Deluxe Ltd v. Club Metropolitan Ltd and Ors [1995] 2 HKLR 69.

CMY v. Tam Siu Wing [2008] 4 HKLRD 604.

Coco v. AN Clark [1969] RPC 41.

Cole v. Turner (1704) 87 ER 907.

Collins v. Wilcock [1984] 3 All ER 374.

Colonial Mutual Life Insurance Society Ltd v. Producers and Citizens Co-Operative Assurance Co of Australia Ltd [1931] 46 CLR 41.

Constantine v. Imperial Hotels Ltd [1944] 1 KB 693.

Cookson v. Knowles [1979] AC 556; [1978] 2 All ER 604 (HL).

Corby Group Litigation Claimants v. Corby BC [2008] EWCA Civ 463; [2009] QB 335.

Corr v. IBC Vehicles [2008] UKHL 13 (HL).

Corsina (Far East) Ltdv and Taipen Yusen Wharf & Godown Co. Ltd. [1976] HKCU 45.

Coventry v. Lawrence [2014] UKSC 13.

Cox v. Ministry of Justice [2016] UKSC 10.

Crofter Hand Woven Harris Tweed Co Ltd v. Veitch [1942] AC 435 (HL); [1942] 1 All ER 142.

Cunard v. Antifyre [1933] 1 KB 551.

Cunningham v. Reading Football Club (1992) PIQR P 141.

Cutler v. Wandsworth Stadium Ltd [1949] AC 398.

D&F Estates Ltd v. Church Commissioners [1989] AC 177 (HL).

Daborn v. Bath Tramways Motor Co Ltd [1946] 2 All ER 333.

Davies v. Mann (1842) 10 M & W 546.

Davies v. Presbyterian Church of Wales [1986] 1 WLR 323.

DBS Bank (HK) Limited v. San-Hot HK Industrial Co Ltd & Anor [2013] 4 HKC 1.

De Beers Abrasive Products Ltd v. International General Electric Co of New York [1975] 2 All ER 599.

De Keysers Royal Hotel Ltd v. Spicer Bros Ltd (1914) 30 TLR 257.

Dennis v. Ministry of Defence [2003] EWHC 793.

Dense Billion Ltd v. Hui Ting-Sung & Others and Lam Siu-Hung [1996] 2 HKC 110 (CA).

Derbyshire County Council v. Times Newspaper Ltd [1993] AC 534 (HL).

Derry v. Peek [1889] 14 App Cas 337.

Dobson v. Dobson [1999] 4LRC 291.

Donoghue v. Stevenson [1932] UKHL 100.

Doughty v. Turner Manufacturing Ltd [1964] 1 QB 518.

Dubai Aluminium Co Ltd v. Salaam [2002] UKHL 48.

Duchess of Argyll v. Duke of Argyll [1967] 1 Ch 302.

Dutton v. Bognor Regis Urban District Council [1972] 1 All ER 462 (CA).

Dyer v. Munday [1895] 1 QB 742.

Dymond v. Pearce [1972] 1 All ER 1142.

East Asia v. Tsien Wui Marble Factory Ltd & Ors [2000] 1 HKLRD 268.

East Suffolk Rivers Catchment Board v. Kent [1941] AC 74 (HL).

Eastern and South African Telegraph Co Ltd v. Cape Tramways Co Ltd [1902] AC 381 (PC).

Ellison v. Ministry of Defence [1997] 81 BLR 101.

Emerald Construction Co Ltd v. Lowthian [1966) 1 WLR 691.

Emperor (China Concept) Investment Ltd v. SBI E-2 Capital Securities Ltd and Another [2005] HKLRD L13.

Everitt v. Martin [1953] NZLR 298.

Ex parte Island Records Ltd [1978] 3 All ER 795 (CA); [1978] 1 Ch 122.

Exchange Telegraph Co v. Gregory & Co [1896] 1 QB 147.

F v. Berkshire Health Authority [1981] QB 432.

Fagan v. Metropolitan Police Commissioner [1969] 1 QB 439.

Fairchild (suing on her own behalf) etc v. Glenhaven Funeral Services Ltd and Others etc [2002] UKHL 22.

Fan Hung Shing v. Hang Fung Shipping Company Ltd (HCPI 1192/1995).

Far East Engineering Services Ltd v. Choy Yau Chiu [2005] HKCU 1400 (unreported HCA 2146 of 2004, 7 October 2005).

Fardon v. Harcourt-Rivington [1932] All ER Rep 81, (1932) 146 LT 391 (HL).

Fitzgerald v. Lane [1987] QB 781 (CA).

Flavius v. MPC (1982) 132 NLJ 532.

Fok Chik Yeung Apple v. I-Cable Telecom Ltd [2015] HKCU 2414.

Formerly Known as v. Eton Properties Limited [2012] HKCU 1268.

Fouldes v. Willoughby [1841] 151 ER 1153.

Fowler v. Lanning [1959] 1 QB 426.

Froom v. Butcher [1976] QB 286 (CA).

Fu Cheung Chun Tom v. MTR Corp Ltd [2009] HKCU 336.

Fu Lok Man James v. Chief Bailiff of the High Court [1998] 2 HKC 1.

Fung Wai Han v. Hui Chik Keung [2006] 4 HKLRD 549.

Gee v. Metropolitan Railway Co [1873] LR 8QB 161.

General and Finance Facilities Ltd v. Cooks Cars (Romford) Ltd [1963] 2 All ER 314.

Ghulam Rbani v. Secretary for Justice for and on behalf of Director of Immigration [2012] HKCU 364 (unreported, DCCJ 531/2010, 16 February 2012).

Gillingham Borough Council v. Medway (Chatham) Dock Co Ltd [1993] QB 343.

Glasgow Corp v. Muir [1943] 2 AC 448.

Godfrey v. Demon Internet Ltd [2001] QB 201.

Goldman v. Hargrave [1967] 1 AC 645.

Goldsmith v. Bhoyrul [1998] QB 459.

Grant v. Australian Knitting Mills Ltd [1936] AC 85.

Green v. DP Group Services (UK) Ltd [2006] EWHC 1898 QB.

Gregg v. Scott [2005] 4 All ER 812.

Groves v. Lord Wimborne [1898] 2 QB 402.

H West & Son Co Ltd v. Shepherd [1964] AC 326.

Hale v. Hants & Dorset Motor Services Ltd & Anor [1947] 2 All ER 628.

Hale v. Jennings Bros [1938] 1 All ER 579 (CA).

Hale v. London Underground Ltd [1993] PIQR Q30.

Haley v. London Electricity Board [1965] AC 778 (HL).

Halsey v. Esso Petroleum Co Ltd [1961] 2 All ER 145.

Hambrook v. Stokes Bros [1925] 1KB 141.

Harris v. James [1876] 45 LJQB 545.

Harris v. Wyre Forest District Council [1988] Q.B. 835 (HL).

Harrison v. British Railways Board [1981] 3 All ER 679.

Hastie v. Magistrates of Edinburgh [1907] SC 1102.

Haynes v. Harwood [1935] 1 KB 146.

Hedley Byrne & Co Ltd v. Heller & Partners Ltd [1964] AC 465 (HL).

Henderson v. Merrett Syndicate Ltd [1995] 2 AC 145 (HL).

Her 'Majesty's Revenue & Customs v. Hashu Dhalomal Shahdadpuri & Anor [2010] 5 HKLRD 690.

Hicks v. Chief Constable of South Yorkshire [1992] 2 All ER 65 (HL).

Hill v. Chief Constable of West Yorkshire [1988] 2 All ER 238 (HL).

Ho Ka Yin v. Express Security Ltd [2011] 4 HKRLD 395; [2011] HKCU 1398.

Ho Kwai-Loy v. Leung Tin-Hong & Another [1978] HKLR 72.

Ho Wing Cheung v. Liu Sin Fun & Another [1980] HKLR 300.

Holliday v. National Telephone Co [1899] 2 QB 392 (CA).

Hollins v. Fowler [1875] LR 7 HL 757.

Hollywood Silver Fox Farm v. Emmett [1936] 2 KB 468.

Home Office v. Dorset Yacht Co Ltd [1970] AC 1004; [1970] 2 All ER 294.

Hsu Li Yun v. Incorporated Owners of Yuen Fat Building [2000] 1 HKLRD 900 (CA).

Hudson v. Ridge Manufacturing Co. Ltd [1957] 2 QB 248.

Hughes (Russell McDonald) v. Lord Advocate [1963] AC 837(HL).

Hung Sau Fung v. Lai Ping Wai [2016] 1 HKLRD 106.

Hunter v. British Coal [1999] QB 140.

Hunter v. Canary Wharf Ltd [1997] UKHL 14; AC 655 (HL).

Hutchins v. Maughan [1947] VLR 131.

Hyett v. Great Western Railway Co [1948] 1 KB 345.

Ideal Construction Ltd v. Maeda Corp [1992] 1 HKC 528 (HC).

Incorporated Owners of Fu Fai Court, Tin Hau Temple Road v. Henble Ltd [2003] HKEC 1254.

Innes v. Wylie (1844) 174 ER 800.

Intel Corporation Intell Ltd v. Daw [2007] EWCA Civ 70.

International Business Machines Corporation & IBM United Kingdom Limited v. Web-Sphere Limited [2004] EWHC 529.

Inverugie Investments Ltd v. Hackett [1995] 1 WLR 713 (PC).

Investasia Ltd & Anor v. Kodansha Co Ltd & Anor [1999] 3 HKC 515.

Irving Matthew William and Anor v. Man Chun Yeung and Anor [2016] HKCU 689.

J Bollinger v. Costa Brava Wine Co [1961] 1 WLR 277.

J T Stratford & Son Ltd v. Lindley [1965] AC 269.

Jaensch v. Coffey [1984] 54 ALR 417.

Jameel v. Wall Street Journal Europe SPRL (No.3) [2007] 1 AC 359 (HL).

James Mc Naughton Papers Group Ltd v. Hicks Anderson & Co [1991] 2 QB 113; [1991] 1 All ER 134 at 145 (CA).

Janvier v. Sweeney [1919] 2 KB 316 (CA).

Jeffries v. Great Western Rly Co (1856) 5 E & B 802.

Jiang Zhong v. Yeung Chun Leung (formerly t/a Dream Home Workshop, and Others) (05 February 2016, DCEC1267/2010).

Jobling v. Associated Dairies Ltd [1982] AC 794.

Jolley v. Sutton London Borough Council [2000] 1WLR 1082.

Jones v. Livox Quarries Ltd [1952] 2 QB 608; [1952] 1 TLR 1377 (CA).

Junior Books v. Veitchi [1983] 1 AC 520 (HL).

KBC Bank NV v. Automotive Communications Ltd [2011] HKCU 1686.

Kau Chun Wing v. Main Shine Development Ltd [2010] HKEC 216 .

Khorasandjian v. Bush [1993] 3 WLR 476; [1993] QB 727.

Kiddle v. City Business Properties Ltd [1942] 1 KB 269.

Kirk v. Gregory [1876] 1 Ex D 55.

Kirkham v. Chief Constable of Greater Manchester [1990] 2 QB 283 CA.

Knight v. Home Office [1990] 3 All ER 237.

Knupffer v. London Express Newspaper Ltd [1944] AC 116 (HL).

Kralj v. McGrath [1986] 1 All ER 54.

Kristan Bowers Phillips v. Initial Environmental Services Ltd and Ors [1996] HKCU 594; (1998) HKEC 1011 (CFI).

Kubach v. Hollands [1937] 3 All ER 907.

Kuddus (AP) v. Chief Constable of Leicestershire Constabulary [2001] UKHL 29 (HL).

Kuwait Oil Tanker Co SAK v. Al Bader [2000] 2 All ER (Comm) 271.

Kwoon Chung Motors Co Ltd (冠忠遊覽車有限公司) v. Kwok Cheuk Kin & Ors [2014] HKCU 2750 (CFI).

L v. David Roy Burton [2010] 5 HKLRD 397.

Lagden v. O'Connor [2004] 1 All ER 277.

Lai Ping Wah v. China Insurance Co Ltd & Anor [1999] HKCU 1371 (unreported, HCPI 874/97, 25 November 1999).

Lai Sai Kee & Anor v. Yim Ping Wai [1997] HKLY 578 (HC).

Lai Tai Tai v. Lam Pak Lo & Another [2000] 1 HKLRD 499.

Lam Cheuk Leung v. Erawan Co Ltd & Ors [2004] 1 HKLRD 778.

Lam Mo Bun v. Hong Kong Aerosol Co Ltd & Others [2001] 1 HKLRD 540.

Lam Wing Ching & Ors v. Chow Kum Wing [1985] 1 HKC 189.

Lam Yuk-fong v. Attorney General [1987] HKLR 263.

Lamb v. Camden LBC [1981] QB 625 (CA).

Lane v. Holloway [1968] 1 QB 379.

Langridge v. Levy [1837] 2 M & W 519.

Latimer v. AEC Ltd [1953] AC 643.

*Lau Che Ping v. Hoi Kong Ironwares Godown Co Ltd [*1988] 2 HKLR 650.

Lau Kwai Kiu v. Bian Xintian and Another [2012] 2 HKLRD 954, [2012] 4 HKC 313, [2012] HKCA 169 (CA).

Lau Oi Kiu v. Man Chun Shing & Anor [2015] 4 HKC 73.

League Against Cruel Sports v. Scott [1985] 2 All ER 489.

Lee Cooper Ltd v. C. H. Jeakins & Sons Ltd. [1967] 2 QB 1.

Lee Ting and Another v. Wei Sau-Hung [1977] HKDCLR 17.

Lee Ting Sang v. Chung Chi Keung [1990] 1 HKLR 764 (PC).

Lee Yam Kan v. Ng Pui Kuen t/a Wing Sun Scaffolding Engineering and Another (15/03/2016, HCPI196/2014).

Letang v. Cooper [1965] 1 QB 232 (CA).

Leung Sin Fai v. Perfect World Co Ltd & Ors [1998] 2 HKLRD 115.

Leung Tsang Hung v. Incorporated Owners of Kwok Wing House [2007] 10 HKCFAR 480.

Leung Tsang v. Tse Yin Piu [2004] HKCU 515 (unreported, HCPI 595/2002, 12 May 2004).

Lewis v. Daily Telegraph Ltd [1963] 2 All ER 151.

Li Chung-I v. Li Man-yuen [1991] 2 HKC 230; [1991] 2 HKLR 138.

Li Fook Chu v. HH & Co [2006] 3 HKC 433.

Li Wai Ying & Another v. West Global Ltd & Others (2001) (HCA 1810/2000).

Li Wei v. Brightec Ltd [2001] HKCU 96; 1 HKLRD A18.

Li Yau-Wai v. Genesis Films Ltd [1987] QB 237 (CA); [1987] HKLR 711.

Li Yuen Yi Irene v. Law Wai Chung & Another (02/05/2007, DCCJ2919/2004).

Liao Kuo Chun v. Win Capital (HK) Ltd [2010] 4 HKLRD 257.

Lin Chun Yuen & Anor v. Kwong Kam Chuen & Anor [2002] HKEC 1472.

Lister v. Hesley Hall [2001] UKHL 22; [2002] 1 AC 215 (HL).

Liu Tsz Wah v. Lui Kwok Fai [2015] 1 HKLRD 566.

Livingstone v. Ministry of Defence [1984] N. I 356 (N. Ireland C. A).

Lloyd v. Grace, Smith and Co [1912] AC 716 (HL).

Lloyd v. Osborne [1899] 20 LR (NSW) 190.

Lloyd's Bank Ltd v. Savory & Co [1933] AC 201.

Lochgelly Iron and Coal Co Ltd v. M'Mullan [1934] AC 1 (HL).

Lonrho Ltd. v. Shell Petroleum Co. Ltd. (No.2) [1982] AC 173.

Lonrho Plc. v. Fayed (No. 5) [1992] 1 AC 448; [1993] 1 W.L.R. 1489.

Luen Hing Fat Coating & Finishing Factory Ltd v. Wan Chuen Ming 61 (2011) 14 HKCFAR 14; [2011] 2 HKLRD 223.

Lumley v. Gye [1854] 3 E & B 114.

Macnab v. Richardson [2008] EWCA Civ 1631.

Mainstream Properties v. Young Mainstream [2007] UKHL 21 (HL).

Majrowski v. Guy's and St Thomas' NHS Trust [2006] UKHL 34 (HL).

Malone v. Laskey [1907] 2 KB 141.

Manton v. Brocklebank [1923] 2 KB 212.

Marc Rich & Co AG v. Bishop Rock Marine Co Ltd [1996] AC 211 (HL).

Marcic v. Thames Water Utilities Ltd [2004] 1 All ER 135.

Mason v. Levy Auto Parts [1967] 2 QB 350.

Maxson Transportation Ltd v. Poon Wai Hang [2007] HKEC 133.

McFarlane v. E.E. Caledonia Ltd [1994] 2 All.

McGhee v. National Coal Board [1973] 1 WLR 1.

McHale v. Watson (1965) 111 CLR 384; [1996] 115 CLR 866.

Mckay v. Essex Area Health Authority [1982] 2 QB 116.

McKinnon Industries Ltd v. Walker [1951] 3 DLR 577 PC.

McLoughlin v. O'Brian [1983] 1 AC 410.

McPhail v. Persons (Names Unknown) [1973] Ch 447.

McWilliams v. Sir William Arrol & Co Ltd [1962] 1 WLR 295 (HL).

Menfond Electronic Art & Computer Design Co Ltd v. Wong Wang Tat Victor [2013] 2 HKC 259.

Merkur Island Shipping v. Laughton [1983] 2 All ER 189 (HL); [1983] 2 AC 57.

Mersey Docks & Harbour Board v. Coggins & Griffith (Liverpool) Ltd [1947] AC 1.

Midland Bank Trust Co Ltd v. Hett Stubbs & Kemp [1978] Ch 384, [1978] 3 All ER 571, [1978] 3 WLR 167.

Miller v. Jackson [1977] 3 All ER 338 (CA); [1977] 3 WLR 20 (CA).

Ming An Insurance Co (HK) Ltd v. Ritz- Carlton Ltd [2002] 2 HKLRD 844 (CFA).

Ministry of Housing and Local Government v. Sharp [1970] 2 QB 223.

Mobil Oil Hong Kong Ltd and Dow Chemical (Hong Kong) Ltd v. Hong Kong United Dockyards Ltd, The 'Hua Lien' [1991] 1 Lloyd's Rep 309.

Mogul Steamship Co Ltd v. McGregor, Gow & Co [1892] AC 25.

Mohammed Said v. Secretary for Justice sued for and on behalf of Director of Immigration [2012] HKCU 2036 (unreported, DCCJ 1717/2010, 21 October 2011).

Mohammed Yaqub Khan v. Attorney General [1987] HKLR 145; [1990] HKCU 0269.

Mohamud v. WM Morrison Supermarkets plc [2016] UKSC 11.

Mok Ka Yin v. Tsang Hing On [2007] 2 HKLRD 858, [2007] HKCU 1006.

Mok Lai Fong v. Ng Po Sui [2011] 3 HKLRD 67.

Moorgate Mercantile Co Ltd v. Finch and Read [1962] 1 QB 701 (CA).

Moreland Timber Co v. Reid [1946] VLR 237.

Morris v. CW Martin [1966] 1 QB 716 (CA).

Morris v. Murray [1990] 3 All ER 801 (CA).

Mourton v. Poulter [1930] 2 KB 183.

Muirhead v. Industrial Tank Specialities (1986) QB 507.

Mujiati v. Chong Wai Kwan [2004] HKCU 1226.

Mulcahy v. R [1868] LR 3 HL 306.

Mullin v. Richards [1998] 1 WLR 1304

Murphy v. Brentwood District Council [1990] 2 All ER 908; [1991] 1 AC 398.

Murray v. Ministry of Defence [1988] 2 All ER 521 (HL).

Musgrove v. Pendelis [1919] 2 KB 43 (CA).

Mutual Life Citizen Assurance Co v. Evatt [1971] 1 All ER 150.

N v. Agrawal [1999] PNLR 939.

Nettleship v. Weston [1971] 2 QB 691 (CA).

Newstead v. London Express Newspapers [1940] 1 KB 377 (CA).

Newton v. Edgerley [1959] 1 WLR 1031.

Ng Ching Ying v. Lee Siu Yeung & Another [2001] HKLRD (Yrbk) 646.

Ng Hoi Sze v. Yuen Sha Sha & Anor [1999] HKCU 1583 (CACV 93/1999).

Nickerson v. Hodges [1920] 84 Sol Jo 37.

Nicrotherm Electrical Co Ltd v. Percy [1956] RPC 272.

North Glamorgan NHS Trust v. Walters [2002] EWCA Civ 1792 (CA).

OBG v. Allan [2007] UKHL 21; [2008] 1 AC 1 (HL).

Ogwo v. Taylor [1987] 3 WLR 1145.

On Hang Chu v. Chan Ngun [2003] HKCU 814.

On Park Property Management Ltd v. The Incorporated Owners Of Kwan Yick Building Phase II [2014] HKCU 221.

Oriental Press Group Ltd v. Hong Kong Daily News Ltd & Anor [1997] 3 HKC 622.

Ormrod v. Crosville Moter Service Ltd [1953] 1WLR 1120.

Overseas Tankship (U.K.) Ltd. v. The Miler Steamship Co. and anor (The Wagon Mound No. 1) [1961] AC 388 (PC).

Overseas Tankship (UK) Ltd v. The Miller Steamship Co and Anor (The Wagon Mound No. 2) [1967] 1 AC 617.

Page v. Smith [1996] AC 155 (HL).

Paris v. Stepney Borough Council [1951] 1 All ER 42 (HL).

Parker v. British Airways Board [1982] QB 1004.

Parkinson v. Liverpool Corporation [1950] 1 All ER 367.

Pasley v. Freeman (1789) 3 TR 51.

Paul v. Summerhayes [1878] 4 QBD 9.

PBL Publication (Hong Kong) Ltd v. Marks Hundred Co Ltd [1987] 2 HKC 157.

Peek v. Gurney [1873] LR 6 HK 377.

Penfolds Wines v. Elliott (1946) 74 CLR 204 (Australia).

Perrett v. Collins [1998] 2 'Lloyd's Rep 255 (CA).

Peter Geoffrey De Krassel v. Vincent Julia Chu & Ors [2010] 2 HKLRD 937.

Peter P F Chan v. Hong Kong Society of Accountants [2001] 1 HKLRD 687 (CA); leave to appeal refused in [2001] 1 HKLRD 779 (CFA).

Phillips v. Britannia Hygienic Laundry Co Ltd [1923] 1 KB 539.

Phipps v. Rochester Corp [1955] 1 ALL ER 129; [1955] 1 QB 450.

Pickford v. Imperial Chemical Industries plc [1998] ICR 673.

Pido v. Compass Technology Company Ltd [2010] 2 HKLRD 537 (CA)

Pitts v. Hunt [1991] 1 QB 24 (CA).

Polaroid Far East Ltd v. Bel Trade Co Ltd & Ors [1990] 2 HKLR 447.

Police v. Greaves [1964] NZLR 295.

Ponting v. Noakes [1894] 2 QB 281.

Poon Chau Nam v. Yim Siu Cheung [2007] 10 HKCFAR 156.

Prison Service v. Johnson [1999] ICR 275.

Quinn v. Leathem [1901] AC 495 (HL).

Quinn v. Leathem [1901] AC 495.

R v. Brown [1993] 2 All ER 75.

R v. Chan Wing Kuen [1995] 1 HKC 470.

R v. Deputy Governor of Parkhurst Prison ex parte Hague [1992] 1 AC 58.

R v. Governor of Brockhill Prison, ex p Evans (No. 2) [2000] 4 All ER 15; [2001] 2 AC 19 (HL).

R v. Rimmington [2006] 1 AC 459.

Rabies Ordinance (Cap 421) ss 2 & 24, 25 & 26.

Rainfield Design & Associates Ltd v. Siu Chi Moon [2000] 3 HKCFAR 134.

Rainham Chemical Works Ltd v. Belvedere Fish Guano Co [1921] 1 AC 465 (HL).

RCA Corp v. Pollard [1983] Ch 135.

Re an Arbitration between Polemis and Furness, Withy & Co Ltd [1921] All ER 40.

Re Tran Quoc Cuong & Anor [1995] 5 HKPLR 208.

Read v. Croydon Corporation [1938] 4 All ER 631.

Read v. Lyons [1946] 2 All ER 471 (HL); [1947] A C 156.

Ready Mixed Concrete (South East) Ltd v. Minister of Pension and National Insurance [1968] 2 QB 497, 517.

Reality Harvest Ltd v. Gold Margin Development Ltd [2000] HKEC 588.

Reckitt & Colman Products Ltd v. Borden Inc [1990] RPC 340.

Reed & Bull Information Systems v. Stedman (1999) IRLR 299

Reeves v. Metropolitan Commissioner of Police [2000] 1 AC 360 (HL).

Revenue and Customs Commissioners v. Total Network SL [2008] UKHL 19; [2008] 1 AC 1174 (HL).

Rickards v. Lothian [1913] AC 263.

Riddick v. Thames Board Mills [1977] QB 881.

Rigby v. Chief Constable of Northamptonshire [1985] 2 All ER 985.

Robert Addie & Sons (Collieries) Ltd. v. Dumbreck [1929] AC 358.

Roberts v. Ramsbottom [1980] 1 WLR 823.

Robinson v. Kilvert (1889) 41 Ch D 88 (CA).

Rogers v. Night Riders [1983] RTR 324.

Ronia Ltd v. William Clarke [2005] HKCU 261; (CFI, HCA 3972/2000).

Rookes v. Barnard [1964] AC 1129; [1964] UKHL 1.

Rose v. Plenty [1976] All ER 97.

Ross v. Caunters (1980) Ch 297.

Rothwell v. Chemical & Insulating Co Ltd [2008] 1 AC 281, [2007] 4 All ER 1047 (HL).

Rylands v. Fletcher (1868) LR 3 HL 330; [1868] UKHL 1 (HL).

Salmon v. Seafarer Restaurants (1983) 1 WLR 1264.

Salsbury v. Woodland [1971] QB 324.

Saltman Engineering Co Ltd v. Campbell Engineering Co Ltd [1948] 65 RPC 203.

Sanfield Building Contracts Ltd v. Li Kai Cheong (FACV No. 16 of 2002, 12 June 2003); (2003) 6 HKCFAR 207.

Scott v. London and St Katherine Docks [1865] 3 Hurl. & C 596.

Scott v. Shepherd [1773] 2 W Bl 892; [1558-1774] All ER Rep 295.

Sedleigh-Denfield v. O'Callaghan [1940] UKHL 2.

Shan He Electronics Components Co Ltd v. Skybo International Food Co Ltd & Anor (2002) HKCU 212.

Shelfer v. City of London Electric Lighting Co [1895] 1 Ch 287.

Shenzhen Fuhaitong Precision Industry Co Ltd v. Byd Company Ltd [2010] HKCU 1813.

Sidaway v. Board of Governors of the Bethlem Royal Hospital [1985] AC 871 (HL).

Sim v. Stretch [1936] 2 All ER 1237.

Simms v. Leigh Rugby Football Club Ltd (1969) 2 All ER 923.

Simon v. Helmont [2012] UKPC 5.

Sinodental Investments Ltd and Others v. Sin Chung Yin Ronald and Others (HCA2176/2012)

Slater v. Clay Cross Co Ltd [1956] 2 All ER 625.

Smith v. Charles Baker & Sons [1891] AC 325 (HL).

Smith v. Kenrick [1849] 7 CB 515.

Smith v. Leech Brain & Co [1962] 2 QB 405.

Smith v. Littlewoods Organisation Ltd [1987] AC 241.

*Smith v. Eric S. Bus*h [1990] 1 AC 831; [1989] 2 All ER 514.

Snowball v. Gardner Merchant Ltd [1987] LRLR 397.

So Kai Hau v. YSK2 Engineering Co Ltd. [2010] 5 HKLRD 278.

Sorrell v. Smith [1925] AC 700 (HL).

Southport Corp v. Esso Petroleum Co Ltd [1954] 2 QB 182.

Spartan Steel And Alloys Ltd v. Martin & Co (Contractors) Ltd [1973] QB 27.

Spring v. Guardian Assurance Plc [1994] UKHL 7.

St. Helen's Smelting Co v. Tipping [1895] 11 HL Cas 642.

Star Ferry Co Ltd v. The Owners of The Ship or Vessel 'Argonaut' & Anor [1980] HKLR 921.

Star Industrial Co Ltd v. Yap Kwee Kor [1976] FSR 256.

Stennett v. Hancock [1939] 2 All ER 578.

Stephen v. Myers (1830) 4 C & P 349.

Stevenson Jordan & Harrison v. Macdonald & Evan [1952] 1 TLR 101.

Stovin and another v. Norfolk County Council [1996] UKHL 15.

Stovin v. Wise (1996) AC 923.

Sturges v. Bridgman [1879] 11 Ch D 852 (CA).

Sunface International Ltd & Others v. Meco Engineering Ltd [1990] 2 HKLR 193.

Susan Field v. Barber Asia [2003] HKCU 712; [2004] 3 HKLRD 871.

Sutherland Shire Council v. Heyman (1985) 60 ALR 1 at 55-56, Aust HC.

Sze Ha Kam Carly v. Chum Chi On (DCPI1658/2009).

T v. Kan Ki Leung & Anor [2002] 1 HKLRD 29 (CFI).

Ta Xuong v. Incorporated Owners of Sun Hing Building [1997] 4 HKC 171.

Tai Hing Cotton Mill Ltd v. Liu Chong Hing Bank Ltd [1985] 2 All ER 947 (PC); [1986] AC 80.

Tai Ping Yeung Motors Ltd. v. Man Kan Heung and ors., (unrep. DCCJ14620/2000, 27 July 2001).

Tai Yip Dyeing Factory Ltd v. Kong Hoi Sang (21/02/2007, HCA2917/2004).

Tarleton v. M'Gawley (1790) 1 Peake NPC 270.

Taylor v. Glasgow Corporation [1922] 1 AC 448 (HL).

Tennent v. Earl of Glasgow [1864] 2 M (HL) 22.

The Catholic Child Welfare Society and others (Appellants) v. Various Claimants (FC) and The Institute of the Brothers of the Christian Schools and others (Respondents) [2012] UKSC 56.

The Chamber of Hong Kong Computer Industry Company Limited v. Hong Kong Computer Association Limited (06/12/2013, HCA621/2010).

The Pool Co Ltd v. Sino Rise Realty Ltd & Anor. [2014] HKCU 2266.

Theaker v. Richardson [1962] 1 WLR 151 (CA).

Thomas Brown & Sons Ltd v. Fazal Deen (1962) 108 CLR 391.

Thompson and Hsu v. Commissioner of Police of Metropolis [1998] QB 498.

Thompson v. MPC [1997] 3 WLR 403 (CA).

Thomson & Co Ltd v. Deakin [1952] 2 All ER 361 (CA); *GWK Ltd v. Dunlop Rubber Co Ltd* [1926] 42 TLR 376.

Tin Tin Yat Pao (International) Ltd (in Liq) v. Tin Tin Publication Development Ltd [2000] 3 HKC 1.

Tinsley v. Milligan [1994] 1 AC 340 (HL).

Titchener v. British Railways Board [1983] UKHL 10.

Tomlinson v. Congleton Borough Council [2003] UKHL 47; [2004] 1 AC 46, HL.

Topp v. London Country Bus (South West) Ltd [1993] 3 All ER 448 at 460, [1992] RTR 254.

Torquay Hotel v. Cousins [1969] 1 All ER 522 (CA); [1969] 2 Ch 106.

Transco Plc v. Stockport Metropolitan Borough Council [2003] UKHL 61; [2004] 2 AC 1 (HL).

Tsang Hon Chu v. Wong Kwok Leung [2005] DCCJ 3917 of 2003.

Tsang Mei Ying & Anor v. Lam Pak Chiu & Anor [1999] 2 HKLRD 807; [2000] 1 HKLRD 883 (CA).

Tse Fung Sin v. Tung Wah Group of Hospitals [2007] HKEC 1899.

Tse Soon Cheung v. William McIntyre Ross & Anor [1965] HKLR 258

Tse's Forex Investment Co Ltd v. Man Yuk Lan & Anor [1995] HKLY 1001 (CA).

Tsun Fat Finance Co Ltd v. Commissioner of Police [2002] 3 HKC 232 (CFI).

Tuberville v. Savage (1669) 91 ER 1072.

Turbo Top Ltd v. Lee Cheuk Yan [2013] 3 HKLRD 41.

Ultramares Corp v. Touche (1931) 255 NY 170, (1931) 174 NE 441 (NYCA).

Vaughan v. Menlove (1837) 132 ER 490 (CP).

Vaughan v. Taff Vale Rly Co (1860) 5 H & N 679.

Vento v. Chief Constable of West Yorkshire Police [2003] ICR 318.

Victorian Railway Commissioner v. Coultas (1888) 13 App Cas 222.

Videan v. British Transport Commission [1963] 2 QB 650.

Vowles v. Evans [2003] 1WLR 1607.

Wagner v. International Railways Co [1921] 133 NE 437 NY 176.

Wainwright v. Home Office [2004] 2 AC 406 (HL).

Walker v. Northumberland County Council [1995] 1 All ER 737.

Walter v. Selfe [1851] 4 De G & Sm 315; (1850) 20 LJ Ch. 433.

Watson v. British Boxing Board Control [2001] QB 1134.

Wayfoong Credit Ltd v. Tsui Siu-man Plastics [1984] HKLR 259.

Wells v. Cooper [1958] 2 QB 265.

Wells v. Wells [1999] 1 AC 345.

West London Commercial Bank Ltd v. Kitson [1884] 13 QBD 360.

Western Counties Manure Co v. Lawes Chemical Manure Co [1874] LR 9Ex 218.

Westlands Estates Ltd & Another v. Swilynn (HK) Ltd [1985] HKLY 1005.

Wheat v. E Lacon & Co Ltd [1966] AC 552.

Wheeler v. JJ Saunders Ltd [1995] 3 WLR 466; [1996] Ch 19.

White or Frost v. Chief Constable of South Yorkshire Police [1999] 2 AC 455 (HL).

White v. Jones [1995] 2 AC 207 (HL); [1995] AER HL 691 (HL).

Wilkinson v. Downton [1897] 2QB 57; [1895-99] All ER Rep 267.

William Alan Terence Crawley v. Attorney General [1987] HKLR 379, HC.

William Allan v. Messrs Ng & Co. (a firm) & Anor (HCA10844/1994, (24 December 2010).

Williams v. Holland [1833] 10 Bing 112.

Wilsher v. Essex Area Health Authority [1986] 3 All ER 801; [1987] QB 730 (CA); [1988] 2 WLR 557 (HL).

Wilson v. Lombank Ltd [1963] 1 WLR 1294.

Wilson v. New Brighton Panelbeaters [1989¬] 1 NZLR 74.

Wilsons & Clyde Co Ltd v. English [1938] AC 57 (HL).

Wing On Travel Services Ltd v. Hong Thai Citizens Travel Services Ltd [2001] 2 HKLRD 481.

Wise v. Kaye [1962] 1 QB 638.

Wong Ching Chi & Anor v. Full Yue Bleaching & Dyeing Co Ltd [1994] 3 HKC 606, HC.

Wong Chun Tak v. The Registrar of High Court [2015] HKCU 1255.

Wong Kam v. Shum Yuk Fong [2001] HKEC 1220.

Wong Kwai Fun v. Li Fung [1994] 1 HKC 549 (HC).

Wong Kwok Tung v. Tsang Hin Ping (unrep. HCPI 725/1997)

Wong Kwok-mui v. Lee Yuen-tim [2001] HKEC 249 (DC).

Wong Sai-yee v. Kong Kwan [1988] 1 HKLR 367 (CA)

Wong Tak-hing v. Tai Sang Industrial Co Ltd [1975] HKLR 375.

Wong v. Parkside Health NHS Trust [2003] 3 All ER 932.

Wong Wai Hing and Anor v. Hui Wei Lee [2001] 2 HKLRD 736 (CA).

Wong Wai Ming v. Hospital Authority [2000] 3 HKLRD 612.

Wong Wai Tak Belinda & Anor v. Smart Team International Investment Ltd [2011] 3 HKC 322.

Wong Wai-chun, Administratrix of the Estate of Cheung Chung Wai Deceased v. the China Navigation Co Ltd [1969] HKLR 471.

Wong Wing Ho v. The Hong Kong Housing Authority and Another (28/12/2007, CACV28/2007).

Wong Yiu Ming v. To Chark Wah & Anor [1993] 1 HKC 510.

World Wide Stationery Manufacturing Co Ltd v. Fong Chi Leung [1994] 2 HKC 449 (CA).

Wringe v. Cohen [1940] 1 KB 229.

X (Minors) v. Bedfordshire Council [1995] 2 AC 633.

X v. Y [1988] 2 All ER 648.

*Xiang Si Hua v. Bailey Record Co Lt*d [1987] HKLY 409; [1987] HKCU 18.

Yachuk v. Oliver Blais Co Ltd [1949] AC 386 (PC).

Yang Yee Man, the Administratrix of the Estate of Lam Lok Kin, *Deceased v. Leung Hing Hung* (HCPI 443/2010).

Yapp v. Foreign and Commonwealth Office [2013] EWHC 1098 (QB).

Yeung Kam Fuk v. Len Shing Construction Co Ltd [1986] HKC 160.

Yeung Shea Chun v. Director of Legal Aid [2000] HCA 8439 of 1999.

Yeung Yu v. Wong Yung [1986] HKC 5.

Yien Yieh Commercial Bank Ltd v. Kwai Chung Cold Storage Co Ltd [1988] 2 HKLR 569 (CA).

Youssoupoff v. Metro-Goldwyn Pictures [1934] 50 TLR 581.

Yu Yu Kai v. Chan Chi Keung (2009) 12 HKCFAR 705.

Yue Xiu Finance Company Ltd & Another v. Dermot Agnew and Others (formerly t/a Deloitte Haskins and Sells) [1996] 1 HKCU 0467.

Yuen Chi Man Daniel v. Cheng Pui Man [2015] HKCU 3025.

Yuen Kun-yeu v. Attorney General of Hong Kong [1987] 2 All ER 705 (PC).

Yuen Sha Sha v. Tse Chi Pan [1999] 1 HKC 731 (DC).

Zenuna Ltd v. Progress Year International Ltd & Others [2003] 2 HKLRD G5.

Ordinances

Banking Ordinance (Cap 155).

Building Ordinance (Cap 123).

Civil Aviation Ordinance (Cap 448).

Consumer Council Ordinance (Cap 216).

Consumers Goods Safety Ordinance (Cap 456).

Control of Exemption Clauses Ordinance (Cap 71).

Conveyancing and Property Ordinance (Cap 219).

Criminal Procedure Ordinance (Cap 221)

Dangerous Dogs Regulation (Cap 167D).

Defamation Ordinance (Cap 21).

Dogs and Cats Ordinance (Cap 167).

Factories & Industrial Undertakings Regulations (Cap 59 A).

Factories and Industrial Undertakings (Guarding and Operation of Machinery) Regulations (Cap 590).

Fire Services Ordinance (Cap 95).

High Court Ordinance (Cap 4).

Hong Kong Airport (Control of Obstructions) Ordinance (Cap 301).

Hong Kong Basic Law.

Hong Kong Bill of Rights Ordinance (Cap 383).

Hong Kong Reunification Ordinance (Cap 2601).

Law Reform (Contributory Negligence) Act 1945.

Limitation Ordinance (Cap 347)

Mining Ordinance (Cap 285)

Motor Vehicle Insurance (Third Party Risks) Ordinance (Cap 272).

Occupational Safety and Health Ordinance (Cap 509).

Occupier's Liability Ordinance (Cap 314).

Offence Against the Persons Ordinance (Cap 212).

Prevention of Bribery Ordinance (Cap 201).

Sale of Goods Ordinance (Cap 26).

Sex Discrimination Ordinance (Cap 480).

Shipping and Port Control Ordinance (Cap 313).

Supply of Services (Implied Terms) Ordinance (Cap 457).

Town Planning Ordinance (Cap 131).

Toys and Children's Product Safety Ordinance (Cap 424).

Unconscionable Contracts Ordinance (Cap 458).

Waterworks Clauses Act 1875.

Index

The numbers here refers to paragraph numbers.

Made in the USA
Monee, IL
18 October 2026

66037584R10129